RHETORICAL MEMORY AND DELIVERY
Classical Concepts for Contemporary Composition and Communication

RHETORICAL MEMORY AND DELIVERY
Classical Concepts for Contemporary Composition and Communication

Edited by

John Frederick Reynolds
Old Dominion University

1993

LAWRENCE ERLBAUM ASSOCIATES, PUBLISHERS
Hillsdale, New Jersey   Hove and London

Lawrence Erlbaum Associates, Inc., Publishers
365 Broadway
Hillsdale, New Jersey 07642

Library of Congress Cataloging-in-Publication Data
Rhetorical memory and delivery : classical concepts for contemporary
  composition and communication / edited by John Frederick Reynolds ;
  with an introduction by Winifred Bryan Horner.
        p.   cm.
  Includes bibliographical references (p.) and index.
  ISBN 0-8058-1292-X (cloth). — ISBN 0-8058-1293-8 (pbk.)
  1. Rhetoric.   2. Memory.   3. Elocution.   I. Reynolds, John
Frederick, 1952–
P301.R472   1993
808—dc20   93-12528
                                                         CIP

Books published by Lawrence Erlbaum Associates are printed
on acid-free paper, and their bindings are chosen for strength
and durability.

Printed in the United States of America
10 9 8 7 6 5 4 3 2 1

Contents

Preface

The classical rhetorical canons of memory and delivery have interested me ever since I was an undergraduate student double-majoring in speech communication and English at Midwestern State University in Texas in the early 1970s. My teachers there in both departments were among the finest I have known, wonderful and inspiring, but they kept sending mixed messages about the official canon count. I remember being puzzled even as a first-semester college freshman by the fact that there were *five* classical canons in my 9:00 a.m. rhetorical theory class, *four* in my 10:00 a.m. public speaking class, and only *three* in my 11:00 a.m. composition class. It took me far too long to get to the bottom of that mystery, and even longer to realize how much it mattered.

I have assembled this volume of diverse chapters exploring various aspects of classical rhetoric's "problem canons" for two reasons. First, because I think that it is long overdue: rhetorical memory and delivery have always been important, and yet they have never received the kind of widespread critical attention they deserve. Second, because I am convinced that much might be at stake where memory and delivery issues are concerned. Theoretical accuracy, context, and coherence, certainly. The longevity of the rhetoric revival, perhaps. A clearer sense of just how much common ground composition studies' various camps (cognitivists, classicists, developmentalists, and such) actually share. Maybe even a better sense of just how closely the various divisions of rhetorical inquiry (composition, speech communication, media studies, and such) are connected to each other. My thinking here borders, I know, on something akin to the Beatific Vision but, much to my good fortune, Hollis Heimbouch at Lawrence Erlbaum Associates understood my mission and supported it almost immediately, and I am very grateful to her for that.

Lots of people already know this, but I want to acknowledge here in print for anyone who does not that I have long been and continue to be enormously indebted to my friend, colleague, and mentor, Kathleen Welch. Kathleen did not introduce me to classical rhetoric, but she certainly electrified it for me, and I will forever thank her for that. Sincere thanks are due to all of my other memory/delivery contributors, as well. Their enthusiasm for helping me assemble this volume when they all had plenty of other important things to do is probably the best evidence in support of my contention that this book has long needed doing. I greatly admire them all, and am proud to be in their company. In my own professional life, I aspire to be as courageous as Win Horner and Joyce Middleton; as enthusiastic as Sheri Helsley; as provocative as Jay Bolter and David Marc; as prolific as Bob Connors and Bruce Gronbeck; as dependable as Sam Dragga; as humble as Virginia Allen; and as honest as Sharon Crowley.

This volume is dedicated to those for whom it was primarily written, our graduate students in rhetoric. I especially want to dedicate it to the gifted group of graduate students who participated in my summer 1992 writing seminar at the University of Oklahoma. Blake Scott and Melody Bowdon, in particular, gave me three things that summer in Oklahoma that I will always treasure: "Canon-Man," "PlaTroll," and—along with the other members of their group—ample reason to be enthusiastic about the next generation of teacher-scholars in rhetoric.

Finally, I would be remiss not to thank my research assistant, Clayann Gilliam Panetta, and our college's research supportperson, Elaine Dawson, for their valuable assistance with this project; also my family, Vickie and Mattie, for putting up with my faulty memory and excessive delivery.

One Editorial Note: Readers will notice, no doubt, that several of the contributors to this volume extensively review the orality/literacy/secondary orality work of Marshall McLuhan, Walter J. Ong, and Eric A. Havelock in constructing their arguments. Because I knew that readers might choose to read the chapters of this book according to their own ordering preferences rather than mine, I encouraged my contributors to feel free to rehearse this key information in their individual chapters even if they felt certain that other contributors might tackle it also.

Fred Reynolds

Introduction

Winifred Bryan Horner
Texas Christian University

This book marks a turning point in the history of rhetoric. Through its revival of the classical canons of memory and delivery, it reaches into the past to explain the present and suggest possibilities for the future. It explores orality and literacy within a secondary orality that blends written and spoken and visual and aural language.

What Fred Reynolds calls "the five-part construct at the core of the body of work called 'classical rhetoric'" has altered and been altered over the years, but it has never been entirely abandoned. Rhetorical systems often called "new" have never quite given up the classical canons, arguing either for or against them. Modern composition textbooks have continued to make use of the precepts of classical rhetoric without acknowledging or realizing their debt to Aristotle or Cicero. Rhetoric has historically evidenced a tendency to reduce itself to one or two of its canons. For example, Renaissance rhetoric limited itself largely to figures of speech, and eighteenth-century rhetoric was concerned with the last canon in its emphasis on elocution, where style became delivery. In the nineteenth century, rhetoric became the study of English literature, largely confined to the study of style. In spite of these truncations, the classical canons have persisted over the years, enlarging or diminishing to accommodate the latest fads.

This current study recognizes that there can be no complete rhetoric without a consideration of all five of its canons. All of them—invention, arrangement, style, memory, and delivery—are necessary for a full understanding of a communication act, whether it be written, spoken, electronic, or some combination of any or all of these. This collection of chapters looks at memory and delivery as they work in synergistic relation with the other rhetorical canons and take on new importance for the study of rhetoric in the twenty-first century.

Fred Reynolds' chapter opens the discussion with a salvo against modern rhetorical theory for its tendency to "abandon, remove, neglect, ignore, limit, simplify, misrepresent, and/or misunderstand both memory and delivery." He offers a reinterpretation of the classical canon of memory, citing the works of Frances Yates, Mary Carruthers, and Patrick Mahony to challenge the concept of classical memory as merely "memorizing." He offers modern composition theorists four possible reinterpretations of memory for their consideration: memory as mnemonics, as memorableness, as data bases, and as psychology. In the closing chapter, Bruce Gronbeck offers a further overview of the canon of memory, starting with Aristotle's view from his *De Memoria et Reminiscentia,* through Longinus, Bacon, and Campbell, concluding with Toni Schwartz's resonance theory of communication. Gronbeck then moves through literacy/orality considerations, as many of these chapters do, to an enlargement of Ong's concept of secondary orality, to a phonocentric/ocularcentric rhetoric of discourse in television.

Kathleen Welch follows Reynolds' opening chapter with her argument for a return to the canons of memory and delivery, and warns that writing courses must "stop their erasure of electronic discourse from the domain of school rhetoric." Sharon Crowley's chapter is a celebration of the canon of memory, looking to a postmodern rhetoric that would be community- and ethics-bound. Virginia Allen demonstrates important connections between Aristotle and nineteenth-century empiricism, with a close look at Alexander Bain. All of these studies reread the history of the canon of memory in the light of a contemporary rhetoric. Joyce Middleton's chapter does not have the same historical slant as the others, but it is valuable in exploring the importance of oral memory as "storing and passing on cultural memory." She argues persuasively for the inclusion of the "significant relationships between memory, literacy and orality" in contemporary pedagogy.

The remainder of the chapters deal primarily with delivery and, finally, with the blending of the two neglected canons. Robert J. Connors treats delivery in written discourse as print fonts and paper types, and Sam Dragga explores the ethics of presentations in technical writing, a topic that he contends requires more research. One of the most thought-provoking chapters is by Jay David Bolter, who explores the impact of electronic media on memory and delivery, and the resulting merging of the five canons. For example, in hypertext, which he discusses at length, arrangement becomes invention and, in contrast to the old rhetoric in which the writer or speaker exercised tight control, the writer cedes some control to readers who select their own links.

The exciting part of these chapters for me was not always the points that they made or the contentions that they supported, but the problems that they suggested and the questions that they posed. As I read, doors in my mind opened on new vistas in modern rhetoric which emerge with a rereading of the history of memory and delivery in light of electronic media. To begin with, in order to look at the new electronic media, we need to reinterpret the canons of memory and delivery in the historical documents. At best we have misinterpreted that history; at worst we have ignored it. As these chapters suggest and, as our study of history has demonstrated, we need to know the history of rhetoric in order not to repeat the errors of the past or to offer as new theory work that has already been done. Also, we find that the ideas of the great minds of the past are often rich and expandable and can be applied fruitfully to contemporary problems.

And so the first question I would ask is: How do the rhetorics of the past affect our understanding of the canons of memory and delivery? The second set of questions that comes to my mind are those that have to do with the impact of electronic media on rhetoric. Today, memory as a cultural phenomenon preserved in our data bases, in our oral histories, and in our own minds needs to be explored under these new rubrics. What effect does this kind of communal memory have on invention and on contemporary literature and composition? What kind of an effect will it have on libraries and on books and journals, the traditional storehouses of information? Finally, what kind of an impact will it have on our epistemologies and on our thinking processes? As we look at delivery in an electronic age, what impact will screens and windows, as opposed to familiar pages, have on our thinking processes? Will those processes be unalterably changed and, if so, how?

Another set of questions concerns the social and economic effects of electronics on cultures. Will electronic media further separate the underdeveloped nations from the richer ones of the world? I cannot help but wonder how societies such as China, with its different and far more complex graphic systems, will adapt to computers. Will computers further dichotomize our own society and our schools—between the rich who can afford their own expensive hardware and the poor who have only limited access?

All of these questions about memory in its fullest sense and electronic delivery will need further exploration, of course, as Sheri L. Helsley, a graduate student, outlines in the concluding chapter:

> Memory and delivery, like many of the concepts in classical rhetoric, can be especially difficult and challenging because so many different translations, interpretations, and misrepresentations are available. Whereas some may see this as limiting, or as a reason for avoiding or dismissing classical rhetoric itself, I have come to see it as intellectually exciting. I now see rhetorical memory and delivery as ambiguous zones that are unusually rich with opportunities for important new scholarly work by graduate students in composition, speech communication, media studies, and rhetoric.

A final set of questions that occurred to me as I read this volume involved the impact of electronic media on pedagogy—an essential part of any rhetorical theory. How do the new electronic media affect our teaching, as surely they must? How will a reexamination of memory and delivery affect our courses? And, finally, what are our responsibilities as scholars and teachers? Bemoaning the evils of television sounds remarkably like Plato's objections to writing, and like the many complaints about the proliferation of books and journals in the eighteenth and nineteenth centuries. Television and computers are with us and, just as there have always been poor writing and bad books, so do we have bad television. Our responsibility is not to turn our backs on the new media but to respond to them—even to embrace them and to explore their infinite possibilities.

There have been many turning points in the history of rhetoric. Each has been influenced by changes in communication media and inevitably accompanied by dire warnings. With the advent of writing, Plato foretold the loss of memory. People were equally uneasy with the introduction of print. Both fears linger in our reluctance "to put it in writing." Computers and television raise essentially the same fears, and David Marc voices many of them in his chapter. He attributes to the new media such ills as "the chronic epidemic of clinical depression, the rising rates of murder, suicide and random violence, the now chronic threats to the family of divorce and child abandonment, the appearance of whole new psychosomatic ailments (notably Epstein-Barr syndrome)." These fears may be well-founded, but our response to the new media, as scholars and teachers, is really what is important.

We are indeed faced with responsibilities as we enter the latest language revolution. We will need to understand memory and delivery as important parts of a full rhetoric. We will need to develop what I. A. Richards called a "defensive rhetoric" to guard against the obvious evils of the new media. But more importantly, we will need to learn how to draw on its resources to enlighten and enrich our own and others' lives. And before we can do either, we will have to turn our attention to the nuances of rhetorical memory and delivery in light of the new electronic media if we are to understand how they affect our lives and the many messages that we send and receive.

1 Memory Issues in Composition Studies

John Frederick Reynolds
Old Dominion University

> *Now let us turn . . . to the custodian of all the parts of rhetoric, memory.*
> —*Rhetorica Ad Herennium*

COMING TO TERMS WITH THE "PROBLEM" CANONS IN CLASSICAL RHETORIC

If the five-part construct at the core of the body of work called "classical rhetoric" is not the most *essential* feature of "the most complete critical system that has ever been devised for the analysis and production of discourse" (Welch, "Classical" 3), then certainly it is the most *tenacious*. For nearly 2,500 years it has survived attacks and misrepresentations, accomodated the views of the strictest constructionists and most liberal interpreters, and managed to remain pertinent to Western rhetorical theory despite fundamental cultural transitions from orality to literacy to electronic technology. On this an unusually wide range of scholars seem to agree.

The five classical canons (alternatively called the parts, faculties, functions, categories, or divisions) of rhetoric emerge as "the most constant and recurring features in systematic treatments of the art" (Scaglione 14). They continue to constitute "the basic pattern of all theoretical and critical investigations into rhetorical art and practice" (Thonssen et al. 86). These five fundamental rhetorical issues—invention (content, discovery), disposition (arrangement, organization), style (diction, elocution), memory (mnemotechniques), and delivery (voice/gesture, presentation)—were canonized in Latin rhetoric as *inventio, dispositio, elocutio, memoria,* and *pronuntiatio* or *actio,* and were known in Greek rhetoric as *heurisis, taxis, lexis, mneme,* and *hypokrisis.* Their exact origin is unknown, but the five recur in rhetorical treatises from antiquity to the present, where they always seem to command—individually, if not collectively—the most serious scholarly attention.

The study of rhetoric, most seem to agree, is essentially the study of rhetoric's five canons. They are "the sub-disciplines of the main, the lesser arts of the greater" (Connors 64). They provide a structure that allows rhetors and rhetoricians to analyze and study separately the various parts of a complete rhetorical system (Murphy, *Synoptic* 83). In classical rhetoric, the canons represented the process followed by rhetors as they composed pieces of discourse (Crowley 1). In modern rhetoric, they represent "the aspects of composing which work together in a recursive, synergistic, mutually dependent relationship" (Welch, "Platonic" 5–6). A "classical" theory of composition is, ultimately, a theory of composition based on invention, arrangement, style, memory, and delivery (Murphy, *Short History* 225).

The canons have both practical and theoretical aspects (Crowley 2; Kennedy 63); they apply to both encoding and decoding, forming a complete system for both generating and analyzing discourse (Welch, "Ideology" 270). They represent "not only the concepts with which rhetors must deal and which they must master, but also the aspects of rhetorical acts which critics examine and evaluate" (Thonssen et al. 86). In part, the very history of rhetoric can be characterized by shifts in the relative importance of the various canons (Crowley 1), by "changing relationships and interrelationships between them" (Mahony 14). Throughout Western history, given rhetorical systems have concentrated on one or more of the canons and virtually ignored the others (Crowley 1). In speech studies, "minor changes in the meanings of the five terms have been developed in various treatises over the years, but the pattern remains the same" (Thonssen et al. 86). In composition studies, the five canons are one of two primary theories that dominate the discipline (Welch, "Ideology" 269)—the other being the modes of discourse.

Both disciplines' textbooks, however, have for too many years presented unconscious, imbedded, implicit, partial, or oversimplified versions of the canons (Reynolds, "Teaching" 70), as if it did not matter. Chronically, perhaps unintentionally, the authors of these textbooks have for decades promoted a truncated version of the five classical canons—a version focusing enormous attention on invention, arrangement, and style issues, but ignoring, misrepresenting, or failing to engage memory and delivery issues.[1] Almost never is the original five-part scheme presented completely or explicitly in any of the hundreds of textbooks used to teach oral and written communication. (The sole exception to the rule appears to be Winifred Bryan Horner's 1988 composition

---

[1]Conventional textbook treatments of memory and delivery issues are thus quite consistent with the three "interpretive options" for classical issues in general which Kathleen Welch describes in "The Platonic Paradox" and *The Contemporary Reception of Classical Rhetoric:* (a) ignore them, (b) reduce/misrepresent them, or (c) engage them.

textbook for St. Martin's Press, *Rhetoric in the Classical Tradition*.[2]) In speech studies, the fourth canon—memory—has virtually been dropped from the textbooks, and delivery usually receives incidental treatment, if any (Thonssen et al. 87). In composition studies, the first three canons—invention, arrangement, and style—are used to organize the materials presented in the vast majority of the textbooks, but the last two—memory and delivery—are typically ignored or, worse, deleted without a word of explanation (Welch, *Contemporary;* "Ideology" 270; "Platonic" 5). This deletion, when it *has* been acknowledged, discussed, and explained (elsewhere, of course, not in the textbooks themselves), has been attributed to changed conditions in the law courts (Kennedy 105); to memory's absorption under disposition (Crowley; Kennedy 210; Mahony 14)[3]; and, most often, to the Western world's transition from orality to literacy.[4]

Largely because of this long-standing textbook tradition, the tendency has been for modern rhetorical theory to abandon, remove, neglect, ignore, limit, simplify, misrepresent, and/or misunderstand both memory and delivery. On the other hand, though, memory and delivery have always been problematical (Connors 64; Welch, "Electrifying" 31) and, of the five canons, memory has always been the canon that received the least attention (Carruthers 8, 160; Corbett 38)—despite the fact, ironically, that memory was regarded by the ancients as "the noblest of the canons, the basis for the rest" (Carruthers 9).

In composition studies of late, memory issues have been ignored or dismissed even more so than delivery issues (at least explicitly). To some extent this is not especially surprising; delivery is the more readily revived of the two "problem canons," both theoretically and practically. It is easier to reconceptualize and employ "delivery" issues in composition studies than it is to reconceptualize and

---

[2]As of this writing, Horner's *Rhetoric in the Classical Tradition* is the only writing textbook on the market that overtly and explicitly employs the complete five-part canonical construct. Sam Dragga and Gwendolyn Gong's award-winning *Editing: The Design of Rhetoric* employs "the canons of rhetoric" as its organizing device, but only four canons are presented: Memory is never mentioned, even though "memorableness" is analyzed as an aspect of delivery (16).

[3]In her award-winning book *The Methodical Memory,* Sharon Crowley offers a rich, detailed, and compelling analysis of how "canon absorption" climaxed in current-traditional rhetoric. Crowley argues that memory, "a crucial component of any introspective theory of invention" (21), became "a theory of composing" when combined with "method" (45). The resulting "methodical memory" combined memory, invention, and arrangement and led to "EDNA," the modes of discourse, the "situations which become genres" (134), the essence of current-traditional rhetoric. Crowley shows that at one point in this process memory, invention, and arrangement were all absorbed by style (121).

[4]See Crowley (1), Corbett (39), Welch ("Platonic" 9), and Reynolds ("Computer-Assisted" 101) for representative examples of variations on this theme. See Carruthers (10–12, 17–18, 170), however, for an important and well-argued challenge to the whole orality-to-literacy hypothesis. Carruthers offers at least one alternative explanation for memory's demise: The classifying of memory and delivery as "technical" (rather than "philosophical") parts of rhetoric by historians "may have contributed to the impression that *memoria*, being merely technical, was limited in its applicability to the conditions of oral debate, as was Delivery" (13).

employ "memory" issues. Rethinking delivery requires less of an interpretive leap, and there are fewer interpretive options. Rethinking delivery simply requires that one see equivalencies between oral, written, and electronic *pronuntiatio* and *actio*—analogies between voice/gesture and layout/typography, for example—something that composition specialists focused on technical and computer-assisted writing have been doing with considerable ease for some time now.[5] Rethinking memory, however, requires that one first correct the record and challenge the firmly entrenched and faulty assumption that memory issues are limited to "memorizing the speech," and therefore without written or electronic equivalents. At least part of the responsibility for that assumption must be borne, ironically, by classical rhetoric's best-known and most distinguished modern advocate, Edward P. J. Corbett.

CORRECTING THE RECORD
ABOUT CLASSICAL MEMORY

> *How greatly we misunderstand when we reduce ancient and medieval memoria to our word "memorization."*
> —Mary Carruthers, *The Book of Memory*

Corbett's *Classical Rhetoric for the Modern Student* (1965) marked the beginning of renewed interest in classical rhetoric and, consequently, renewed interest in all of its rhetorical canons, including memory and delivery. Ironically, in all editions of his influential book (1965, 1971, 1991) Corbett revived the canon of memory only long enough to dismiss it, to define it as "memorizing," and then to exclude it from further analysis and consideration:

The fourth part of rhetoric was *memoria* (Greek, *mneme*), concerned with the memorizing of speeches. Of all the five parts of rhetoric, *memoria* was the one that

---

[5]Examples of recent work on layout/typography/design issues in writing and the teaching of writing are abundant, most especially when the focus is on technical or computer-assisted writing. See Rosemary Hampton's article on graphics in the Fall 1990 issue of the *Rhetoric Society Quarterly,* Sam Dragga's article on pictorial illustrations in the Spring 1992 issue of the *Technical Communication Quarterly,* and the entire December 1990 issue of *College English* for representative examples. Clearly there is an emerging consensus that "the meaning of a text derives not only from its verbal content, but also from its graphic devices—script, page layout, the surface written upon" (Chartier). Horner (*Rhetoric*), Dragga and Gong (*Editing*), and Reynolds ("Computer-Assisted") explicitly refer to these concerns as "delivery" issues. Sullivan openly considers the possibility: "Can word publishing be usefully described as a contemporary resurgence of the ancient rhetorical canon of delivery?" ("Taking"). Lanham ("Digital") argues that typography/design issues inevitably revive classical concerns, but he does not specifically refer to classical delivery. The earliest contemporary reconsideration of delivery issues in composition studies appears to have been Robert Connors's 1983 article "*Actio:* A Rhetoric of Manuscripts" for *Rhetoric Review.*

received the least attention in the rhetoric books. The reason for the neglect of this aspect of rhetoric is probably that not much can be said, in a theoretical way, about the process of memorizing; and after rhetoric came to be concerned mainly with written discourse, there was no further need to deal with memorizing. . . . There will be no consideration in this book of this aspect of rhetoric. (38)

Corbett's discussion of the canon of delivery was somewhat more elaborate, but similar in its interpretive stance: "Understandably enough, discussions of delivery, as well as of memory, tended to be even more neglected in rhetoric texts after the invention of printing, when most rhetorical training was directed primarily to written discourse" (39). Given his enormous status and influence in composition studies,[6] his awareness of the interest in memory issues that had been sparked in large part by his work, and his discussion elsewhere of some of the new thinking about memory (and delivery) issues that had emerged since the publication of his first and second editions,[7] Corbett's unrevised and repeated dismissal of memory in his third edition was most unfortunate and really quite curious.

Important work by Frances Yates, Mary Carruthers, and Patrick Mahony, however, has fundamentally challenged the notion that classical "memory" was limited to "memorizing." Frances A. Yates's *The Art of Memory* (1966) gave the fourth rhetorical canon one of its most thorough and expansive analyses to date. Yates traced complex, multiple, interrelated notions of rhetorical memory to antiquity. The classical art, she explained, had involved much more than memorizing: It had included improving the memory (2), imprinting on the memory (3), memorizing in order (3, 7), making memorable (9), holding in memory (12), retrieving from memory (34), delivering from memory (6), and preserving in memory (45). Memory, she noted, had been viewed in antiquity as being critical to invention (5, 12, 34, 45), arrangement (3, 4, 7), style (8), and delivery (6, 7). Memory was the *loci* of the *topoi* for Aristotle (31), and the connection to the divinity of the soul for Plato (36, 37). Memory was the custodian of all the parts

---

[6]To cite only one example of Ed Corbett's influence, Sharon Crowley dedicated *The Methodical Memory* to him, cited his *Classical Rhetoric for the Modern Student* as a marker of "the revival of interest in classical rhetoric," and even attributed the "stimulation" of the "process" movement to that revival (181).

[7]In his foreword to Win Horner's *Rhetoric in the Classical Tradition,* for example, which he described as "the most sensible and fruitful adaptation of classical rhetoric available today for the undergraduate classroom" (vii), Corbett had this to say about the textbook's treatments of memory and delivery: "Horner has found a way to restore attention to memory and delivery, even in a writing class. . . . [She] shows us how we can resort to [sources] other than our own memory banks . . . [and] she shows us the written equivalent of the oral delivery system for the ancient Greeks and Romans" (vi). These remarks, which clearly demonstrate Corbett's awareness and approval of approaches to memory and delivery other than his own, were published in 1988—three years before the publication of the third edition of *Classical Rhetoric for the Modern Student.* How puzzling it is, then, that his third edition did not acknowledge, include, challenge, or react in some way to these developments.

of rhetoric to the author of *Ad Herennium* (5), proof of the soul's divinity to Cicero (45), the source of oratory's power to Quintilian (43), the "groundwork of the whole" to Plato (37), and the key to invention to Aristotle (34). Yates's work encouraged and historically validated complex, multidimensional notions of memory as a rhetorical canon.

Similarly, Mary Carruthers's *The Book of Memory* (1990) confirmed that for "the ancients and their medieval heirs" (29) the art of memory had involved much more than rote memorization techniques (106, 208). The classical art, she showed, was rooted in a complex "neuropsychology of storage and recollection" (46) involving both encoder and decoder (13) in highly visual coding and ordering strategies. Memory work was seen as being critically important to invention (20, 26, 197), arrangement (33), delivery (208), *ethos* (68, 182), *logos* (104), and audience (181). Classical discussions of memory, Carruthers noted, consistently reveal that the ancients had a highly sophisticated awareness of the complex interrelationships between writing/reading, collecting/recollecting, and composition/division (19, 25, 27, 30, 72, 166, 189–92, 243). These discussions, she revealed, persistently relied on two metaphorical models, both of them traceable to Plato (21, 33)—perhaps even to the Presocratics (221)—and both of them steeped not in orality but in *literacy:* memory as "a tablet for *writing*," and memory as "a storehouse for *books*." These metaphors, Carruthers wrote, are "so ancient and so persistent that [they] must, I think, be seen as a governing model or 'cognitive archetype'" (16); they "change slightly over the centuries to reflect the most common form of writing materials, but [their] tenacity in Western thought is remarkable" (28).[8]

Patrick Mahony's "McLuhan in the Light of Classical Rhetoric" (1969) offered one of composition studies' first analyses of rhetorical memory as more than memorizing. Mahony argued that Marshall McLuhan had contributed to the evolution of the canons by revealing a vital alliance between memory and delivery: "In terms of videotapes, phonograph records, and indexed books, to go no further, memory or information storage has been exteriorized into new media or forms of pronunciation" (14). Mahony insisted that McLuhan had revealed memory to be not only storage but also psychology. "He sees," Mahony wrote (citing a McLuhan discussion of Yates that had referred to the unconscious as "the greatest of all possible memory theatres"), ". . . a oneness of memory, electronic technology, and the human unconscious" (15). Mahony's analysis foreshadowed

---

[8]Composition studies specialists would do well to closely examine some of the fascinating parallels between ancient *memoria* and contemporary composition traced by Carruthers in her book—for example, that the classical ability to "compose" was both process and product of rhetorical education (44), that the process had to be individualized (64), that the "composer" had to learn multiple strategies and styles (206), and that "composing" training focused on multiple rather than final "drafts" (205). *The Book of Memory* even suggests classical analogues to Connors's "manuscript *actio*" (256), Flower's "chunking" strategy (84), Bolter's work on hypertext (194), and Welch's dialectical vision of writing (169).

the subsequent emergence of at least four interrelated approaches to memory in modern composition studies: memory as mnemonics, memory as memorableness, memory as databases, and memory as psychology.

FOUR INTERPRETIVE OPTIONS
FOR RESTORING THE CANON OF MEMORY
TO COMPOSITION STUDIES[9]

Memory is the gathering together in the soul of words and themes for composition.

—Julius Victor, *Ars Rhetorica*

Memory as Mnemonics

The classical art of memory included the study of, and the use of, mnemonics or "mnemotechnics" (Yates xi) to facilitate thinking, retention, and recall. These mnemonics were employed for both macro- and microrhetorical purposes. As Yates noted, rhetors of antiquity employed mnemonics designed to remind them of points and sequences (3, 8), as well as mnemonics designed to remind them of words (8). The former were primarily architectural in nature (4); the latter, as Walter Ong and Eric Havelock sought to demonstrate, were primarily acoustic. Ong hypothesized the oral ("pre-literate") poet's dependence on both types of mnemonics, with the acoustic dominating:

> In a primary oral culture, to solve effectively the problem of retaining and retrieving carefully articulated thought, you have to do your thinking in mnemonic patterns, shaped for ready oral recurrence. Your thought must come into being in heavily rhythmic, balanced patterns, in repetitions or antitheses, in alliterations and assonances, in epithetic and other formulary expressions, in standard thematic settings (the assembly, the meal, the duel, the hero's "helper," and so on), in proverbs which are constantly heard by everyone so that they come to mind readily and which themselves are patterned for retention and ready recall, or in other mnemonic form. Serious thought is intertwined with memory systems. Mnemonic needs determine even syntax. (34)

Both Ong and Havelock argued that the Western world's transition from oral dominance to writing dominance altered, rather than eliminated, the use of mnemonics. Ong described the alphabet, for example, as "a major bridge between oral and literate mnemonics" (100). Havelock called the transition from

---

[9]What I have tried to do here is offer a representative cross-section of implicit/explicit, practical/theoretical, textbook/nontextbook treatments illustrating each of the interpretive options at work. My collection of examples is by no means exhaustive.

orality to literacy a transition from echo to sequence (*Muse* 73), from oral syntax to literate syntax (108), from ear-and-mouth to eye (99).[10] His work theorized that literacy prompted not the decline of architectural and acoustic mnemonics but, rather, "an alteration in the ratio" (*Literate* 9).

The rhetorical trend toward "sight mnemonics," as Havelock referred to them, had major implications for writers: "Put in terms of compositional technique . . . the process is one in which language managed acoustically on echo principles is met with competition from language managed visually on architectural principles" (*Literate* 9). The difference between oral and written discourse is "essentially a shift from sound to visual space," with the use of visual space becoming "the central, though not the only, focus of attention" (Ong 117). Writers set up sequences defined not by sound but by space: beginnings, middles, and ends of words, lines, paragraphs, and texts; pages of lines moving top to bottom and left to right; headings, chapters, and references; aboves and belows. "All this is quite a different world of order," Ong insisted, "from anything in the oral sensibility" (100).

A number of people in modern composition studies now call for training writers and readers in this visual sensibility. Some suggest heightening reader consciousness of space-defined sequence; others call for training writers in the use of sight mnemonics. Connors, for example, has imagined "a rhetoric of manuscripts," one in which writers use visual mnemonics to ensure reader attention, interest, and comprehension (69–71). I have reported success teaching writers "to notice extra-textual features in others' work and to use them in their own . . . to provide a mnemonic dimension for readers" (Reynolds, "Computer-Assisted" 104).[11] Marilyn Sternglass's textbook *Reading, Writing, and Reasoning* (1983) was built on the thesis that "perceptive writing derives from effective reading"—that clearly "there is a relation between reading and writing . . . not only from the standpoint of *what* is read but of *how* a given piece is read" (ix)—and, consequently, on a reading/writing model rooted in the retrieval of prior knowledge, the comparison of text and expectations, and the stimulation of prediction strategies (x). Winifred Bryan Horner's *Rhetoric in the Classical Tradition* (1988) teaches mnemonic strategies (explicitly for readers, implicitly for writers) in its "memory" chapter:

> Topic sentences and thesis statements introduce main segments of discourse and contain main ideas that are developed through examples and details. By skimming such sentences, you can usually ascertain the writer's basic arguments. Often an introduction will state the proposition or main idea just as the conclusion will

---

[10]Again, see Carruthers for a well-developed challenge to the acoustical-to-architectural, earmindedness-to-eyemindedness hypothesis.

[11]Sullivan ("Desktop") has reported similar results: "This emphasis on the visual dimension of writing [has] improved the quality of my students' work and their ability to discuss the visual dimensions of meaning" (346).

present a summary of the author's arguments. Scanning such elements can help you to eliminate material germane to your subject. So, it helps to read first and last paragraphs and to search out theses and topic sentences that introduce main ideas and sections. . . . Also, visual signals such as indentation for paragraphs, headings in different type size or color, numeral or letter headings all indicate introduction of a new idea. Topic and thesis sentences are often found at these junctures. (347)

Connors's notions about manuscript *actio,* my own about extratextual features, Sternglass's about writer/reader text expectations, and Horner's about skimming and scanning were all early manifestations of an approach to memory in composition studies which imagines memory as the use of mnemonics. A second but related approach imagines *memoria/mneme* as making written texts memorable.

Memory as Memorableness

Mnemonics make written words, ideas, phrases, and arrangements memorable so that they might, as Yates put it, "help memory" (10). Yates traced this concept of memory, too, to antiquity, to "one of the most curious and surprising passages" (9) in *Ad Herennium:*

> Now nature itself teaches us what we should do. When we see in every day life things that are petty, ordinary, and banal, we generally fail to remember them, because the mind is not being stirred by anything novel or marvellous. But if we see or hear something exceptionally base, dishonorable, unusual, great, unbelievable, or ridiculous, that we are likely to remember for a long time . . . ordinary things easily slip from the memory while the striking and the novel stay longer in the mind. . . . Thus nature shows that she is not aroused by the common ordinary event, but is moved by a new or striking occurrence. Let art, then, imitate nature. (9–10)

Ong also confirmed the interrelationship between the memorable and the mnemonic in his work analyzing oral-formulaic poetry: "How could you ever call back to mind what you had so laboriously worked out? The only answer is: Think memorable thoughts" (34). Today, many of the voices advising student writers echo Ong's advice.

A notion of memory as making writing memorable resonates, for example, throughout the various editions of *The St. Martin's Guide to Writing.* Rise Axelrod and Charles Cooper's best-selling textbook begins with multiple exercises in writing about memorable persons and events. Writing memorably, it argues, is an essential strategy in both college and professional writing, because every type of nonfiction prose relies to some extent on storytelling (20). The key to mastering this essential narrative strategy, it advises, then, is to "shape the experience into a story that is entertaining and memorable" (45). In one chapter

Axelrod and Cooper tell their readers/writers that they must search their memories for memorable situations (50), include memorable details (54) that will paint memorable pictures (55), highlight memorable phrases (56), and revise for more memorable language (58). In another they recommend that writers keep journals of memorable sentences and passages (377). Imbedded throughout the various chapters of many currently popular writing textbooks like *The St. Martin's Guide* is an implicit notion of memory as the development of memorable subjects, words, phrases, sentences, passages, and texts. Similarly imbedded is a notion of memory as a set of information databases.

Memory as Databases

The St. Martin's Guide, for example, defines invention as "searching your memory and discovering the possibilities for your subject" (88). It recurringly recommends, as an invention strategy, the use of questions designed to stimulate memory (5, 90). Yates traced this approach to memory, too, to antiquity, to *Ad Herennium*'s distinction between natural and artificial memory: "The natural memory is that which is engrafted in our minds" (5) and "the artificial memory [is that which is] used, not only to memorize speeches, but to hold in memory a mass of material which can be looked up at will" (12).[12] The classical distinction between natural and artificial memory continues to be of interest in contemporary composition studies, as work like Rick Cypert's "Memory: A Step Toward Invention" (1987) has shown. In his work, Cypert identified "two essential types of memory in freshman composition students": the natural memory, which leads to narrative, and the artificial memory, which encourages the analytical. "The two forms of memory prove interdependent," Cypert reported, "and students need to be aware of that and encouraged to regard memory as an essential part of the inventive process."

In addition to a natural/artificial memory distinction, a short-term/long-term memory distinction has also proved useful in contemporary composition research examining memory's relationship to invention. Richard Young and Patricia Sullivan, for example, suggested that our very motive for writing lies in limits on the capacity of our short-term memory, and that "a modern art of memory might provide explicit strategies for increasing the power of short-term memory and accessing long-term memory more effectively" (225).[13] George Hillocks's important 1986 research compilation and meta-analysis, *Research on Written Composition,* reported bodies of research suggesting that in the composing process short-term memory contains information that guides style (59, 60, 226) and long-

---

[12]As I thank my linguist colleague Charles Ruhl for pointing out, the imitation of models in classical rhetorical instruction (most especially the imitation of stylistic tropes and figures) was based on the belief that imitation would internalize these structures and patterns in artificial memory.

[13]Young and Sullivan offer the disclaimer, however, that "a 'modern art of memory' might be only another name for an art of invention approached from a new and interesting direction" (225).

term memory preserves information that guides ideas and structures (19, 21). Linda Flower and John Hayes's research has been especially revealing about a vital link between memory and composing. It has suggested the presence in long-term memory of generalized writing plans which appear to be important in guiding discourse production (Hillocks 19). Their work has argued that both short- and long-term memory play critical roles in the composing subprocesses: planning, goal-setting, translating, and generating, for example (21).

Much of the research on memory's function as a repository for information guiding intervention, arrangement, and style has been translated into contemporary composition pedagogy—in Flower's *Problem-Solving Strategies for Writing,* for example. Flower's textbook advises its writer/reader to resist the temptation to invent by "memory dump" (83–84), to rely instead on "memory networks" that can function as "the raw material for later planning" (68–69). In addition, it makes explicit distinctions between short- and long-term memory, and offers a "chunking" strategy that writers can use to help their readers compensate for the limitations of short-term memory (168–71).

Memory also proves to be "inextricably bound" to creativity and invention in Horner's *Rhetoric in the Classical Tradition.*[14] Horner's textbook advises students that memory is central to writing:

> Writers can draw on their own personal experiences in their writing. So enlarging and enriching what you store in your memory is important. Modern rhetoric, however, must add another dimension to the concept of memory. In addition to the individual memory, there are a number of sophisticated ways of storing cultural knowledge in books, libraries, computers, and databases. (338)

Rhetoric in the Classical Tradition then generates pedagogy from an approach to memory issues that derives from an explicit distinction between

> two kinds of memory: the cultural memory and the individual memory. As the classical rhetoricians devised ways to store and retrieve information from the human memory, the modern rhetorician must also consider ways to retrieve information from books, libraries, and computers. (339)

What especially distinguishes Horner's treatment of memory from others like it, though, is her overt use of the five-part canonical scheme as the organizing principle for her textbook.[15]

---

[14]See Enos ("Review"): "Horner's view that technology has externalized the storage of information from within the writer does not diminish her emphasis of memory's importance but rather extends its parameters. In fact, students will be struck by the observation that memory is inextricably bound to creativity (373) and, correspondingly, familiarization with and access to information as the basis for invention" (170).

[15]Horner's overt restoration of memory and delivery was nothing short of a "unique contribution" (Enos 170) that made "rhetorical history" (Reynolds, "Redefining" 202).

Memory as Psychology

"Perhaps the most important connection that memory as a canon of rhetoric gives us," Kathleen Welch has argued, "is its explicit pointing to psychology" ("Platonic" 7). "While the canon of memory is certainly not the only approach to psychology and discourse," Welch has acknowledged, "it remains an important one." In contemporary composition studies, memory and psychology now resonate in at least three important ways since Mahony first suggested the connection in 1969. First, Carruthers's work and Flower and Hayes's work have demonstrated an important connection between memory and cognitive/neuropsychology. Second, Ong's work, as well as Havelock's, has speculated about connections between memory changes and subsequent alterations in the formation of psychological consciousness. Third, Welch has argued that memory is central to Plato's rhetoric as a sort of collective psychological unconscious linking present to past (8), that it is memory that creates the "systematic connection between rhetoric and psychology" (7).

This third relationship between memory and psychology is complex, Welch admits, but she has argued that it is critical to recognizing Plato's special contribution to contemporary rhetoric:

> We cannot simply excerpt a few lines—as we do so nicely with Aristotle—and provide a definition of Platonic rhetoric. We have to consult the rhetorical form of Plato's work, the interaction of rhetoric and dialectic, and the psychological activity of the speaker or writer with the listener or reader. The medium of writing (that is, Plato's use of the canon of delivery) and the psychology of discourse (Plato's use of the canon of memory) combine with the canons of invention, arrangement, and style to provide a Platonic definition of rhetoric. (10)

According to Welch's work, to ignore or delete the memory-as-psychology option, either implicitly or explicitly, is to ignore or misunderstand Plato's unique contribution to composition studies (5).[16]

SOME FINAL THOUGHTS

These various interrelated approaches to memory issues individually and collectively demonstrate that the classical canon of memory is still central to writing

---

[16]See Patrick Hutton's "The Art of Memory Reconceived: From Rhetoric to Psychoanalysis" (1987) for its resonance with Welch's stance on Plato's special contribution: "In the Aristotelian tradition the art of memory was merely instrumental. . . . In the Platonic tradition, however, the powers of memory were judged to be more substantive. Plato taught that mnemic images were directly expressive of a transcendental reality. For the mnemonist who shared these views, the value of a mnemic image was directly tied to the ideal reality that it was empowered to represent. The art of

and reading, that memory remains as important to contemporary composition studies as it was to rhetorical studies in antiquity. With rare exceptions, though, the contemporary connection to the classical scheme is still largely ignored, underestimated, or misunderstood. Discussions of memory issues regularly appear in our writing textbooks and other disciplinary discourses in a variety of forms, but they appear mostly in unconscious, imbedded, or implicit treatments. Most composition teachers today rely on one or more aspects of the classical canon of memory, whether they realize it or not, and this reliance, conscious or unconscious, certainly reconfirms the case for the vitality, flexibility, and relevance of classical rhetoric.[17]

But any discipline's continued reliance on a classical system of five recursive, interrelated, interactive rhetorical canons ought to be a conscious one. Where composition studies are concerned, there are at least two reasons why. First, as Welch has noted, no other system for the production and reception of texts possesses the completeness of classical rhetoric and its definitive connection to systems of education and to cultures ("Electrifying" 32). Second, classical rhetoric offers the added benefit of "its central insight—that the generation and deployment of discourse is intimately related to the possession of cultural power" (Crowley 168).

The "margins" between writing and memory are being "redrawn" (Bolter 57) even as I write or you read this sentence. Those of us working right now in composition studies have a unique historical opportunity to contribute to the redrawing of those margins. We need only keep remembering that memory issues matter.[18]

WORKS CITED

Axelrod, Rise B., and Charles R. Cooper. *The St. Martin's Guide to Writing*. 2nd ed. New York: St. Martin's, 1988. (3rd ed. 1991.)

Bolter, Jay David. *Writing Space: The Computer, Hypertext, and the History of Writing*. Hillsdale, NJ: Lawrence Erlbaum Associates, 1991.

Carruthers, Mary. *The Book of Memory: A Study of Memory in Medieval Culture*. Cambridge: Cambridge UP, 1990.

Chartier, Roger. "Meaningful Forms." *Times Literary Supplement* Oct. 6, 1989: 8–9.

---

memory, therefore, was a way of establishing correspondences between the microcosm of the mind's images and the macrocosm of the ideal universe, which were believed to be congruent structures" (374–75)

[17]See Knoblauch and Brannon, of course, for a wholly alternative view, one asserting that classical rhetoric is as irrelevant to modern life as "witches," "ether," and "foretelling the future from animal entrails" (22). But see also Susan Jarratt's terse response to that view (qtd. in Reynolds, "Teaching" 67), as well as Crowley's explanation for Knoblauch and Brannon's stance (173–74).

[18]An earlier version of this chapter appeared in different form in the *Rhetoric Society Quarterly* in 1989 (see Reynolds "Concepts").

Connors, Robert J. "*Actio:* A Rhetoric of Manuscripts." *Rhetoric Review* 2 (1983): 64–73.

Corbett, Edward P. J. *Classical Rhetoric for the Modern Student.* New York: Oxford UP, 1965. (2nd ed. 1971, 3rd ed. 1991.)

Crowley, Sharon. *The Methodical Memory: Invention in Current-Traditional Rhetoric.* Carbondale: Southern Illinois UP, 1990.

Cypert, Rick. "Memory: A Step Toward Invention." Conference on College Composition and Communication, Atlanta, Mar. 1987. ED280036.

Dragga, Sam, and Gwendolyn Gong. *Editing: The Design of Rhetoric.* Amityville: Baywood, 1990.

Enos, Richard Leo. "Review of Winifred Bryan Horner's *Rhetoric in the Classical Tradition.*" *Rhetoric Review* 7 (1988): 169–70.

Flower, Linda. *Problem-Solving Strategies for Writing.* 3rd ed. San Diego: HBJ, 1989.

Havelock, Eric A. *The Literate Revolution and Its Cultural Consequences.* Princeton: Princeton UP, 1973.

———. *The Muse Learns to Write.* New Haven: Yale UP, 1986.

Hillocks, George, Jr. *Research on Written Composition: New Directions for Teaching.* Urbana: NCRE/ERIC, 1986.

Horner, Winifred Bryan. *Rhetoric in the Classical Tradition.* New York: St. Martin's, 1988.

Hutton, Patrick H. "The Art of Memory Reconceived: From Rhetoric to Psychoanalysis." *Journal of the History of Ideas* 48 (1987): 371–92.

Kennedy, George A. *Classical Rhetoric and Its Christian and Secular Tradition from Ancient to Modern Times.* Chapel Hill: U of North Carolina P, 1980.

Knoblauch, C. H., and Lil Brannon. *Rhetorical Traditions and the Teaching of Writing.* Upper Montclair: Boynton/Cook, 1984.

Lanham, Richard A. "Digital Rhetoric: Theory, Practice, and Property." *Literacy Online: The Promise (and Peril) of Reading and Writing with Computers.* Ed. Myron C. Tuman. Pittsburgh: U of Pittsburgh P, 1992. 221–43.

Mahony, Patrick. "McLuhan in the Light of Classical Rhetoric." *College Composition and Communication* 20 (1969): 12–17.

Murphy, James J., ed. *A Short History of Writing Instruction: From Ancient Greece to Twentieth-Century America.* Davis: Hermagoras, 1990.

———. *A Synoptic History of Classical Rhetoric.* Davis: Hermagoras, 1983.

Ong, Walter J. *Orality and Literacy: The Technologizing of the Word.* New York: Methuen, 1982.

Reynolds, John Frederick. "Classical Rhetoric and Computer-Assisted Composition: Extra-Textual Features as 'Delivery.'" *Computer-Assisted Composition Journal* 3 (1989): 101–07.

———. "Classical Rhetoric and the Teaching of Technical Writing." *Technical Communication Quarterly* 1 (1992): 63–76.

———. "Concepts of Memory in Contemporary Composition." *Rhetoric Society Quarterly* 19 (1989): 245–52.

———. "Redefining 'the Classical Tradition' in a New Writing Textbook." Rev. of Winifred Bryan Horner's *Rhetoric in the Classical Tradition. Rhetoric Society Quarterly* 18 (1988): 201–03.

Scaglione, Aldo. *The Classical Theory of Composition.* Chapel Hill: U of North Carolina P, 1972.

Sternglass, Marilyn S. *Reading, Writing, and Reasoning.* New York: Macmillan, 1983.

Sullivan, Patricia. "Desktop Publishing: A Powerful Tool for Advanced Composition Courses." *College Composition and Communication* 39 (1988): 344–47.

———. "Taking Control of the Page: Electronic Writing and Word Publishing." *Evolving Perspectives on Computers and Composition Studies: Questions for the 1990s.* Eds. Gail E. Hawisher and Cynthia L. Selfe. Urbana: NCTE, 1991. 43–64.

Thonssen, Lester A., A. Craig Baird, and Waldo W. Braden. *Speech Criticism.* 2nd ed. New York: Ronald, 1970.

Welch, Kathleen E. "Classical Rhetoric and Contemporary Writing Pedagogy: Orality, Literacy, and the Historicizing of Composition." Conference on College Composition and Communication, St. Louis, Mar. 1988.

————. *The Contemporary Reception of Classical Rhetoric: Appropriations of Ancient Discourse.* Hillsdale, NJ: Lawrence Erlbaum Associates, 1990.

————. "Electrifying Classical Rhetoric: Ancient Media, Modern Technology, and Contemporary Composition." *Journal of Advanced Composition* 10 (1990): 22–38.

————. "Ideology and Freshman Textbook Production: The Place of Theory in Writing Pedagogy." *College Composition and Communication* 38 (1987): 269–82.

————. "The Platonic Paradox: Plato's Rhetoric in Contemporary Rhetoric and Composition Studies." *Written Communication* 5 (1988): 3–21.

Yates, Frances A. *The Art of Memory.* Chicago: U of Chicago P, 1966.

Young, Richard, and Patricia Sullivan. "Why Write: A Reconsideration." *Essays on Classical Rhetoric and Modern Discourse.* Eds. Robert J. Connors, Lisa S. Ede, and Andrea A. Lunsford. Carbondale: Southern Illinois UP, 1984. 215–25.

2 Reconfiguring Writing and Delivery in Secondary Orality

Kathleen E. Welch
University of Oklahoma

> *The students who come to us now exist in the most manipulative culture human beings have ever experienced. They are bombarded with signs, with rhetoric, from their daily awakenings until their troubled sleep, especially with signs transmitted by the audio-visual media. And, for a variety of reasons, they are relatively deprived of experience in the thoughtful reading and writing of verbal texts. They are also sadly deficient in certain kinds of historical knowledge that might give them some perspective on the manipulation that they currently encounter.*
> —Robert Scholes, *Textual Power*

THE SUPPRESSION OF MEMORY, DELIVERY, AND IDEOLOGY

The five functions (*erga* in Greek, *officia* in Latin) or canons of classical rhetoric have, remarkably, maintained a long life in different guises, a life I have examined elsewhere as having exerted an enormous and largely unrecognized claim on the issues that drive the teaching of writing in North America and the positioning of Plato in current rhetoric and composition theory.[1] Invention, arrangement, style, memory, and delivery (the standard English translations of the *erga*) have recurred in different forms and with different emphases in varying historical eras. Their tendency toward completeness, interaction, and interdependence in both

---

[1]See "Ideology and Freshman Textbook Production: The Place of Theory in Writing Pedagogy," in which I analyze the canons of rhetoric as they are repeated in writing textbook after textbook, and *The Contemporary Reception of Classical Rhetoric* (95–100), in which I examine some of the consequences of removing memory and delivery from Plato's rhetoric. In both places, I attempt to show what happens to a strong theory when it is unacknowledged and how this absence of recognition leads to major interpretive problems, in one case for theory-unconscious textbooks and in the other case for understanding Plato's rhetoric in current rhetoric and composition studies.

Greek and Roman classical rhetoric provided one of the sources of rhetoric's power in those eras and cultures. Later, however, individual canons were more frequently incorporated, according to one particular ideology or another, into other canons and then seemed to disappear. In our own century, the canons' enormous and largely unacknowledged power has occurred in the reliance of writing pedagogy on textbooks that truncate the five canons from five to three, so that invention, arrangement (form), and style repeatedly colonize the last two—memory and delivery—and then eradicate them.

It is crucial to an understanding of Western literacy at this millenium to recognize that the disappearance of memory and delivery is not a benign removal; rather, it is part of a larger movement in the United States to pablumize the humanities in general, and to vitiate writing in particular by behaving as if it were a mere skill, craft, or useful tool. The writing-as-tool metaphor, in fact, recurs in composition textbooks, in many discussions of writing, and in many generally held assumptions about why writing is "good for you." It occurs even in discussions among some writing specialists in the discipline of English. If writing is a tool, then it is part of the Cartesian reality in which we all continue to live. A tool is a thing out there in the world, a palpable object that one can store in the garage and retrieve as necessary. A tool can be put aside; language cannot. The persistence of the tool metaphor reveals a great deal about how language is regarded; it is a metaphor that needs to be examined and replaced.

Many issues of culture, ideology, society, and the construction of public and private lives reside in the functions of memory and delivery; public and private realms are routinely and tacitly regarded not as a construction, but as palpably, "obviously" separate entities. The elimination of memory and delivery in the majority of student writing textbooks constitutes the removal of student-written language from the larger public arena. The removal reinforces the common, dualistic idea that students live outside ideology if they choose to do so, just as they are outside language if they choose to be. The memory and delivery exision fits well, as I have noted elsewhere, with the formalist appeal of much twentieth-century writing instruction, especially current-traditional writing. In addition, it accomodates well the formalist approaches to the study of literary texts (Literature with a capital L), removing Great Books from the taint of "real life" and the murkiness that exists there in the formation of power relations and in other ways. The come-let-us-glow-together school (sometimes called the Truth and Beauty School) of literary interpretation cannot allow the public, the contested, the political, to enter the study of the Great Books, except insofar as those issues appear as dead (that is, resolved) conflicts. This school's proponents claim that the study of literary texts is apolitical.

Although traditionalists in literary studies do not, as far as I know, explicitly treat the canons of rhetoric (truncated or otherwise), they do tend to suppress questions of ideology and the ways that all writers and readers are entwined in it. So do many teachers of writing. In a persistent call to the aim of the moment, the revision-is-good-for-you rhetorical stance, and other hallmarks of skill-bound writing instruction (in its current-traditional manifestation and in the more powerful and helpful "process" schools), student writers and the teachers who share this stance tend to place themselves outside, not inside, of language. It is this suppression of ideology and the attempt to stand outside language that provide two of the connections between traditional literary study and the traditional study of writing. Memory and delivery interfere with the writing process and its privileging of invention and the thoughts and feelings of the writer; to this extent they are dangerous to the status quo of the process movement, both expressivist and cognitivist.

A standard explanation for the removal of memory and delivery from the five canons relies on a simplistic idea that the burgeoning power of writing made memory and delivery less relevant because those two canons are said to be more powerful in orally dominant cultures. This is not the case. Memory and delivery do not wither with the growing dominance of writing; rather, they change form. The interiorization of writing did in fact have profound effects, but the split between the oral and the written is not as convenient as many commentators would have it. With the increasing empowerment of writing, memory and delivery took on different attributes. Elsewhere I have connected memory to psychology and delivery to medium (see, for example, Welch, *Contemporary* 98–100). It is crucial to note that memory and delivery were not afterthoughts as they gradually developed in Greek rhetoric and found fuller expression in, for example, Hermagoras's lost work [which can be construed from later references to it (Kennedy 304)] and in Cicero (particularly in *On the Character of the Orator*).

THE INFLUENCE OF WRITING TEXTBOOKS

Writing textbooks maintain the destructive commitment to three of five canons partly through connection and repetition; the books frequently repeat material that has occurred in other books, partly because new textbooks are contracted according to the publishing genres of the rhetoric, the reader, and the argument book. (Handbooks that provide rules for the writing of dominant-culture English are a separate issue, and do not share the problems discussed here.) These publishing genres have the conventions, constraints, and "rules" that all genres have. They operate in the world of textbook production and consumption, but they do not operate outside of it; in fact, they appear to be hermetically sealed, as other genres can be. Most writing textbooks are based not on new, energizing, and important writing theory but on, simply, the genres of other textbooks. One successful textbook leads to many competitors, each vying for a portion of an already proven market. These markets are based on tried material, on issues that have already worked according to the number of sales they have generated. The room for newness, particularly for the newness of writing theories, is small. As I have argued elsewhere, composition textbooks appear to be driven by publishers who believe that writing teachers desire constructions such as the three canons (or the modes of discourse, or the process-is-terrific stance). However, as Arthur Applebee has pointed out, the textbooks teach the teachers first (127). The putative "desires" of imagined writing teachers are in fact the desires inculcated by theory-unconscious textbooks which too often trivialize writing into a tool marketed to large numbers of paying students, many of whom are taught by instructors with little or no training in the writing theory which would lead them away from the dominant notion of writing as a mere skill.

In these ways and others, the repetition of the truncated canons has taken on a life of its own. Dozens of textbooks present the first three canons—invention, arrangement, and style—as the center of writing concern, a center that is presented as just "there" and not susceptible to examination. The textbooks' continuing reliance on the truncated structure speaks to the tenacity of the canons as a way of producing discourse, and to the mesmerizing effect that theory unconsciousness continues to have on the textbook industry.[2] Other reasons can be found to explain the tenacity of the first three canons. The rigorous suppression of memory and delivery (to provide one historical example) connects as well to the cordoning off of rhetoric enacted by Ramus in the sixteenth century, when he constructed rhetoric in a way that made invention, arrangement, and memory central parts of dialectic and not of rhetoric (Ong).[3] With the removal of these functions from rhetoric, style and a narrow idea of delivery then received more emphasis. The long journey of rhetoric as attenuated style or language decoration gathered great momentum that continues today. In Ramus's powerfully influential construction, rhetoric was diminished by removing canons that were central to it. We continue to work with the results of this legacy.

RECONSTRUCTING MEMORY AND DELIVERY

The construction in this volume and much of the discussion of the five canons link memory and delivery, but a great deal of the research (probably most of it)

---

[2]Fortunately, in recent years, many excellent textbooks have been published that acknowledge the theory that always operates. The problem lies in the continuation of the truncated canons in many of the theory-unconscious textbooks, a symptom of the desire to deprive students and their teachers of the dynamic theory that is taking place now, and to replace it with formulaic guidelines that are boring and that teach student writers to distance themselves from their own writing.

[3]Ong's analysis of Ramus has a great deal to teach us about the rearrangement of power between dialectic (Ramus's version of "logic") and rhetoric. Ong writes: "Ramus' influence is in school or university textbooks, and is perpetuated as part of that great deposit of textbook literature dealing with the most familiar of our ideas which is rewritten in every generation, while remaining so much a part of the universal heritage that no one can believe it has ever changed or even derived from a particular source" (*Ramus* 9).

exists separately. The place of memory has received powerful new interpretations by, among others, Mary Carruthers in *The Book of Memory,* and Jody Enders in "Memory and the Psychology of the Interior Monologue in Chretien's *Cligés*" and "Music, Delivery, and the Rhetoric of Memory in Guillaume de Machaut's *Remède de Fortune.*" And of course Frances A. Yates's *The Art of Memory* remains central. These writers have worked to revise some of the standard arguments about the nature of parts of medieval thought by analyzing the pivotal role of memory in epistemology and so have taught us a great deal about this frequently neglected canon. Sharon Crowley, in *The Methodical Memory: Invention in Current-Traditional Rhetoric,* has analyzed systems of invention and how constructions of memory enabled those systems to operate forcefully. Work on memory and writing in our own era needs careful attention, as other chapters in this volume indicate. The idea of memory as consciousness and the connection of memory to psychology (cognitive and depth, to name two kinds) continues to be an important area in the theory, practice, and production of discourse.[4] Nevertheless, memory largely has been forgotten. One site of the erasure of memory has been in most of the writing textbooks that remain so powerful in our culture. I will not forget memory here but will instead go on to treat delivery (Latin *actio,* Greek *hypokrisis*) and its status as medium.

The ways in which I want to think about delivery here center on the ways that it has been reconstructed through electronic forms of discourse. Delivery in its life as medium has acquired enormous power in the twentieth century. I want to suggest connections between the canon and the (mostly unconscious) theory of representative writing textbooks. In addition, I hope to offer some suggestions about one strategy for reorganizing the humanities—one that is dangerous in many ways—rather than perpetuating its current life as a wizened, toothless being that is acknowledged as important and then sharply ignored. In other words, I hope to make the connection between the crucial placement of writing as a central form of articulation in our time and dominant culture and as a center for the re-creation of the humanities away from the pabulumized, weekend diversion that it now appears to be in the dominant culture.

Delivery is weakened if it refers only to the gesture, physical movement, and expression that many commentators have dismissed it as doing. It includes this aspect of communication in person, but it includes much more as well. Elsewhere, following Patrick Mahony's explication of Marshall McLuhan in "Marshall McLuhan in the Light of Classical Rhetoric," I have elaborated on the canon of delivery as medium. This issue is central to an understanding of the striking revivification of classical rhetoric in the second half of the twentieth

---

[4]I avoid the standard and, in my opinion, destructive binary opposition of theory and practice. Aristotle, of course, emphasized this threesome, and it has been articulated and historicized by James L. Kinneavy. See also Janet Atwill. The dominance of the theory/practice split damages new work in writing studies and other disciplines as well.

century. To understand the extraordinary importance of delivery in the last 100 years or so, and its probable importance in the coming decades, an understanding of the connection between delivery and kinds of literacy is important. For many readers, the material I treat next is familiar; I have treated it extensively elsewhere, and various other people have as well. I rehearse it here for readers who have interpreted material on primary orality, literacy, and secondary orality differently, or for those who are not yet familiar with it.

SECONDARY ORALITY AND DELIVERY

Delivery is a site for excavating how electronic forms of discourse have changed the ways that rhetoric operates now and how strong-text theorists (to use Deborah Brandt's term from *Literacy as Involvement*) have not taken account of it.[5] Delivery now *is* secondary orality in the sense that Walter J. Ong develops it in *Orality and Literacy: The Technologizing of the Word*. He defines it there as "present-day high-technology culture, in which a new orality is sustained by telephone, radio, television, and other electronic devices that depend for their existence and functioning on writing and print" (11). This concept, which depicts a stage of consciousness rather than the mere use of tools with various skills, relates to Ong's and Eric A. Havelock's conceptualization of two related stages of consciousness, primary orality and literacy. Primary orality is characterized by an emphasis on speaking not only for communication but also for the transmission of cultural values, norms, behaviors, and ideologies. Primary orality indicates a kind of consciousness in which the dynamism of the spoken word is powerful but evanescent; its very burst of energy plays it out. It ends. Only spoken repetition keeps it going. The standard version of primary orality that we have (although literate cultures cannot really understand it) are the Homeric epics. Ong relies on and extends the work of Milman Parry and Albert Lord, as well as of other scholars, and shows the oral features not only of the Homeric poems but of orally dominant texts from other cultures as well.

Literacy, the second part of Ong's three stages, began in about 720–700 BCE and contributed to the development of abstraction and therefore the burst of abstract writing that characterized fourth-century BCE Greece.[6] Literacy accelerated in the fifteenth century with the establishment of print discourse. Secondary orality, Ong's third stage, began in the nineteenth century, when various electron-

---

[5]To a remarkable extent, Brandt's strong-text account of literacy corresponds to formalism. For many people, calling someone a formalist constitutes *argumentum ad hominem/ad feminam*. Brandt's construction may allow us to talk about the same thing without name-calling.

[6]The designation of 720–700 BCE as the time that the phonetic Greek alphabet we recognize emerged is from Rhys Carpenter. Alternative formulations include Denise Schmandt-Bessarat's and Martin Bernal's. See also I. J. Gelb (176–89).

ic devices revolutionized communications.[7] We are now well into secondary orality, in which there is a new emphasis on the ear and a change in emphasis on the eye (with screens of various kinds requiring our attention, as well as the linearity of pages of print). The spoken word is now frequently electrified, instantaneous, repetitive, and so familiar that we take it for granted or, more usually, cordon it off into another Cartesian category out there in the world, retrievable and usable as necessary but not an inherent part of human beings. Contrary to this dominant notion, however, is the idea that group consciousness now depends to a great extent on secondary orality. Like air, it exists and sustains us.

There is no point in arguing about the human need for air; nor is there any point in arguing about the presence of electronic forms of discourse, including their relationship to writing. Ong makes this point. Nevertheless, many people—intellectuals inside and outside the academy, the enlightened, the unenlightened, all kinds of people—complain bitterly about the ubiquity of electronic discourse, or secondary orality. The familiar cries about illiteracy (children will not read books) and the attendant proclamations that U.S. culture is about to disintegrate because of television (or, similarly, regrets about the use of the telephone as a replacement for letter writing) reveal a sense of loss. Sometimes this loss converts to anger.

I suggest here—and I want to carry the suggestion over to writing pedagogy, a cultural practice that needs to reflect culture as well as change it or offer possibilities for subverting it—that there is not so much a loss as there is a change. We have many ways of communicating. The reading and writing of texts and the formation of consciousness based on written communication—literacy—have not been displaced by anything; rather, they have grown even more powerful, as the record number of published books indicates. Writing has changed irrevocably because of secondary orality; composition needs to take account of this change with more thorough theories that will inform composition textbooks.

Our classroom, or institutional, practices have been deeply conditioned by secondary orality, and so this chapter urges deeper examination of the new power of the spoken word in its electronic manifestations, particularly in film and television. The computer is, of course, a central issue in secondary orality. Jay David Bolter, in *Writing Space: The Computer, Hypertext, and the History of Writing,* and Michael Heim, in *Electric Language: A Philosophical Study of Word Processing,* treat changes in thought brought about by our interactions with computers. Their work is central and pathbreaking in the understanding of computers and secondary orality. All of the technologies of secondary orality require individual investigations. Here, however, I focus on secondary orality and how it relates to television.

---

[7]For standard explanations of this development see, for example, McLuhan, Eisenstein, Couturier, and Innis.

SECONDARY ORALITY AND TELEVISION

Secondary orality as it occurs in television shares many properties with the characteristics of primary orality that Ong shows us (*Orality* 33–49) and that he treats as suggestions rather than as rigid categories (36).[8] According to Ong, primary orality is "additive rather than subordinative," "aggregative rather than analytic," "redundant or 'copious,'" "conservative or traditionalist," "close to the human lifeworld," "agonistically toned," "empathetic and participatory rather than objectively distanced," and "homeostatic." In addition to these characteristics, primary oral cultures are formulaic. These characteristics can be applied to television texts because secondary orality shares many properties with primary orality even though it differs substantially. The following are three similarities:

1. *Secondary orality is repetitive.* Televised texts can be screened endlessly. The phenomenon of the sound bite depends for its existence on its repeatability. Its essence can be said to lie in its repetition. Televised advertising, obviously, depends on repetition for part of its power.

2. *Television texts in secondary orality are formulaic.* For example, the 30-minute text of the "NBC Nightly News" (22 minutes of news and 8 minutes of commercials) is comprised of lead stories, secondary stories, filler, and "humor," all slotted according to the lengths and requirements of advertisements, which, in the United States, control this form of delivery.

3. *Television texts in secondary orality are additive.* For example, a television station can stay on the air for 16 hours, 20 hours, or 24 hours a day; it need only add material, usually material that has been conveyed previously.

According to these three characteristics, the forms of secondary orality are like the forms of the *Odyssey*.[9] The texts from both kinds of orality rely on formula, repetition, addition, and so on. More significantly, perhaps, the ancient poem and the modern news show appear because of these characteristics to be in some ways simple, elementary, and not really sophisticated. They seem to many literate minds to be superficial. The "depth" that we are conditioned to respond to in a novel such as George Eliot's *The Mill on the Floss* does not seem to be there. The texts from primary and secondary orality appear to be centered on big

---

[8]Joyce Middleton, in *Confronting Lingering Questions in Plato's Phaedrus: How Textbook Authors Draw on Historical Speech Strategies to Teach Writing,* has shown a useful way of appropriating Ong's categories in his section "Some Psychodynamics of Orality."

[9]See Ong: "Diachronic study of orality and literacy and of the various stages in the evolution from one to the other sets up a frame of reference in which it is possible to understand better not only pristine oral culture and subsequent writing culture, but also the print culture that brings writing to a new peak and the electronic culture which builds on both writing and print. In this diachronic framework, past and present, Homer and television, can illuminate one another. But the illumination does not come easily" (*Orality* 2).

events. In the *Odyssey,* a journey orders the big events. On the journey big events occur—the encountering of Circe, the Cyclops, the Sirens, and so on; the storyteller (recreater) could remember the poem by stringing together the big events. On "NBC Nightly News," the 30-minute text is constructed in a similar way. Parallel big events provide the form: disasters, assassinations, hurricanes, floods, Mideast tensions, battles in ongoing wars, and so on. Parallel to these are the big events of the commercials (which have changed form in the last decade because of the formal demands of cable technology, the proliferation of channels, and the phenomenon of zapping). Just as Homer (or the Homeric poets) provided contrast between the big events of the Cyclops, Circe, the Sirens, and other figures by providing relief (the development of Telemachus as he faces the problem of the absent father, Penelope's manipulation of the suitors, and so on), so the evening news provides lulls, or breaks from the big events by giving us a graphic of stock market movement (with accompanying music-as-sedative) or a fast weather map with the following day's highs, and so on. In other words, in the collaboratively written Homeric text and the collaboratively written Nightly News text, the formula requires some contrast between the presentation of big events; otherwise, readers/spectators would be exhausted. The Homeric text and the television text have an extraordinary amount of common material. They are repetitive, formulaic, and additive. (In fact, television producers refer to "segments" in their ordinary discussions; segments are easily added or subtracted according to various demands.)

SECONDARY ORALITY AND LITERACY

I want to discuss at this point some of the things that secondary orality is not. First of all, secondary orality is not a destroyer of literacy. It is, instead, an extension of literacy. The fact that many intelligent and sensitive people believe—really believe—that secondary orality threatens literacy is a phenomenon that needs more investigation. Henry Sussman's *High Resolution: Critical Theory and the Problem of Literacy* shares this sadness about the low quality of television, which he dismisses as *kitsch* (a term he does not really probe), and is a recent and significant example of the characteristic response. Second, literacy and secondary orality are not in opposition. Conventionally, in the public and academic imaginations, they are held to be opponents. This false opposition leads to the formulation that reading is good and viewing is bad. Robert Scholes's designations in *Textual Power* are useful here; he identifies three phases, which he names skills, in confronting a text: reading, interpretation, and criticism (21–41). *Reading* in Scholes's formulation is "largely unconscious" and "based upon a knowledge of the codes that were operative in the composition of any given text and the historical situation in which it was composed" (21). *Interpretation* concerns the finding of meaning in a text. Scholes uses the example of reading a parable for its story but interpreting it for its meaning (22). *Criticism* involves a response based on being a member of a group. Criticism requires going beyond the merely personal. It is a critique of the themes and the codes in a text.

I suggest that much viewing of television texts stops at Scholes's first phase: passive reading, in which spectators lose themselves to a certain extent, and during which little reflection takes place. I further suggest that the video response that stops with passive reading typifies not only general spectatorship, but the spectatorship of intellectuals as well. People are simply not in the intellectual habit of critiquing a video text. Frequently, people respond that the televised text is not worthy of this kind of investigation. Television texts, rock music texts, radio texts, and so on are dismissed. In fact, they frequently are not textualized. The sophisticated explication of these texts—which to a large extent promote, defend, and extend corporate capitalism, sexism, racism, and other aspects of the status quo—is not only necessary but crucial. Electronic texts abound; refraining from analyzing their operations as part of secondary orality, as powerful sources of delivery, means that decoders are going to be less sophisticated in dealing with the powerful forms of the newly powerful delivery systems of secondary orality.

DELIVERY IN WRITING TEXTBOOKS

In spite of the centrality of delivery and its reconfiguration in secondary orality, a strange erasure of the forms of secondary orality has taken place in writing textbooks. I have examined 45 recently published first-year writing textbooks to determine the extent to which these powerful sources account for the forms of secondary orality. A number of textbooks now on the market are theoretically sensitive, pedagogically sound, and attractive in many other ways, but the vast majority (the readers, the rhetorics, the argument books, and the hybrids) do not substantially account for the powerful new kinds of delivery. Rather, they treat the forms of electronic discourse not as issues that affect consciousness but as new sources of content. Textbook excerpts from professionally produced writing regularly include essays or parts of longer works "about" some aspect of television or film. Students are shown how to cite electronic forms of discourse, but they are not taught anything about the new forms of consciousness brought about by those kinds of texts. In fact, a distressingly high number of the books continue to repeat the truncated canons, the modes of discourse, and an attenuated version of "process." The highly oral features of our students' discourse—the repetition, the formulism, and the additive qualities, for example—are not accounted for. Students enter a world in most of these textbooks that assumes enormous changes in delivery have not happened at all or, if they have, that they have nothing to do with student writing. These textbooks—with some exceptions—act as if secondary orality has not changed delivery, and that we are not all conditioned by these forms. A duality develops. Electronic discourse is for "real" life. Print discourse, including students' own writing, is for school culture (which, it goes without saying, is a central site for the promulgation of official culture). In this duality, school discourse is not a place to pour one's passions, to engage one's life force. It is something to get through; or it is something to get by with. Real life and school life are disconnected and students are not shown what they need: how the discourses of real life and school life partake of the same thing. When we fail to make these connections in our writing courses, we give up the most powerful of the available means of persuasion in the particular case of wising up our students and ourselves, to echo Aristotle vaguely.

When we erase the forms of secondary orality, we erase what we know is there. A pretense therefore takes place. The uncritical reception of electronic texts is promoted. Students are implicitly instructed not to interpret texts outside of school and outside of print. This need not, and must not, continue. In a writing class that acknowledges the existence of secondary orality, students could interpret an apparently throwaway text, such as a Coke advertisement, and probe its ideological positioning as it emerges from the canon of delivery. Six issues, for example, could be addressed in class discussion and then used as a basis for students to script their own soft drink commercials (in a different class, students could videotape their own commercials): (a) Where are the cameras? (b) What is the nature of the medium (is it videotape or film, black and white or color, or both)? (c) What is the *mise en scène;* for example, the placement of the people in the frame, the space taken up by various people or objects, the interaction of color or light and shade and line and form? (d) How does editing influence the interpretation (the self-conscious editing, the use of wipes, the length of takes, and so on)? (e) How are light and shadow manipulated? (f) What are the production values (the relationship of television advertisements to the high Hollywood gloss that we expect from the Classic Hollywood Cinema)?

FINAL THOUGHTS

I would finish this analysis with a reference to Raymond Williams, from his book *Television: Technology and Cultural Form:*

> So many uses of the medium have been the transmission . . . of received forms . . . that it is often difficult to respond to some of its intrinsic visual experiences, for which no convention and no mode of description have been prepared or offered. Yet there are moments in my kinds of programme when we can find ourselves looking in what seem quite new ways. To get this kind of attention it is often necessary to turn off the sound. . . . What can then happen, in some surprising ways, is an experience of visual mobility, of contrast of angle, of variation of focus, which is often very beautiful. . . . I see it as one of the primary processes of the technology itself . . . [but when] I have tried to describe and explain this, I

have found it significant that the only people who ever agreed with me were painters. (77)

The means of interpretation we are talking about here invoke a grammar of television. Two writing assignments can derive from such a grammar: an exegesis of the video text in writing (which we can juxtapose with and analogize to the exegesis of a sonnet in a traditional English class), and then the writing of a script for a commercial (or the actual production of one, a text that can be used to develop the analytic ability discussed previously).

Students who are able to interpret electronic texts in sophisticated ways will be more likely (and able) to interpret other texts that constitute their lives. For example, the text of a university (how the structure of the university determines who we are, in Foucault's sense): If students cannot read the text of their university, then it is less likely that the students will succeed in it. A second example lies in the way that Kathleen Hall Jamieson reads the text of a presidential campaign (see, for example, *Eloquence in an Electronic Age*).

In *High Resolution,* Henry Sussman contends that "the greatest extension of literacy thus involves the very careful reading of the relationships that configure all organized systems, not only the linguistic and imagistic codes of artworks but also systems of production, distribution, management, communication, education," and so forth (224). But Sussman does not take the issue far enough. Reading is not enough. Writing, encoding, is required to understand adequately how texts operate in secondary orality. Students need to know how to write manipulative discourses as well as straightforward discourses. They need to know how to write what Jasper Neel, in *Plato, Derrida, and Writing,* calls "antiwriting," writing in which a student hides out, not making any kind of connection.

Students from orally dominant cultures—Native Americans, for example—can especially benefit from applications of orality/literacy/secondary orality theory in the classroom. Texts from their literatures (for example, "The Origin Myth of Acoma" from the Acoma tribe in New Mexico) are especially formulaic, repetitive, additive, situational, and so on. They especially resemble the Homeric poems and the texts of electronic discourse. By examining the dynamism of the spoken word, we can better include non-European groups that have historically been excluded and marginalized, left to lament that they are not understood by the dominant university culture. Orality/literacy/secondary orality theory offers us one way of better understanding, including, and empowering students from these cultures.

Empowerment in writing can take place with the use of orality/literacy/secondary orality theory. This empowerment can derive from making writing courses locations for the training of cultural critics who understand the pressures and possibilities of delivery in its newly revivified manifestations. Writing courses can show students how to produce and evaluate texts of many kinds.

Theories of secondary orality can comprise one critical part of this urgent project. But, first, writing textbooks must account for delivery as it exists in secondary orality. They must stop their erasure of electronic discourse from the domain of school rhetoric. If they did, the tedium that comprises so much writing instruction would convert to thrilling intellectual energy.

WORKS CITED

Applebee, Arthur N. *Tradition and Reform in the Teaching of English.* Urbana: NCTE, 1974.

Atwill, Janet M. "Toward Posthumanist Rhetorics: Aristotle and Productive Knowledge." Paper presented at the Conference on College Composition and Communication, Seattle, Mar. 1989.

Bernal, Martin. *The Fabrication of Ancient Greece 1785–1985.* New Brunswick, NJ: Rutgers UP, 1987. Vol. 1 of *Black Athena: The Afroasiatic Roots of Classical Civilization.* 3 vols.

Bolter, Jay David. *Writing Space: The Computer, Hypertext, and the History of Writing.* Hillsdale, NJ: Lawrence Erlbaum Associates, 1991.

Brandt, Deborah. *Literacy as Involvement: The Acts of Writers, Readers, and Texts.* Carbondale: Southern Illinois UP, 1990.

Carpenter, Rhys. "The Antiquity of the Greek Alphabet." *American Journal of Archeology* 37 (1933): 8–29.

Carruthers, Mary. *The Book of Memory: A Study of Memory in Medieval Cultures.* Cambridge, Eng.: Cambridge UP, 1990.

Cicero. "De Oratore; or, On the Character of the Orator." *Cicero on Oratory and Orators.* Trans. J. S. Watson. Carbondale: Southern Illinois UP, 1970.

Couturier, Maurice. *Textual Communication: A Print-Based Theory of the Novel.* London: Routledge, 1991.

Crowley, Sharon. *The Methodical Memory: Invention in Current-Traditional Rhetoric.* Carbondale: Southern Illinois UP, 1990.

Eisenstein, Elizabeth L. *The Printing Press as an Agent of Change: Communications and Cultural Transformations in Early-Modern Europe.* 2 vols. Cambridge: Cambridge UP, 1979.

Enders, Jody. "Memory and the Psychology of the Interior Monologue in Chretien's *Cligés.*" *Rhetorica* 10 (1992): 5–23.

———. "Music, Delivery, and the Rhetoric of Memory in Guillaume de Machaut's *Remède de Fortune.*" *PMLA* 107 (1992): 450–64.

Gelb, I. J. *A Study of Writing.* Chicago: U of Chicago P, 1952.

Heim, Michael. *Electric Language: A Philosophical Study of Word Processing.* New Haven: Yale UP, 1987.

Homer. *The Odyssey of Homer.* Trans. Richmond Lattimore. New York: Harper, 1965.

Innis, Harold. *Empire and Communications.* Toronto: U of Toronto P, 1972.

Jamieson, Kathleen Hall. *Eloquence in an Electronic Age: The Transformation of Political Speechmaking.* New York: Oxford UP, 1988.

Kennedy, George A. *The Art of Persuasion in Greece.* Princeton: Princeton UP, 1963.

Kinneavy, James L. "Theory, Theories, No Theories." Paper presented at the Conference on College Composition and Communication, Cincinnati, Mar. 1992.

Lord, Albert B. *The Singer of Tales.* New York: Atheneum, 1976.

Mahony, Patrick. "McLuhan in the Light of Classical Rhetoric." *College Composition and Communication* 20 (1969): 12–17.

McLuhan, Marshall. *The Gutenberg Galaxy: The Making of Typographic Man.* Toronto: U of Toronto P, 1962.

Middleton, Joyce I. *Confronting Lingering Questions in Plato's Phaedrus: How Textbook Authors Draw on Historical Speech Strategies to Teach Writing*. Diss. U of Maryland, 1988.

Neel, Jasper. *Plato, Derrida, and Writing*. Carbondale: Southern Illinois UP, 1988.

Ong, Walter J. *Orality and Literacy: The Technologizing of the Word*. New York: Methuen, 1982.

———. *Ramus, Method, and the Decay of Dialogue: From the Art of Discourse to the Art of Reason*. Cambridge: Harvard UP, 1958.

Parry, Milman. *The Making of Homeric Verse: The Collected Papers of Milman Parry*. Ed. Adam Parry. Oxford, Eng.: Clarendon, 1971.

Schmandt-Besserat, Denise. "The Envelopes that Bear the First Writing." *Technology and Culture* 21 (1980): 357–85.

Scholes, Robert. *Textual Power: Literary Theory and the Teaching of English*. New Haven: Yale UP, 1985.

Sussman, Henry S. *High Resolution: Critical Theory and the Problem of Literacy*. New York: Oxford UP, 1989.

Welch, Kathleen E. *The Contemporary Reception of Classical Rhetoric: Appropriations of Ancient Discourse*. Hillsdale, NJ: Lawrence Erlbaum Associates. 1990.

———. "Ideology and Freshman Textbook Production: The Place of Theory in Writing Pedagogy." *College Composition and Communication* 38 (1987): 269–82.

Williams, Raymond. *Television: Technology and Cultural Form*. New York: Schocken, 1975.

Yates, Frances A. *The Art of Memory*. Chicago: U of Chicago P, 1966.

3 Modern Rhetoric and Memory

Sharon Crowley
Northern Arizona University

THE GRIP OF MODERNISM

Timothy Reiss opens his study of modern thought with an observation made by Mircea Eliade in 1956: "For almost two centuries, the European mind has put forward an unprecedented effort to explain the world, so as to conquer and transform it."[1] In Europe and America, modernism was the age of science, enlightenment, and liberal politics. It was also the age of colonization, world war, genocide, and systematic destruction of the environment. Reiss comments:

> Only recently has this European mind—at least commonly—become aware that something may be amiss in this desire for conquest, dominion, and possession. Yielding in part before the growing evidence of its own impotence, we are beginning to realize that the expression and implementation of this desire is the mark of a particular epistemological inflection that is far from the only one possible, or even available. (21)

As we emerge from modernism, we are able to see its limits more clearly.

Here's a vest-pocket definition of modernism: It is the congeries of intellectual assumptions that privileges individuals over social collectivities.[2] Modern-

---

[1]Eliadé's observation appeared in *Forgerons et alchimistes* (Paris, 1956, 12).

[2]Of course the terms *modern* and *modernism* have multiple uses depending on who is using them and for what purposes. Modernism began to lose its hold on Western intellectual habits during the early- or mid-twentieth century, depending on whether you are talking about science or the arts or politics. In science, it ended with the discovery of relativity theory and quantum physics. In art and aesthetics, modernism is a more specific development of much shorter duration. Aesthetic modern-

31

ism assumes that each person is an integrated, coherent self, and whereas this self undergoes changes as it experiences new situations, it remains relatively stable throughout its lifetime. In order to insure that some social order prevails in this wilderness of rampant individualism, modernism privileges reason over all other human faculties and posits that all rational persons think alike, at least when they are thinking rationally. Human reason is transcendental and universal and, as such, it functions independently of an individual human's social station or experiences. The preeminent instrument of reason is the scientific method. When this is rigorously followed, it can produce true knowledge. Language is the medium through which selves express the fruits of their reason, and it is utterly transparent to the expression of meaning; that is, if humans use language carefully, they can make it represent their meanings and intentions. Michel Foucault called modernism an age of representation, because its adherents believed that human reason repeated the truth of nature (including human nature), and accurately represented this truth to itself.

I place the beginnings of modernism in the seventeenth century. The publication of John Locke's *Essay on Human Understanding* in 1694 is a handy marker, because this work offered a popular description of modernist beliefs about how people think and express themselves. Equally arbitrarily, I place the end of modernist dominance of Western thought in the 1960s, when student demonstrations erupted in Europe and America. I choose these markers not because they are true or accurate, but because they roughly indicate the heyday of modern rhetorical theory.

My pocket chronology places the first adaptations of rhetorical theory to modern thought in the eighteenth century. Adam Smith lectured on rhetoric during the 1760s at Edinburgh; he was also, not coincidentally, the author of an influential treatise on modern economics called *The Wealth of Nations*. Joseph Priestley published a modern rhetorical theory in 1762 entitled *Lectures on Oratory and Criticism* and, again, not coincidentally, he was an innovative experimenter in chemistry and related sciences. The consummate modern rhetoric is George Campbell's *Philosophy of Rhetoric,* composed during the heady intellectual ferment now known at the Scottish Enlightenment, and published in 1776. This work, like Smith's and Priestley's, reflects modern interest in empiricism both as a means of proof and as a kind of reasoning.

---

ism extends from the late nineteenth century roughly through the 1950s. The world wars can be read as modernist enterprises; the cold war, however, became eerily postmodern (and thoroughly rhetorical) once nuclear weaponry was sophisticated enough and widely dispersed enough to kill every living being and render the planet uninhabitable for thousands of years. For accounts of modernism that treat it in the way I do here, as a cultural phenomenon that includes scientific, rhetorical, philosophical, and political thought, see Foucault, Habermas, and Reiss. For accounts and criticisms of aesthetic modernity, see Eagleton and Huyssen. For a fuller account of modern rhetorical theory and my dissatisfaction with it, see *The Methodical Memory*.

The rhetoricians who wrote these treatises were aware that they were doing something new. They explicitly rejected classical rhetoric, and they interwove the modern respect for reason and method, along with its disrespect for language, throughout their texts. According to modern rhetorical theory, the point of rhetoric is to lay out the truth so plainly and clearly that other reasonable persons are required to accept it. Rhetoric begins with rational inquiry, which occurs in the reflective mind of an individual and purposive inquirer. Inquirers translate their findings into language that faithfully represents reality and minds that perceive it. Because reason is universal and language is a transparent reflection of reality and/or reason, reasonable persons can understand the fruits of rhetorical investigation. In understanding, these persons accept them, because their truth is guaranteed by the rationality of the inquiry and the utter transparency of language.

Modern rhetorical theories were written throughout the nineteenth century; Alexander Bain's *English Composition and Rhetoric* (1866) is typical. A few modern rhetorical theories appeared during the first half of the twentieth century (I. A. Richards's *Philosophy of Rhetoric,* for example), and they continued to be published through the 1950s—witness J. L. Austin's *How to Do Things with Words* (1955), Chaim Perelman and Lucy Olbrechts-Tyteca's *A New Rhetoric* (1958), and Stephen Toulmin's *The Uses of Argument* (1958).[3] During the 1960s, stirred by student dissatisfaction with their teaching, academic rhetoricians lamented the sterility of the rhetoric they had inherited. They hoped for the advent of "new" rhetorics, but none appeared. (I discount "process" pedagogy as a "new" rhetoric because, for all its supposed borrowing from ancient rhetorical theories, its epistemology is solidly grounded in modernism.)

Modernism still maintains its grip on rhetorical theory. Although postmodern rhetorical practices have emerged in politics, in advertising, in law, in popular argument about religion and ethics, and even in accounting, only a few rhetoricians have tried to describe them.[4] No rhetorician, as far as I am aware, has

---

[3]What these works have in common is their subscription to the notion of *commensurability,* a term I borrow from Richard Rorty. The hope of commensurable rhetorical systems is that disagreement between persons is a product of failure to follow the current procedure, or of misunderstanding the meanings of words. They assume as a basic premise that a set of rules can be found "which will tell us how rational agreement can be reached on what would settle the issue on every point where statements seem to conflict. These rules tell us how to construct an ideal situation, within which all residual disagreements will be seen to be 'noncognitive' or merely verbal, or else merely temporary—capable of being resolved by doing something further" (316). Eighteenth- and nineteenth-century rhetoricians looked for these rules in the methodical operation of reason. Twentieth-century rhetoricians looked for them in rule-governed uses of language intended to make language behave itself. However, because disagreements are always occasional and local, a set of universal rules for reaching agreement will never be found, nor can such rules be universally applied, short of coercion.

[4]See, for example, Kathleen Hall Jamieson's investigations of television's transmogrification of traditional rhetorical practices, or Barry Brummett's work on popular culture.

developed a self-consciously postmodern rhetorical theory. Modern rhetorics continue to serve as mainstays of the canon used in the graduate study of rhetoric. And despite the work of theorists and teachers who advocate the use of alternative pedagogies, the school versions of modern rhetoric continue to dominate instruction in the composition of both oral and written discourse.

I believe that rhetoricians and teachers of composition need to unthink modernism in order to break its grip on our theorizing about rhetoric and the teaching of writing. I am not trying merely to be trendy. We can now see that the modern period was not a time of continuing intellectual progress and increasing enlightenment, as its adherents maintained. Its emphasis on reason, although liberating to those who invented modernism in the seventeenth century, has been used since then to exclude or secondarize women, children, and people of color—anyone who could be labeled "irrational." Liberalism is the politics of modernism, with its emphasis on individual rights and the power of reason to find solutions to social problems. That liberalism is currently unable to deal with today's social realities is yet another sign of modernism's demise. Liberal emphasis on the sovereign self has given Americans a rights-based politics that, although capable in the past of increasing the sphere of social democracy, has been reduced in recent times to the ongoing adjudication of competing rights. Modernism has no ethics beyond its valuing of individual rights, and consequently it is incapable of envisioning the sorts of collectivist or duty-centered ethics that we need to move us away from our current political impasse.

The rhetorical theory I described earlier follows modernism in its emphasis on reason and individualized inquiry, its preference for method, and its devaluation of ethics. I have argued elsewhere that because it does so, it is not a rhetoric at all; it is, rather, a philosophy or a metaphysics based on a transcendentalized definition of human intellect. It prescribes for the use of all a process of inquiry that was first put forward by middle-class men as a description of their ideal thought process. I think that the transcendentalizing impulse of modernism, along with its emphasis on individual rights rather than on collectivist or commu nal knowledge, is inimical to rhetorical theory.

Rethinking modern rhetoric is hard to do in the absence of postmodern rhetorical theories. However, ancient and medieval accounts of composing do present us with dramatic alternatives to modernist accounts, and hence they can serve as sources for understanding the workings of human communication in nonmodern ways. For one thing, ancient and medieval accounts of composing point up, by contrast, the linear economy of modern composing practices. For another, the existence of alternative models of composing demonstrates the ahistoricity of modern attempts to prescribe a universalized composing process based on literate skills. For another, they problematize modern connections of intelligence to literacy. Ancient and medieval composing processes could involve writing, but they did not require it. Last of all, comparison of older models of composing to the model suggests why modern thought is inimical to rhetoric as this art was understood in ancient thought.

MEMORY AND INVENTION
IN ANCIENT RHETORIC

Until the modern period, memory held a central place within rhetorical theory—and in lots of other intellectual endeavors as well. In ancient times even people who could write easily (like Cicero, for instance) relied on their memories, not merely as storage facilities for particulars, but as structured heuristic systems. In other words, memory was not only a system of recollection for ancient and medieval peoples; it was a means of invention.

I have long suspected that the ancient inventional scheme called "commonplaces" or "topics" is related to the "places" recommended as mental storage facilities by ancient authorities on memory. Long before the time when writing was readily available to most people, rhapsodists traveled about the Greek countryside reciting epic and lyric poetry and telling stories of the gods. These wandering bards could recite long poems whenever the need arose. They apparently accomplished this partly by relying on bits of lines or images that they could insert into any recitation wherever they needed a transition or a description or a way to fill out the meter of a line. Homer probably repeated phrases like "rosy-fingered dawn" and "the wine-dark sea" to help him remember what came next while he recited lengthy poems.

It is somewhat riskier to suppose that these stock or tag lines could also be used to trigger the rhapsodist's memory, because we have no evidence of the practice of artificial memory prior to the fifth century BCE. However, rhapsodists must have used some relatively organized means to remember long poems, and it is not unreasonable to assume that such techniques might have resembled more fully conceptualized fifth-century arts of memory. Perhaps rhapsodists also connected tag lines to the vivid sorts of mental images that are recommended as a mnemonic technique by later rhetoricians; the Homeric poems certainly provide plenty of these.

Fifth-century rhetors might have used topics in the same way that rhapsodists used tag lines, memorizing a stock of arguments that were general enough to be inserted into any speech. In *Menexenus,* Plato gives us a glimpse of how this might have been done:

> Yesterday I heard Aspasia composing a funeral oration about these very dead. For she had been told, as you were saying, that the Athenians were going to choose a speaker, and she repeated to me the sort of speech which he should deliver—partly improvising and partly from previous thought, putting together fragments of the

funeral oration which Pericles spoke, but which, as I believe, she composed. (236b)

Because Plato nowhere suggests that Aspasia worked from a written text or that she produced one, it is likely that she held her arguments in memory. If so, the "fragments" from which she created the oration were not parts of pieces of an already written discourse; they were instead what would later be called "commonplaces." These would include typical arguments in praise of the dead, such as Aspasia needed for her funeral oration.

Plato's narrator is not shocked to discover that Aspasia actually composed a discourse widely attributed to Pericles. His lack of comment is a bit surprising, given the gender politics of ancient Athens. However, his response is consonant with the attitudes toward authorship that prevail in memorial cultures, where compositions are not thought to be "owned" by their authors but are generated from a common store of knowledge. In such cultures, individual memories are stocked with information and relations that are important enough to remember and use often. As Mary Carruthers remarks in her study of medieval memory arts, classical and medieval thinkers assigned "a crucial role to a notion of communal memory accessed by an individual through education. . . . This notion is basic to Aristotle's view of politics as the life of the individual completed in society. Such assumptions put the civic bond on a historically continuous basis" (24). Persons were citizens of their cultures by virtue of their knowledge about that culture and its history, stored in memory. To put this another way, memories are constituted by things everyone knows—they are truly common places.

Almost all ancient authorities credit a fifth-century magician named Simonides with the invention of artificial memory. This term refers to the trained ability to remember long lists of items or names by associating each item or name with a carefully ordered set of mental images. According to Cicero, Simonides taught "that persons desiring to train this faculty must select localities and form mental images of the facts they wish to remember and store those images in the localities, with the result that the arrangement of the localities will preserve the order of the facts, and the images of the facts will designate the facts themselves" (*De Oratore* II.lxxxvi.354). In other words, Simonides concluded that a mental construction, consisting of a series of images of places that were somehow orderly, would assist people in remembering lists of names or items if they simply associated each name or item with a mental "place." A person has only to review each of the places, in order, to remember the items or names associated with it. The expression "in the first place" may originate from this memory practice.

This memory system took the notion of place literally. Its teachers recommended that students visualize a street or a house with which they were familiar. They were then to identify points along the street (say, houses or buildings) or rooms inside the house with the items they wished to remember. Teachers recommended that the images be striking or strange enough to be easily remembered. For example, if I wanted to remember the five arguments I was making in a talk, I could associate the first of these with the entryway to my home. But because the entryway to my house is not very memorable, I would place some striking or memorable item within my mental image of the entryway–say, a large yellow umbrella stand. I would then associate the second argument of my talk with some image located in the next room that I enter in my house—the living room. And so on. The system works even better if the images I use are identified in some way with the arguments I want to remember. If my first argument, for instance, had to do with the necessity of stopping acid rain, I might imagine that an umbrella with large holes stands in the imaginary yellow umbrella stand in the imagined entryway to my house.

During Simonides's lifetime, sophistic rhetoricians began to assemble lists of commonplaces for use in public argument. The oldest rhetorical treatise we possess, the *Dissoi Logoi,* consists mainly of a list of variations on topics such as "what is true for one person is true for another." Rhetors who memorized this topic and "placed" its variants in some orderly way in their memories would be ready to invent arguments for use on any occasion simply by combining and expanding on the appropriate variations. A trained memory could house many such topics, along with their associated variations, if these were placed in some orderly manner. Composition would then amount to selection, combination, and amplification of appropriate topics and their variations to suit a particular occasion.

After writing became readily available, lists of topics that had been stored in memory could be preserved in manuscript as well, as they apparently were in the *Dissoi Logoi* and in the lists of sophistic topics referred to as "handbooks" in Aristotle's *Rhetoric*. Characteristically, the topics in these collections are arranged in contradictory pairs, because the sophists taught their students how to argue both sides of any question. The contradictory-pairs arrangement may also have been a memory aid.

We possess a set of sample proofs for the courtroom, called the "Tetralogies" and supposedly composed by the sophist Antiphon. Their title derives from the fact that the samples are arranged in sets of four speeches, two for a prosecutor and two for a defendant. Here is the beginning of the prosecutor's first speech from the third tetralogy:

(1) It is rightly prescribed that, in murder trials, the jury should take the greatest pains that the prosecution and the presentation of evidence should be just, and that they should neither let the guilty go free nor bring the innocent to trial. (2) For when the gods desired to make humankind and created our first ancestors, they provided earth and sea to feed and [preserve] them, so that we should not die before the term of old age through lack of the necessities of life. Whoever, then, un-

lawfully kills one of those whom the gods have found worthy of such provision, he is guilty of sin against the gods and throws the principles of human society into confusion. (3) The dead man, deprived of the gifts of the gods, naturally leaves behind as their punishment the hostility of avenging spirits, which those who judge or bear witness contrary to what is just, joining the doer of the deed in his impiety, bring on to their own households—a pollution which does not belong to them. (4) If we, the avengers of the dead, prosecute the innocent out of some malice, we shall, since we are not avenging the dead, be haunted by terrible avenging spirits, the suppliant souls of the dead; and if we unjustly put to death the guiltless, we are liable to the penalties for murder; and if we persuade you to act lawlessly, we too become responsible for your error. (5) This is what I fear; and so I bring the sinner before you, while I stand clear of reproach. Taking due account of what has just been said, do you accordingly attend to the legal verdict and pass upon the criminal a sentence fitting the crime. In so doing you will render the whole city clear of pollution. (Sprague 156–57)

The first commonplace reminds the jury of the seriousness of their duty, and of the procedures connected with jury trials. The second section contains a sophistic commonplace, also used by Protagoras, concerning the relation of humans to the gods (Plato, *Protagoras* 320d.ff). This section, along with sections 3 and 4, reminds the jury about the serious religious consequences of murder. The last part of section 4 emphasizes the legal penalties for juries and prosecutors who fail to punish the guilty, and section 5 charges the jury to do the right thing.

The commonplaces in this sample speech are so general that they could be used verbatim (which would be unlikely if they were retained in memory rather than in writing), or they could be altered to fit a given occasion more closely. Of course, rhetors could use some or all of them, as the situation warranted. Even though these topics are recorded in writing, they lack the sort of internal logic (called "cohesion") that is expected in modern discourse and prescribed by modern rhetorical theory. In other words, their ordering principle is not what moderns might call "discursive." Perhaps that ordering reflects some ancient memory art.

The centrality of the term *place* to both ancient memory arts and ancient inventional theory is tantalizingly suggestive. In each art, a place is a mental storage facility, a pigeon hole in which a trained memory locates a line, an argument, an image—anything that might be useful during composition. My suspicion about the connection or identity between memory and topical systems of invention has been strengthened by Mary Carruthers's research on medieval memory systems. In *The Book of Memory,* Carruthers argues that "all mnemonic organizational schemes are heuristic in nature. They are retrieval schemes, for the purpose of *inventio* or finding" (20). She makes an explicit connection between memory and the topics: "The memory of an orator is like a storehouse of inventoried topics that ideally would contain all previous ways-of-saying ethical truths like 'justice,' 'fortitude,' 'temperance,' from which he draws in order to fit words to yet another occasion, requiring another way-of-saying" (26). If memory and invention are as closely associated as I think they are, it follows that a rhetoric that occults the role of memory will give less attention to invention than one that does not. This is precisely what happened in modern rhetoric.

From Campbell's day forward, modern rhetoricians substituted something they called "experience" for communal memory. This curious entity was presumed to be constituted by an individual's sensory relation to the physical world. Modern rhetoricians simply forgot or neglected the roles played by ideology, communal tradition, and memory in forming a self. This forgetfulness of common knowledge led in turn to the privatization of invention, because its results were thought to be solely the product of "individual experience." This set of moves made invention seem somewhat mysterious to those who were not good at it. Modern rhetoricians explained that some people were better at invention than others because they had had more productive experiences: They had read more, done more, thought harder. The pedagogical response to this impasse was to concentrate on arrangement and style.

THE DEMISE OF MEMORY ARTS

Modern historians have argued that ancient and medieval peoples relied on their memories because they were not literate. But Carruthers's research soundly debunks the "absent-literacy" theory as a reason for the importance of memory to ancient and medieval habits of thought. The medieval process of composing required both memory and literacy, but the composers themselves did not need to be literate. Here is Carruthers's description of the stages that occurred in medieval composing:

> These are, first, *invention,* taught as a wholly material process of searching one's inventory. It involves recollection primarily, and occurs with postures and in settings that are also signals of *meditatio;* indeed, it is best to think of invention as a meditational activity. It results in a product called the *res.* . . . The *res* is the "gist" of one's composition; more complete than what modern students think of as an outline, it should, according to Quintilian, be formed fully enough to require no more than finishing touches of ornamentation and rhythm. In other words, the *res* is like an early draft or even notes for a composition, still requiring much shaping and adjustment.
>
> The post-invention stage is, properly, composition itself. Its products are called *dictamen;* it might, but need not, involve writing instruments. As will become clear, the *dictamen* is most like what we now call a *draft;* a number of versions, each unfinished, could be involved. *Compositio* covers three closely-related activities: *formalization,* or taking one's *res* and giving it final form as a composed piece; *correcting,* both by adding and emending, but also by comparing and adjusting the revisions to make sure the words fit one's *res* in intention and accuracy as

much as possible (changing one's *res* drastically at this stage would indicate a lack of proper invention); *polishing,* artfully adjusting one's expression to make it striking and memorable in all its details (the medieval *ars dictamimis* addresses this specifically). For *compositio,* a set of waxed tablets or other informal (easily correctable) writing support could be used, on which one might write down all or parts of one's *res* to make stylistic tinkering easier. But, depending on one's maturity and experience, this process could, like invention, be completely mental.

When the *dictamen* was shaped satisfactorily, the composition was fully written out on a permanent surface like parchment in a scribal hand; this final product was the exemplar submitted to the public. (Usually . . . the scribal fair-copy was submitted once again for a final corrective collation by the author or author's agent before the exemplar was made available for further copying.) The word "writing" properly refers to this last inscribing process, which the author might do himself, but usually did not. (194–95)

Carruthers notes that the composing process was not considered complete until the written document had been read by others. In medieval memorial culture, to "read" meant to store in memory, to rework, and to comment on the productions of other memories. Sometimes composers themselves reworked their written compositions after they had been glossed by others, thus treating them exactly as they treated material stored in memory—as a source of invention.

Most moderns cannot perform the intellectual tasks Carruthers describes. However, our inability to compose from memory and our ignorance about non-literate methods of composing do not justify the privilege we give to literacy-based models of the composing process. Memory-based models of composing demonstrate that literacy-based models are not natural in the sense that they draw on innate cognitive processes or structures that are always brought into play when people compose. Memorial composition also complicates the debate about orality versus literacy, insofar as this method of composing requires neither speaking nor writing. Finally, ancient and medieval uses of memorial composition problematize the modern connection of literacy to intelligence.

This connection bars Aspasia and Aristotle, Augustine and Aquinas from admission to the ranks of the intelligent. In Aspasia's day, the only people who bothered to become literate were those who could not afford to keep literate slaves or to hire literate scribes. It is doubtful that Aristotle was literate in our modern sense, and so it is equally doubtful that he "wrote" the *Rhetoric* in our sense of writing—sitting down with parchment or wax tablet and quill or stylus. Assuredly he composed it, but he may have done so from memory, and the text we now revere may represent lecture notes taken by his students.[5] If this is the case, modern scholars' attempts to find "order" in the *Rhetoric,* to make its three books cohere and demonstrate "unity," represents yet another imposition of

---

[5]Ironically, the only account we have of Adam Smith's lectures on rhetoric exists in copious notes taken by a student. Did Smith's student have a trained memory?

modern discursive standards on a text whose ordering principles are those of memory, not literacy. Augustine was literate, but he associated intelligence with memory. In Book X of the *Confessions,* he remarked: "Great is the power of memory, sometimes awe-inspiring . . . a deep and endless multiplicity; and this thing is my mind, and this thing am I myself." Aquinas, who reputedly could dictate so profusely from memory that he kept as many as five scribes busy at the same time, utilized the notion of "intellectual memory" to account for the mind's ability to invent concepts (Carruthers 57).

However, respect for the capacities of memory began to ebb during the early modern period. At the same time, books became more widely available, and more so-called ordinary people learned to read (far fewer learned to write). Interestingly enough, the technologies and materials necessary for cheap printing had been known and available since ancient times, but they were not widely exploited until the modern era. I think the demise of memory arts has much to do with the advent of modernism. In other words, I do see a connection between the expansion of literacy technologies and the demise of memory arts, but it is not the connection that is usually made—that literacy offered such an improvement for storing and sorting information that intellectuals immediately abandoned memory in favor of reading and writing. Writing—considered as a recording technology, as a method of composing, and as metaphor—is much friendlier than memorial composition to modern notions like the sovereignty of individuals (and hence of authors), to language conceived as a representative medium for thought, and to method as a preferred means of inquiry.

First of all, from a modern point of view, writing is better suited to the discovery of knowledge than is memory. The knowledge preferred by moderns is not book knowledge; it is "new" empirical knowledge, knowledge gained from reliance on the senses, on observation. Modern knowledge is "new," and because its accuracy depends on a single individual's sense perceptions, it has to be recorded in writing so that others can repeat the observer's mental process and thus verify its accuracy. Thus a profound shift in attitudes toward writing occurred in modernism: The texts themselves, the written pages signed by individual authors, were treated as representations of their minds. They were authoritative insofar as they exactly represented intentions. In contrast, previous ages had located textual authority not in an artifact, but in the composers' communal memory of their culture's verbal productions. For Augustine, knowledge was indeed contained in books, but "books" was an expansive term that included codices and written manuscripts, the everexpanding text that was his own memory, and the remembered intellectual tradition he inherited and shared with other scholars. It also referred to the "book of nature" and it included God's memory as well.

Second, writing is far more suited than memory to the modern notion that individuals produce "original" composition. Writing is done for absent others, and it is often done alone. Writing produces an artifact, a commodity which from a reader's point of view seems to have sprung *ab ovo* from writers' intelligence, particularly if they provide no footnotes. Individuality and the commodification of knowledge are both products of modern thought. Modern models of composition occult the communal or shared nature of composing, because they occult the role of memory in that process (Crowley 22). Memory, on the other hand, is collective; when medieval scholars "read" Aristotle, they memorized him, made Aristotle part of their working memories. (Indeed, they consumed Aristotle; a common set of medieval metaphors for memory conceived of it as "the stomach of the mind.") A trained memory was a hubbub of voices, a highly communal affair. Trained memories were individualized only insofar as the individuals who wished to remember chose the ordering systems and categories with which they designed their memories. They might borrow these from nature or from human inventions such as the alphabet or the streets of their hometowns, and their memories were random and idiosyncratic to that extent.

Third, memory is not representative, as writing was supposed to be in modern rhetoric. In order to exalt the role of a sovereign author in composing, modernism posited that language exactly represented the ideas in a composer's mind— that it was, in other words, subservient to the author's wishes and in the author's control. Modernism denied that language is larger than any of its individual users, that it has meaning only insofar as it has a history and a current community of users. This denial awarded authors sovereignty over their thought processes and the language they used, so the contents of mind could be viewed as an accurate representation of reality.

Memory also utilized a notion of representation, of course, but the places of memory were not conceived as faithful pictures of reality. On the contrary, they were artfully and vividly designed so that they could be remembered more easily. In consequence, memory is more hospitable to the role played by craft in composing than is modern invention theory. The modern turn to the plain style entailed much more than a rejection of the excesses associated with highly ornamented composition; it was an attempt to banish altogether the supplemental play of language from the composing process, to regard writing as a stenograph, an utterly transparent medium for transferring information from a writer to a reader.

Last and most important, writing and method are linear rather than aggregative. Until the advent of electronic composing, writing necessarily progressed in linear fashion, one word after another, one sentence following the next. Revision was difficult. Writers had to cut and paste, to write in between lines and all over margins, to redraft, to copy over. Indeed, a much-revised hand- or typewritten text looks very much like a heavily glossed medieval manuscript; medieval glossing, however, was done by many hands, not just one, and it was done not to revise (that is, to change or eliminate), but to expand and fill out a composition with appropriate allusions and digressions.

Modern invention is economical, spare, methodical; the investigator decides on an object of study, investigates its parts in order, and reports results in a discursive order that re-presents the order of the investigation as nearly as possible. Methodical invention privileges unity and coherence. Memory, on the other hand, is associative, global; it privileges disquisition, repetition, digression, allusion, allegory. In memorial composition, revision does not require ink and paper, but only another visit to the appropriate mental places. Composers working from memory may be led down interesting byways as they mentally walk the paths of their carefully organized memories, and their compositions may be the richer for it. Persons who trained their memories in similar ways would be able to tease out the paths taken by their associations if they cared to do so. Ordering principles governed the composing process, but they were not universally prescribed in advance, as they are for composers who use method.

MEMORY AND RHETORIC

If I seem to sing the praises of memorial composition, I do not do so in order to wish us back into an age that is long gone. Rather, I wish to point up the inconsistency of modern intellectual habits with more rhetorical consciousnesses. A rhetorical consciousness is fully consonant with memory arts, which were designed to facilitate copious accretion of knowledge. A rhetorical attitude toward composition emphasizes copiousness, abundance, plenitude, aggregation, so that a composer will have something to say whenever an occasion arises. Although this necessity of having something to say is occulted in modern rhetoric, it remains a necessity nonetheless. People who know nothing outside their own experience cannot compose discourse that anyone else cares about.

More rhetorical ages were aware that knowledge is partly a product of tradition, of remembrance of human words and works. What people learn from their elders, their teachers, their public media, their clergy, is fully as important to invention as knowledge earned by means of sensory experience. Rhetorical investigation centers on ethics and politics rather than physics and metaphysics because rhetorical knowledge is concerned with the relations that obtain between human beings. The ancients claimed that such knowledge was contained in the commonplaces of human discourse and memory. Modern rhetoricians simply ignored it. Postmodern thinkers are trying to reclaim it. Foucault calls it power/knowledge; Derrida calls it writing; feminist theorists call it patriarchy; ethnic critics call it racism; political theorists call it ideology.

Carruthers remarks that "the valuing of memory training depends more . . . on the role which rhetoric has in a culture than on whether its texts are presented in oral or written forms" (11). I agree. Memory and rhetoric thrive in cultures that celebrate community and plenitude. Perhaps it is safe to say that these things may be more highly valued now than they used to be. At the very least, postmodern writers have rescued writing from the sterile role it played in modernism, reminding us that writing, like memory, is a heuristic, a way of stimulating selection, reworking, and amplification of *all* that writers know.

WORKS CITED

Carruthers, Mary. *The Book of Memory: A Study of Memory in Medieval Culture*. Cambridge, Eng.: Cambridge UP, 1990.

Cicero. *De Oratore*. Trans. E. W. Sutton and H. Rackham. Loeb Classical Library. Cambridge: Harvard UP, 1967.

Crowley, Sharon. *The Methodical Memory: Invention in Current-Traditional Rhetoric*. Carbondale: Southern Illinois UP, 1990.

Eagleton, Terry. *The Ideology of the Aesthetic*. London: Blackwell, 1990.

Foucault, Michel. *The Order of Things: An Archeology of the Human Sciences*. New York: Random, 1973.

Habermas, Jurgen. *The Philosophical Discourse of Modernity*. Cambridge: MIT UP, 1987.

Huyssen, Andreas. *After the Great Divide*. Bloomington: Indiana UP, 1986.

Plato. *Collected Dialogues*. Eds. Edith Hamilton and Huntington Cairns. Princeton: Princeton UP, 1961.

Reiss, Timothy J. *The Discourse of Modernism*. Ithaca: Cornell UP, 1982.

Rorty, Richard. *Philosophy and the Mirror of Nature*. Princeton: Princeton UP, 1979.

Sprague, Rosemary Kent, ed. *The Older Sophists*. Columbia: U of South Carolina P, 1972.

4 The Faculty of Memory

Virginia Allen
Iowa State University

> *Great is the power of memory; it is something terrifying [amazing], my God, a profound and infinite multiplicity; and this [something] is the mind, and I am this myself. What therefore, am I, my God? What is my nature? A life various, manifold, and utterly immeasurable.*
> —St. Augustine, *Confessions*

Although it has been traditional to dismiss the art of Memory or "mnemotechnics" (Yates xi) as a theoretically uninteresting set of tricks for imposing images on places to aid in memorizing the parts of a speech, in fact, when we set out to study the history of memory in rhetorical theory, what we discover is an entangled relationship among the most fundamental problems of philosophy, physiology, psychology, and rhetoric. Regrettably, however, we have become so mindful of the disciplinary boundaries institutionalized at the end of the nineteenth century that we have yielded up essential pieces of our discipline without contest. After the turn of the century, rhetoric (conceived of as written composition) in English departments was reduced to style and arrangement, with invention bootlegged in under the patterns of development, while delivery and a cursory treatment of artificial memory were relinquished to speech communication. Problems about the nature of mind—for which natural memory is an essential consideration—were split into physiological studies of the brain, psychological (experimental) studies of behavior, philosophical studies of meaning, and the quest for latent memory or the unconscious in the scientific aberration of psychoanalysis.

As a rejuvenated study of memory will demonstrate, rhetoricians were at the scene of each of these disciplinary schisms, and efforts to write the history of rhetoric that are not interdisciplinary in focus can succeed only by narrowing the definition and scope of rhetoric. To maintain that the problems of memory are not our concern or that they more properly belong to other disciplines is to accept the premise that rhetoric is only *techne,* appropriately defined by the how-to books of composition cookery. Kathleen Welch goes even further when she argues that "by diminishing its range" to three of the five canons, what has been created "is not an adaptation but a wholly new structure that denies the central language issues of culture and power" (99).

A rhetorical theory that dismisses problems of the nature of mind as uninteresting or that presupposes the workings of memory to be unproblematic is a truncated theory. It is memory that mediates between our perception of the flow of disconnected sense data—what William James called "one big, blooming, buzzing confusion" (*Psychology* 16)—and our knowledge or understanding of reality; when we explain how memory operates within a particular theory of mind, we have gone a long way toward explaining the theory itself. When we fail to examine a theory whole, we run the risk of misconstruing its aims and basic presumptions.

COMPETING THEORIES OF PSYCHOLOGY OF THE MIND

What should be attended to as we sort out competing theories of mind is always the principle that underlies the attempts at explanation. There is an inevitable overlap in terminology from one era to the next as different thinkers try to explain the same data: The soul becomes psyche, "parts" of the soul become functions that then become faculties, or one of the faculties—such as reason—becomes dominant over the rest, but as a critical term is then picked up and explained from a different perspective, it takes on a very different meaning. Nowhere is this more evident than in shifting meanings of the term *faculty*.

Alexander Bain, the Scottish Association psychologist who cast such a long shadow over current-traditional rhetoric, would be somewhat surprised at the particular slant given by rhetoricians to the misunderstanding of his theory of the mind. Toward the end of his life, speaking "On 'Association' Controversies," he addressed the need for a well-defined vocabulary:

> The process of see-saw is eminently called for here. We go on a certain way upon given definitions; we find them open to exception; we go back and correct them, and proceed again, until some new flaws are discovered. But to stay debating ultimate questions, before making any forward movement at all, is a device that may be handed over to the Committee for arranging the debates in Pandemonium. (169)

Richard Sorabji begins the introduction to his translation of *De Memoria et Reminiscentia* with the claim that "Aristotle's account of memory is fuller than that to be found in the best-known British empiricists," and he goes on to maintain that "it therefore serves, for the student, as a better introduction to the subject of memory" (1). Because British empiricism is the "normal science" against which much of our contemporary rhetorical theory develops, it would seem incumbent upon us to understand that tradition; and, given the frequency with which rhetoricians conflate associationism (the main stream of British empiricism flowing from John Locke to David Hume to Alexander Bain) and faculty psychology (sometimes regarded as one of its tributaries, sometimes regarded as the opposing theory) in their characterization of nineteenth-century rhetoric, and because both traditions trace their lineage back to Aristotle, we might best begin with him.

ARISTOTLE'S FACULTY PSYCHOLOGY

Aristotle has been called the "fountainhead of faculty psychology," which Hearnshaw characterizes as "a type of psychology which, in spite of many attempts to kill it, refuses completely to die" (25). Aristotle identified a number of "parts" of the soul that are recognized as cognitive faculties, but he did not use the existence of these so-called faculties as his explanatory concept. For Aristotle, it is the animal that does the perceiving or imagining, not the part (or faculty) of the soul, a move that James referred to as "the orthodox 'spiritualistic' theory of scholasticism and common-sense" (*Principles* 15). Thomas Aquinas, although relying on Aristotle for many of the details, was committed to the immortality of the soul and found it necessary, therefore, to separate Reason or Intellect as a faculty autonomous from bodily functioning in order to explain the preservation of the soul beyond the dissolution of the body. The Scottish School of Common Sense (Dugald Stewart and Thomas Reid) referred to the "inherent powers" (faculties) of the mind as distinct from acquired powers (habit); when conflated with the faculties of the phrenologists and leavened with a liberal dose of mental discipline, faculty psychology became the pop psychology of the nineteenth century, clinging tenaciously to educational theory long after it lost any theoretical credibility among philosophers and a new breed of physiological philosophers called psychologists. It is James's mocking refutation of this sort of "faculty psychology" that has obviously narrowed but also solidified the denotation of that term in the twentieth century:

> In old times, if you asked a person to explain why he came to be remembering at that moment some particular incident in his previous life, the only reply he could make was that his soul is endowed with a faculty called memory; that it is the inalienable function of this faculty to recollect; and that, therefore, he necessarily at the moment must have a cognition of that portion of the past. This explanation by a "faculty" is one thing explanation by association has superseded altogether. If by saying we have a faculty of memory, you mean nothing more than the fact that we can remember, nothing more than an abstract name for our power inwardly to recall

the past, there is no harm done; we do have the faculty; for we unquestionably have such a power. But if, by faculty, you mean a principle of *explanation of our general power to recall,* your psychology is empty. ("Memory" 74–75)

Aristotle used the faculties or "parts" of the psyche as naturalistic descriptions of the capacities of the specimen—man[1]—under analysis, not as a substitute for explanation, and he took exception to earlier thinkers, most notably Plato, who separated the body from the soul.

A central problem for Plato was how to explain the coexistence of the sensible world, which is always in a state of flux, with knowledge, which must be infallible, stable, and real. Plato's solution to the problem is well known and easy for the strict empiricist to dismiss as unfalsifiable or merely quaint: Reminiscence, a faculty of the immaterial soul, has knowledge of the Ideal Forms latent within it. Plato demonstrates that learning is recollection by inducing a young slave boy to solve a problem in geometry[2]; he reasons that the solution must have been latent within the boy because he had not been taught it before (*Meno* 80D–86C). The puzzle for Plato is how knowledge that is infallible and real (the theorems of geometry, for example) exists independently of our perception of it. Our perception of disconnected fragments of sense data adds up to experience, but what must be explained is the mind's capacity to render coherence (or knowledge of reality) out of the blooming, buzzing confusion.

This is the very problem that Hume found insoluble, and that every philosopher since Hume has had to grapple with:

> In short there are two principles, which I cannot render consistent; nor is it in my power to renounce either of them, viz. *that all our distinct perceptions are distinct existences,* and *that the mind never perceives any real connections among distinct existences.* Did our perceptions either inhere in something simple and individual, or did the mind perceive some real connection among them, there would be no difficulty in the case. For my part, I must plead the privilege of a sceptic, and confess, that this difficulty is too hard for my understanding. (Grene 45)

It was Hume's statement of the problem that waked Kant from his dogmatic slumber, and it is the same problem that caused Michael Polanyi to question the very possibility of rational discourse. But, although he has been chastised severely for the neglect, it was not a problem for Aristotle. Marjorie Grene puts the question of Aristotle's negligence with some vigor:

> Twenty years, almost, at Plato's feet, and he never saw it [the problem]. . . . Perception, he agreed, is not knowledge, but it is, obviously, commonsensically,

---

[1]Not always a generic.

[2]The double-square problem: How long will the side of a square be if it contains twice the area of the given square?

the first step to knowledge. Who would puzzle his head with something as clear on the face of it as all this? "Are there real things in the sensible world at all?" "What meeting ground is there, or can there be, between our vision of form and the stream of sense?" For Plato, for post-Humean philosophers, these are serious, even distressing questions. Aristotle never so much as asks them. We shall not inquire, he says in the *Physics,* whether there are natural objects, for that would be to explain *the obvious by the non-obvious,* and only a fool would do that. (46)

Aristotle asked a different sort of question altogether. He saw a world full of creatures of different natural kinds, and he set out to describe them and to distinguish among them on the basis of what could be observed. "It is well known," says Bain, "that the Soul, in Aristotle, was nearly synonymous with life or vitality" ("Historical" 49). The "parts" or "faculties" of the *psyche* for Aristotle refer to general or "vital" functions of the organism: Bain summarizes these functions as "nutrition, growth, decay, as well as movement, sensibility, and thought" ("Historical" 49). Aristotle's method of biological progression is familiar: The lowest or "vegetative" principle common to all living things is growth and nourishment; animals that are "sensitive" have the power to perceive; of those that are capable of perceiving, some perceive the passage of time (they have memory); some of those animals who have memory are able to "recollect" (they can remember their perceptions, their scientific knowledge, and their memories).

The kind of animal who can perceive the passage of time, according to Aristotle, is the kind of animal that can remember: "And they do so by means of that with which they perceive" (449b.24–29). Sorabji includes a long note explaining his choice of the ambiguous translation in preference to "'the perceptive part' . . . because it makes clear that it is the animals which do the perceiving . . . as Aristotle [himself] points out when he is being more careful." Sorabji avoids the "faculty" translation, "because it would wrongly encourage the attribution to Aristotle of the kind of 'faculty' psychology that belongs to later periods" (70–71).

The difference between animals with only memory and those who "recollect" is the power of inference, the power to reason. Aristotle explains:

Now, it has been said in what precedes that it is not the same people who are good at remembering and at recollecting. Recollecting differs from remembering not only in respect of the time, but in that many other animals share in remembering, while of the known animals one may say that none other than man shares in recollecting. The explanation is that recollecting is, as it were, a sort of reasoning [inference]. For in recollecting, a man reasons that he formerly saw, or heard, or had some such experience, and recollecting is, as it were a sort of search. And this kind of search is an attribute only of those animals which also have the deliberating part. For indeed deliberation is a sort of reasoning [inference]. (453a.4–13)

Man is the only one capable of deliberation, and hence the only animal capable of acquiring knowledge; but he is not the only animal capable of memory, nor is there any connection implied between memory and intelligence.

Aristotle opens his treatise on Memory by distinguishing first between "memory" (the ability or tendency) and "remembering" (the act of recollecting), asserting that, in general, slow-witted people have better memories, whereas the quick-witted and those who learn well are better at recollecting (449b.4–8). He takes great care to distinguish between perceiving and/or theorizing about something in the present and remembering something from the past. Likewise, "it is not possible to remember the future, which is instead an object of judgment and prediction" (449b.10–13). Working out a problem (theorizing or exercising scientific knowledge) is not remembering, and this, finally, makes clear his answer to Plato's claim that learning is reminiscence. Memory is not perception or conception (which both take place in the present), but a process subsequent to both:

> For recollection is neither the recovery nor the acquisition of memory; for when someone first learns or experiences something [receives a sense impression], he does not recover any memory since none has preceded. Nor does he acquire memory from the start; for once the state or affection [imprint] has been produced within a person, then there is memory. So memory is not produced within someone at the same time that the experience is being produced within him. (451a.19–24)

Plato had divided into separate spheres "the visible and the intelligible" and then equated the objects of dialectical thought (his example is the hypotheses of geometry) with the Ideal Forms, which are, therefore, separate from the sensible world: "A world which is above hypotheses" (*Republic* 510–11). I must leave the role of imagery in Plato to more sympathetic interpreters: It is occasionally puzzling, not consistent among the dialogues and, as it is expressed in the *Phaedrus,* self-contradictory (see Gulley 194ff). However, for Plato the possibility of thought without images seems clear; this is in sharp contrast to Aristotle, for whom objects of thought need a sensible form, which is inferred from their form in nature. These forms must be "housed" or "stored" somewhere, and Memory becomes that storehouse. Images function as the vehicle for moving perceptions into thought.

All thinking, Aristotle says to the consternation of many commentators, requires an image as the present content of the mind (449b.30–32). Furthermore, in remembering that image is a likeness or a copy of the thing remembered; it is not, however, a symbol:

> For it is clear that one must think of the affection [imprinted image], which is produced by means of perception in the soul and in that part of the body which contains the soul, as being like a sort of picture, the having of which we say is

memory. For the change [perceptual process] that occurs marks in a sort of imprint, as it were, of the sense-image, as people do who seal things with signet rings. (450a.27–31)

Although this explanation does describe one kind of memory, procedural knowledge is the most usual example to demonstrate that his claim is unjustified. Hasty introspection reveals that our knowledge of such things as typing, playing the guitar, and driving a car are not mediated with images. Nor is our general knowledge—stoves are hot; time is money; neighbors are helpful—dependent on images, either accidental or invoked, to guide our behavior. Nor have Aristotle's physiological explanations stood the test of time:

> And this is why the very young and the very old have poor memory, since they are in a state of flux, the former because they are growing, the latter because they are wasting away. Similarly the very quick and the very slow are also obviously neither of them good at remembering. For the former are too fluid [moist], the latter too hard. Therefore with the former the image does not remain in the soul, while with the latter it does not take hold [it makes no impression]. (450a.32–41)

Alongside the intriguing observation that melancholics are particularly sensitive to mental images (453a.16–25)—perhaps anticipating the controversial association of manic depression and creativity—is the absurd notion that "dwarf-like people have poorer memories than their opposites because they have a great weight resting on the perceptive part" (453a.31–34).

In the *Rhetorica Ad Herennium* of the first century, our most detailed source for the ancient art of artificial memory, the power of memory is primarily the power of perception, secondarily the power of imagination in creating vivid images, and only incidentally, if at all, a question of intellect. Thus, the rules for selecting architectural places on which to impose the images have to do with making the images easier to *see:* They should be viewed in a definite order; every fifth locus should be given a distinguishing mark, such as a Golden Hand. Distractions such as a busy street should be avoided. And the places should be of moderate size: If too large, the images are vague; if too small, they quickly become overcrowded. The intervals between places should, likewise, be moderate. Quintilian suggests a large building that you walk through depositing images—a spear in the living room and an anchor in the dining room will enable you to recall that you mean to speak first of war and then of the navy (*Institutio* XI.ii.17–22). The images thus called up in memory and perceived are "read" as ideographs are read and interpreted. Quintilian's examples and the example suggested in the *Ad Herennium* to use the image of a ram's testicles to remind one, punningly, of witnesses (*testes* in Latin) are clearly symbolic[3]; however, as

---

[3]Frances Yates speculates that the ram is actually a "place" on the zodiac, which was a version of the architectural system attributed by Quintilian to Metrodorus of Scepsis.

so much in the memory tradition that comes to us by way of the Roman authors, a provocative suggestion is made but not treated theoretically.

The key point for the mnemonic arts of rhetoric as codified in the *Ad Herennium* is that remembering is perceptual rather than intellectual, and thus, paradoxically, although those who display great feats of memory may be regarded with something akin to awe, it has not been obvious throughout the history of rhetoric that an extraordinary memory is an altogether desirable trait. Especially suspicious has been the memory of words. A mind cluttered with words, it is feared, cannot have adequate room for serious thought.

ARISTOTLE'S ASSOCIATIONISM

Despite his antiquated physiology and conceptual gaps (such as his failure to discuss memory images as symbols), there is considerable sense among the nonsense in Aristotle's treatment of memory. That sense leads directly to the associationist theories of British empiricism, as Howard C. Warren makes plain:

> The notion that one idea or memory image follows another according to certain definite principles was the first step toward a general theory of association among mental states. This fundamental notion is found first, and in quite definite form, in the writings of Aristotle. (23)

One is obliged to pause long enough to note here that Plato had already illustrated the principles of *similarity* and *contiguity* in the *Phaedo:*

> What is the feeling of lovers when they recognize a lyre or a garment or anything else which the beloved has been in the habit of using? Do not they from knowing the lyre form in the mind's eye an image of the youth to whom the lyre belongs? . . . When we perceived something either by the help of sight or hearing or some other sense, there was no difficulty in receiving from this a conception of some other thing, like or unlike, which had been forgotten and which was associated with this. (73–76)

In his chapter on recollection, Aristotle lays out the explanatory principles of memory—*similarity, contrast,* and *contiguity*[4]—that came to be known among the empiricists as the laws of association: "Acts of recollection happen because one change [here an image] is of a nature to occur after another" (451b.10–11).

Images occur after one another, Aristotle says, either out of necessity or out of habit. When the object of your search is similar to, opposite (across from), or next to your starting point, movement (recollection) is facilitated:

> Whenever we recollect, then, we undergo one of the earlier changes, until we undergo the one after which the change in question habitually occurs. And this is

---

[4]Hume, as we will see, included "causality" in the list of fundamental principles.

exactly why we hunt for the successor, starting in our thoughts from the present or from something else, and from something similar, or opposite, or neighboring. By this means recollection occurs. (451b.16–21)

The *Ad Herennium* says the images created to aid in memory can be read off the backgrounds on which they are placed in the same way that letters can be read off a wax tablet or papyrus. Thus it somewhat perfunctorily dispenses with one of the most vexed questions in the study of memory: What, exactly, is an image? Michael Tye dubs the two most popular views, prior to the twentieth century, as "the picture theory" and "the weak percept theory." As the name implies, with the picture theory the mental images are "significantly picture-like in the way they represent objects in the world." With the weak percept theory they are "like perceiving in less than optimal conditions." He amplifies: "The basic claim of the weak percept theory is that the impressions made in memory from data supplied by the senses weaken with time of storage so that mental images generated from these stored impressions are generally less sharp than the corresponding percepts" (1).

Aristotle's assertion that "it is not possible to think without an image" is often cited to illustrate the picture theory, but his next sentence complicates the easy categorization: "For the same effect occurs in thinking as in drawing a diagram." He then proceeds to discuss the differences between the triangle "of a determinate size" that is drawn and the triangle as an object of thought that has no determinate size (449b.30–44).

In laying out the theories of imagery, Tye does not note Aristotle's reference to diagrams, but goes next to Rene Descartes's *Meditation Six* in which he puzzles out the problems involved in distinguishing between a pentagon and a hexagon—both of which can be "imagined" by holding images of their forms as the present content of the mind—and then distinguishing between a chiliagon (a 1,000-sided figure) and a 999-sided figure. We can *conceive* of a figure of that size with one more or less sides; therefore, Descartes concludes, thinking and creating images are different. He agrees with Aristotle that images—which he calls "ideas"—copy the objects they represent, but some ideas—better referred to as "percepts"—"proceed from certain things outside us" and, indeed, copy objects in the external world. Mind, however, operates outside the physical order (matter), and in addition to the "derived ideas" that come to us from experience, there are, for Descartes, innate ideas—the ideas of universal truths, mathematical ideas like those embodied in analytic geometry, which he invented, and the idea of God, which he derived logically from the certainty of his own existence. Thus, memory and the association of ideas were not critical concerns for him. Sensory experiences may remind us of innate ideas, but innate ideas are not produced from them.

Locke objected to Descartes's notion of "innate ideas." To do so, he went back to another idea found in Aristotle, the *tabula rasa*. Locke says:

> Let us suppose the mind to be, as we say, a white paper void of all characters, without any ideas:—How comes it to be furnished? Whence comes it by that vast store which the busy and boundless fancy of man has painted on it with an almost endless variety? Whence has it all the materials of reason and knowledge? To this I answer, in one word, from *experience*. In that all our knowledge is founded; and from it ultimately derives itself. (*Essay*)

Even the blank paper presupposes that what will be "written" is the images of memory by means of which the buzz of experience is stored for retrieval; it is to be "furnished" like the rooms used as the loci for images.

If all learning comes from experience, then the raw material of knowledge must not be innate ideas, as Descartes argued, but sensations. The problem of explaining how the disorganized mass of sensations of our perceptual world achieve structure and meaning is addressed by the natural process of association.[5] If two sensations are frequently linked together, soon one evokes the other. Association, particularly contiguity, is the principle that drives this linkage. The mind not only receives sensations from the outside but reacts by combining and synthesizing in a process called *reflection*. Abstraction is the result.

Berkeley rejects Locke's view of abstract ideas by appealing to introspection. He declares himself unable to form an image of a man or a horse that is not a particular man or a particular horse laden with specific detail. He then ridicules Locke's description of an abstract triangle existing in the mind without specific characteristics: "neither oblique nor rectangle, neither equilateral, equicrural, nor scalenon, but all and none of these at once?" (qtd. from *Essay; Treatise* 13).

Like Aristotle, eighteenth-century empiricists regarded thought as consisting of the manipulation of ideas in the form of simple or complex images built up from simple images mediated through memory and imagination; but Hume is credited as the first person since Aristotle to attempt a classification of the principles of association:

> Though it be too obvious to escape observation that different ideas are connected together, I do not find that any philosopher has attempted to enumerate or class all the principles of association—a subject, however, that seems worthy of curiosity. To me there appear to be only three principles of connection among ideas, namely *resemblance, contiguity in time or place,* and *cause or effect. . . .* The more instances we examine, the more assurance shall we acquire that the enumeration which we form from the whole is complete. (*Enquiry* 3)

For Hume, memory and imagination are not independent faculties but two different ways in which *ideas* (images and thoughts) work. Memory is clearer

---

[5]Locke introduced the phrase "association of ideas" as a chapter heading of the fourth edition (1700) of his *Essay Concerning Human Understanding*. Those who followed the line of reasoning perhaps only implicit there are more responsible for the elaboration of associationism than such hasty summarization may suggest.

and more vivacious than imagination, and the order of memories follows the order of the original impressions. Imagination is not as clear. Tye uses Hume's answer to Berkeley's objection to Locke's description of abstraction as his example of "the weak percept" theory. Interpretation gives an idea its content. As Tye describes the process: "So long as when I use the word 'triangle' I form an idea that I interpret as representing triangles generally and you do likewise, we may understand one another perfectly well even if our ideas *in themselves* have little in common." Thus Hume says: "The image in the mind is only that of a particular object, tho' the application of it in our reasoning be the same as if it were universal" (Tye 10).

The associationist explanation of mental behavior was the mainstream of British empiricism in the nineteenth century. The challenge to it was not from faculty psychology, but from evolutionary theory. Edwin G. Boring refers to James Mill's *Analysis of the Phenomena of the Human Mind* as "the culmination of associationism," a phrase so often used to describe Mill and Bain that it passes nowadays as a descriptor without attribution. Boring's summary is so succinct that it is itself impossible to condense:

> The nineteenth century saw the culmination of associationism in James Mill and its modification from a mental mechanics to a mental chemistry by John Stuart Mill. It saw associationism made over by Bain into a system that was to become the substructure for the new physiological psychology, and it saw the new theory of evolution first brought to bear upon psychology by another associationist, Herbert Spencer. It also saw Wundt use association as the basic principle in his new system of psychology, the system that he built both to guide and to justify the new experimental psychology. (219)

When we look at the rhetoric of the nineteenth century through the lens of memory, the received opinion that it is grounded in something called "faculty psychology" becomes problematic. Especially problematic is the tendency among rhetoricians to make a faculty psychologist of Bain, who is more often designated by histories of psychology as "the culmination of associationism" than James Mill. For an explanation of this peculiar interpretation we must turn to the revival of "faculty psychology" at the end of the eighteenth century.

FACULTIES AS EXPLANATORY CONCEPTS

Here we can pick up the rest of the quotation from James's *Talks to Teachers,* in which he distinguishes the "empty" version of faculty psychology ("We remember because we have a faculty of memory") from associationism:

> The associationist psychology, on the other hand, gives an explanation of each particular fact of recollection; and in so doing, it also gives an explanation of the

general faculty. The "faculty" of memory is thus no real or ultimate explanation; for it is itself explained as a result of the association of ideas. ("Memory" 74–75)

James addressed his explanation to teachers because the faculty theory lingered on in the schools long after it was moot among philosophers and the new psychologists touched by the evolutionary hypothesis.

Unlike the other philosophers so far discussed, Christian von Wolff was an academic, a university professor at Halle during the first half of the eighteenth century, and it has been suggested that it was through his efforts that British empiricism and German rationalism entered the academic tradition. Wolff exemplified a style of reasoning that was highly persuasive to a large number of thinkers, especially those attempting to theorize about pedagogy without offending against religion. It involved a generous mixture of introspection and metaphysics.

Wolff's slippage back and forth between empirical observations and metaphysical explanations was troublesome to Immanuel Kant. Although it was Hume who was credited with waking him from his dogmatic slumber, his *Critique of Pure Reason* was also in part an answer to Wolff's metaphysical rationalism; but it took some time before explanations such as "we remember because we have a faculty of memory" were generally recognized as circular and self-defeating.

Wolff's original and important contribution was the concept of "redintegration," the observation that a memory cue tends to reinstate the entire "past perception" of which it is a part: For example, "Tell me about your accident" calls up the entire event and all its attendant circumstances. Memories, then, are organized or structured clusters, not discrete sensations. As this example shows, however, associationism was felt to be compatible with the faculty explanation and, thus, perhaps, the source of some confusion. The strict associationists did not agree.

Bain's disdain for "the high-flown philosophy that so long prevailed" in Germany is apparent. However, he remarks:

> Spiritualism, as familiar to us, was never the philosophic creed of Germany. Kant, who ridiculed alike materialism and idealism, still less dreamt of bestowing on matter a real existence, by the side of an independent spiritual principle. ("Historical" 61)

Accepting Hume's argument that causality was neither self-evident nor amenable to logical demonstration, Kant extended the same skepticism to all other fundamental principles. He allowed that knowledge begins with experience, but not that it arises from experience alone. The buzz of sensory material impinging on the mind is organized by categories built into the mind (the *a priori* or preexisting categories such as time, space, and causality) and structure the way in which see the world.

The Scottish School of "faculty psychologists" in the late eighteenth and early nineteenth centuries were divided on the issue of the compatibility of association and explanation by faculties but, like Wolff, its objection was to the consequences of the reasoning rather than to the process of reasoning itself. The challenge of Hume's skepticism went to the core of Thomas Reid's staunch Presbyterianism; because he could not fault the reasoning, he concluded that the error was in the premises. Thus, for Reid, ideas are never associated:

> Sensation and memory . . . are simple, original, and perfectly distinct operations of the mind, and both of them are original principles of belief. Sensation implies the present existence of its object, memory its past existence, but imagination views its object naked, and without any belief of its existence or non-existence, and is therefore what the schools call *Simple Apprehension*. (43)

THE CULMINATION OF ASSOCIATIONISM

Bain was himself a determined skeptic. His refusal to take communion was undoubtedly the reason he had trouble getting a university position despite numerous applications. He criticized his friend and mentor John Stuart Mill for regarding poetry as "almost a religion" with Wordsworth as his prophet (*John Stuart Mill* 154). There is irony in Bain's being labeled a faculty psychologist because the closest he came to something akin to religious fervor was in his devotion to associationism (and James Mill was *his* prophet). For example, when Bain says that he derived the modes of discourse "from original principles," he does not mean—as has been charged (Crowley 102)—that he invented them out of whole cloth. The "original principles" are the principles of associationism, the nearest thing to a creed this skeptical and rebellious Scot subscribed to.

Bain's associationism is often referred to as "the beginnings of physiological psychology." He proclaims that "the Brain is the principal, although not the sole, organ of the mind; and its leading functions are mental" (5). The physiological connection was regarded as novel, and—here the explication gets extremely messy—it links him to the phrenologists Gall and Spurzheim, whose pseudo-scientific division of the mind into some twenty-six to thirty-seven faculties may have been derived, Boring suggests, from the faculties of Reid and Stewart (30). This is problematic. The Scottish School recognized memory as one of the fundamental intellectual powers, but Spurzheim omitted it from his list. Although Gall himself questioned whether memory was a unitary faculty, and his division of memory into four different kinds—verbal memory, memory for persons, local memory, and memory for language—is similar to the strategy used in 1816 by Johann Friedrich Herbart (who filled the chair vacated by Kant at Künigsberg) in his convincing refutation of the faculty explanation for mental behavior. No credible theorist argued for the faculty explanation after Herbart.

Lest all this seem frivolous and irrelevant, in the early part of the nineteenth century Gall was an anatomist of some reputation, and his research was in the direct line that led to Paul Broca's verification of cerebral localization in speech loss the same year (1861) that Bain's book, *On the Study of Character Including an Estimate of Phrenology,* appeared. Gall "died rich in Paris" (Garrison 539), but his contemporary reputation has not survived the extravagance of Spurzheim's sensational promotion of the pseudo-science. As a further caveat against the dangers inherent in vocabulary, Bain's rejection of the efforts of "the phrenologists" in 1868 is a rejection of the anatomists[6] in their "attempt to localize the mental functions in special portions of the central mass [of the brain]" (*Senses* 46).

Warren says that Bain's "best piece of analysis is his treatment of the intellectual processes in terms of association, in his first [1855] volume" (104). His worst piece of analysis is certainly *On the Study of Character.* John Stuart Mill, who had looked forward to the book hoping that it would add authority to his own belief in the mental equality of women, was so distressed that he never acknowledged its publication. Robert Young ponders why: "When an intelligent man whose other writings reveal a mind which is at home in careful analysis and systematic presentation writes a rambling and incoherent book, this fact must be explained, and the explanation is likely to be very enlightening." Young's explanation is just as direct: "It is precisely because the book was an abysmal failure that it points out how woefully inadequate the association psychology was for providing the elements of a science of character and personality" (132).

I submit without proof that Bain chafed under his relationship with Mill and that he compared himself to Mill with an intensity that amounted almost to sibling rivalry. He concealed his real feelings about Mill's scandalous relationship with Mrs. Taylor and dared not, in the face of Mill's radicalism on the subject, reveal that in his heart he believed that "the reproductive burden" destined women to mental inferiority. Associationism answered many needs. Mill's intellectual upbringing was, in effect, a scientific experiment, and Bain takes great pains to let the world know that it was a failed experiment and the subject was unworthy.

In his quasi-biography, Bain dismisses his friend's renowned genius as a demonstration of memory without understanding, making an implicit comparison to his own childhood resistance to the memory work involved in learning Latin, which Mill had picked up along with ancient Greek with apparent ease. The role of memory in education remained a central, life-long concern for Bain.

---

[6]A great deal of classical work on mapping the cerebral hemisphere was done in the 1860s and 1870s, and Sir David Ferrier, who studied classics and philosophy under Bain at Aberdeen, was instrumental in moving research from phrenology to physiological psychology. Ferrier found 5 localized centers for various movements in the dog, and 15 different centers in the monkey (see Young).

One of his last political battles at the University of Aberdeen was fought in resistance to requiring the study of classical languages. He argued that languages ought to be learned for their value as languages, not for their value as mental exercise.

Bain's attitude toward memory work is in sharp contrast to the description of "faculty psychology," the belief that the faculties of the mind—imagination, reason, memory, and so forth—are like muscles that can be strengthened with exercise. Therefore, the standard rap goes, abstractions of grammar and rhetoric and the learning of dead languages were deemed useful for their own sake in improving and strengthening the mind (see Applebee 253; Kitzhaber 2–3).

In addition to his refutation of the faculty explanation for mental behavior, Herbart's second contribution had been to initiate a "science" of education. He reasoned that the contents of the mind are ideas, which are never truly lost. To recall a forgotten idea, what is required is the proper association. Therefore, education should be planned to facilitate desired associations. By the middle of the nineteenth century, Bain announced that "the leading inquiry in the art of Education is how to strengthen memory" (*Education* 8), but his ambivalent repugnance for memory work undercut his assertion. Memory, in Bain's Associationist psychology, is reduced to "Retentiveness," synonymous with the principle of contiguity. With Herbart, he agrees that *ideas* are associated, not images, which are more like sensations minus feeling: "They float in a level of their own" (Brett 649). With Aristotle, Bain includes "sensation, memory, physical pleasure and pain, and the desires growing out of these" as being within "the mental sphere of the brutes" ("Historical" 50).

Here is Bain on the subject of "Memory, and Its Cultivation." At first he may sound very much like a faculty psychologist:

> Can we by any artifices cultivate or strengthen the Memory, or the power of Retentiveness as a whole? We may acquire knowledge. Granted. Can we strengthen or increase the natural powers of acquisition? It is, no doubt, said with justice that every faculty can be strengthened by exercise; nevertheless, as regards mental power, the effect is by no means simple. (*Education* 121)

But in the next paragraph, he answers his own question in the unmistakable style of the Associationist:

> The absolute power of Retentiveness in any individual mind, is a limited quantity. There is no way of extending the limit except by encroaching on some of the other powers of the mind, or else by quickening the mental faculties altogether, at the expense of the bodily functions. An unnatural memory may be produced at the cost of reason, judgment, and imagination, or at the cost of the emotional aptitudes. This is not a desirable result. (121)

Anyone who doubted the wisdom of his judgment need only look to the example of John Stuart Mill.

The second volume of the first edition of Bain's psychology was published in 1859 (under Mill's guarantee against financial loss to the publisher), coincidentally with the publication of Darwin's *Origin of Species*. Mill (who himself never dealt with evolutionary theory) declared it a triumph: "The sceptre of Psychology," he said, "has decidedly returned to this island" (Brett 640). Spencer (whose own *Psychology* appeared in 1855) was more astute: And here our story returns again to its Aristotelian roots. Spencer calls Bain's work "a natural history of the mind," as it professed to be, and Bain himself is compared to a naturalist who "collects and dissects and describes species." Its value, according to Spencer, was to be "estimated as a means to higher results. . . . To those who hereafter give to this branch of psychology a thoroughly scientific organization, Mr. Bain's book will be indispensable" (Brett 641).

Bain was as certain in his own mind that associationism was the mechanism for explaining mental behavior as Charles Darwin was that natural selection was the mechanism for explaining evolution. And in the same way that Darwin may occasionally be taken for a progressivist or neo-Lamarckian, Bain occasionally uses the vocabulary or slips into the presuppositions of the opposition. But the differences are serious business. His self-image was at stake.

In his early forties, starting his teaching career in English—a subject for which he had no preparation beyond his background in mental philosophy—Bain spent his next forty years pontificating on the scientific approach to education, writing and revising his genre-setting textbook on *English Composition and Rhetoric,* and presiding over the demise of the association psychology against the onslaught of evolutionary theory and the rise of the experimental method in psychology.

His discussion in *Mental Science* (the popular abridgement of his two-volume psychology) leaves little doubt about his theoretical position. He declares:

> The functions of Intellect, Intelligence, or Thought, are known by such names as Memory, Judgment, Abstraction, Reason, Imagination.
>
> These last designations were adopted by Reid, Stewart, and others, as providing a division of the powers of the Intellect. But, strictly looked at, the division is bad; the parts do not mutually exclude each other. The real subdivision of the intellectual functions is that formerly given, and now repeated.
>
> 2. The primary attributes of Intellect are (1) Consciousness of *Difference,* (2) Consciousness of *Agreement,* and (3) *Retentiveness.* Every properly intellectual function involves one or more of these attributes and nothing else. (82)

Aristotle's principles are retained: Difference is contrast; agreement is similarity; and retentiveness is synonymous with contiguity. And these are the principles around which he wove his rhetoric. Crowley refers to Bain's view of persuasion as "strengthening or loosening the bonds that cement ideas in the mind" as a "rather eccentric innovation" (108), but it epitomizes his whole approach. Her suspicion that he did not really like rhetoric is exactly right. The 1866 text was his *De Inventione* filtered through Associationism.

School rhetoric became inextricably wedded to the faculties of George Campbell, not because Bain was a faculty psychologist—he was not—and not because all the aims of writing could be reduced to Description, Narration, Exposition, Argumentation, and Poetry—they could not—but because his text was there, along with Priestley and Whately and, of course, Aristotle when Bain sat down to do his preparatory cram of rhetorical theory before starting to teach it. Campbell had declared too confidently that the aims of discourse are reducible to four because, he said, we never have as an aim "to remember" (76). "We can see with only a moment of reflection," said Cleanth Brooks and Robert Penn Warren a century and a half later, "that these four types of intention [to inform the reader, to change the reader, to convey the quality of experience to the reader, to tell the reader about an event] correspond to the four basic kinds of discourse: EXPOSITION, ARGUMENT, DESCRIPTION, AND NARRATION" (Britton 4). "In fact it requires only a little more than 'a moment of reflection' to appreciate that these [Bain's] time-honored categories will not serve as a conceptual framework for the study of writing" (4), complained James Britton et al. 200 years later in distinctly hortatory language.

IMPLICATIONS

In the nineteenth century, the overlap between the "faculty psychology" explanation of memory and the "natural kind" explanation is clearly evident in the question of the mental abilities of women. An effective argument in the debate against the education of girls was that their apparent academic ability was attributable to memory, a power of perception (akin to having superior eyesight), and not to intellect. If anything, the otherwise unaccountable equality of girls with their brothers in school work reinforced a belief in the separation of memory and intelligence. The certainty of the inferiority of female intellect could be used to support either view, but whether those who held a low opinion of female intelligence were faculty psychologists, whether they were persuaded that women were of a lower order in the natural world, or whether they felt any need for theoretical consistency at all may be putting too fine a point on the discussion. In an 1873 defense of *The Liberal Education of Women,* a professor of Vassar College pontificates that "while the mental faculties in the two sexes are essentially the same, they are very different in their proportions." Vassar students, he feels certain, have "a memory more quick to receive, if not so retentive as a man's" (Orton 274–75).

Introducing "Associationism" as an alternative explanation did not markedly improve the quality of the debate. The Associationists' harking back to the Aristotelian distinction between memory as an attribute of lower forms of life and recollection as a sign of the more advanced intelligence only encouraged the neo-Larmarckian (progressive) evolutionists in their misguided racism, sexism, and—finally—the class-based elitism that came to characterize the teaching of English. When Harvard professor Barrett Wendell lamented "the clear and definite signs of inferiority" of, as Jean Piche paraphrases, "the hordes of alien and illiterate peasants" upsetting the "ethnic purity" where his "New England Elizabethan forbears worked out their 'unfettered Anglo-Saxon genius'" (18–19), his theoretical justification was *not* faculty psychology.

And so, in the endless see-saw of definition and explanation that separates disciplines, we might say, contra George Campbell, that there is a profound need for a form of discourse addressed to the faculty of Memory.

WORKS CITED

Applebee, Arthur N. *Tradition and Reform in the Teaching of English: A History.* Urbana: NCTE, 1974.

Aristotle. *On Memory.* Trans. Richard Sorabji. Providence, RI: Brown UP, 1972.

Augustine, Aurelius. *Augustine of Hippo: Selected Writings.* Trans. Mary T. Clark. New York: Paulist Press, 1984.

Bain, Alexander. *Autobiography.* London: Longmans, 1904.

———. *Education as a Science* (1878). New York: Appleton, 1884.

———. *English Composition and Rhetoric: A Manual.* New York: American Book Co., 1866.

———. *English Composition and Rhetoric: Enlarged Edition.* New York: American Book Co., 1887.

———. "A Historical View of the Theories of the Soul." *Fortnightly Review* (May 1866): 47–62.

———. *John Stuart Mill. A Criticism with Personal Recollections.* London, 1882.

———. *Mental Science: A Compendium of Psychology and the History of Philosophy Designed as a Text-Book for High-Schools and Colleges.* New York: American Book., 1868.

———. "On 'Association' Controversies." *Mind: A Quarterly Review of Psychology and Rhetoric* 46 (Apr. 1887): 161–82.

———. *On the Study of Character Including an Estimate of Phrenology.* London: Parker, Son, and Bourn, West Strand, 1861.

———. *Senses and Intellect.* 3rd. ed. London: Longmans, 1868.

Berkeley, George. *A Treatise Concerning the Principles of Human Knowledge.* La Salle: Open Court, 1963.

Boring, Edwin G. *A History of Experimental Psychology* (1929). New York: Appleton, 1950.

Brett, George Sidney. *History of Psychology.* New York: Macmillan, 1953.

Britton, James, Tony Burgess, Nancy Martin, Alex McLeod, and Harold Rosen. *The Development of Writing Abilities (11–18).* London: Macmillan, 1975.

Campbell, George. *The Philosophy of Rhetoric.* Ed. Lloyd F. Bitzer. Carbondale: Southern Illinois UP, 1963.

Carruthers, Mary. *The Book of Memory: A Study of Memory in Medieval Culture.* Cambridge: Cambridge UP, 1990.

Cicero. *De Oratore, Books I and II.* Trans. E. W. Sutton and H. Rackham. Loeb Classical Library. Cambridge: Harvard UP, 1967.

Crowley, Sharon. *The Methodical Memory: Invention in Current-Traditional Rhetoric.* Carbondale: Southern Illinois UP, 1990.

Descartes, Rene. *Discourse on Method and the Meditations.* Trans. F. E. Sutcliffe. New York: Penguin, 1968.

Garrison, F. H. *An Introduction to the History of Medicine.* 4th ed. Philadelphia: Saunders, 1929. (Rpt. 1960).

Grene, Marjorie. *A Portrait of Aristotle.* Chicago: U of Chicago P, 1963.

Gulley, Norman. "Plato's Theory of Recollection." *Classical Quarterly* NS 4 (July–Oct. 1954): 194–213.

Hearnshaw, L. S. *The Shaping of Modern Psychology.* London: Routledge, 1987.

Herbart, Johann Friedrich. *Textbook of Psychology.* New York: Appleton, 1891.

Hume, David. *Enquiry Concerning Human Understanding.* Oxford, Eng.: Clarendon, 1975.

James, William. *The Principles of Psychology* (1890). Ed. George A. Miller. Cambridge: Harvard UP, 1983.

———. *Psychology: A Briefer Course* (1892). New York: Henry Holt, 1910.

———. "Memory." *Talks to Teachers on Psychology and to Students on Some of Life's Ideals.* Cambridge: Harvard UP, 1983. 74–87.

Kant, Immanuel. *Critique of Pure Reason.* Trans. N. K. Smith. New York: St. Martin's, 1965.

Kitzhaber, Albert R. *Rhetoric in American Colleges, 1850–1900.* Dallas: Southern Methodist UP, 1990.

Locke, John. *Essay Concerning Human Understanding.* Chicago: Henry Regnery, 1956.

Orton, James. *The Liberal Education of Women.* New York: Garland, 1986. (Facsimile rpt. of 1873 text).

Piche, Jean L. "Class and Culture in the Development of the High School English Curriculum, 1880–1900." *Research in the Teaching of English* 11 (1977): 17–27.

Plato. *The Dialogues.* Trans. Benjamin Jowett. New York: Random, 1937.

Polanyi, Michael. *Personal Knowledge.* London: Routledge, 1958.

Quintilian. *Institutio Oratoria.* Trans. H. E. Butler. 4 vols. Loeb Classical Library. Cambridge: Harvard UP, 1959–63.

Rhetorica Ad Herennium. Trans. H. Caplan. Loeb edition. Cambridge: Harvard UP, 1981.

Reid, Thomas. *An Inquiry into the Human Mind, on the Principles of Common Sense.* 7th ed. Edinburgh, Eng.: Bell and Bradfute, 1814.

Sorabji, Richard. *Aristotle on Memory.* Providence: Brown UP, 1972.

Tye, Michael. *The Imagery Debate.* Cambridge: MIT Press, 1991.

Warren, Howard C. *A History of the Association Psychology.* New York: Scribner's, 1921.

Welch, Kathleen E. *The Contemporary Reception of Classical Rhetoric: Appropriations of Ancient Discourse.* Hillsdale, NJ: Lawrence Erlbaum Associates, 1990.

Wolff, Christian von. *Rational Psychology.* Trans. E. K. Rand. *The Classical Psychologists.* Ed. B. Rand. New York: Houghton, 1912.

Yates, Frances A. *The Art of Memory.* Chicago: U of Chicago P, 1966.

Young, Robert. *Brain, Mind, and Adaptation in the Nineteenth Century.* New York: Oxford UP, 1970.

5 *Actio:* A Rhetoric of Written Delivery (Iteration Two*)

Robert J. Connors
University of New Hampshire

Rhetoric, said Cicero, is one great art composed of five lesser arts: *inventio, dispositio, elocutio, memoria,* and *actio.* Invention, arrangement, style, memory, and delivery are the subdisciplines that go into making an oral speech. We in composition studies have successfully adapted the first three of Cicero's canons to written discourse, but the status of the last two, memory and delivery, has always been problematical. Writers are under different constraints than speakers, for whom the original canons were devised. Writers do not need the traditional mnemonic "art of memory" in order to recall their discourses, and the "art of delivery," usually associated with voice control, elocutionary histrionics, and gestures, seems equally out of place among the writer's skills. Other chapters in this book cover new conceptions of *memoria* that make it central to the writing task, but I carry no brief for it here. In this chapter I wish to examine the concept of *actio* as it relates to the writer. The canon of delivery has to do simply with the manner in which the material is delivered. In written discourse, this means only one thing: the format and conventions of the final written product as it reaches the hands of the reader.

In contrast to the vast literature on oral delivery generated by speech scholars, the field of composition has always dealt with written delivery in a series of terse, mechanical commandments. These are usually found on a page or two of a handbook prescribing (and proscribing) every aspect of writing: "Use 8½" × 11"

---

*This chapter is a revised and updated version of "Actio: A Rhetoric of Manuscripts," which was originally published in *Rhetoric Review* 2 (1983). Given the speed of technological change, it will probably be necessary to update every decade.

white bond paper; double-space the manuscript; do not staple pages; leave margins of 1¹/₂″." These commands represent all we have usually seen of the "rules" of written *actio,* corresponding to the conventions of dress, hygiene, and such, which are preconditions for effective verbal delivery.

Beyond the mere conventions of delivery there are many options, as speakers have always known. Writers, on the other hand, have tended to cling desperately to the letter of their handbook laws, never bestirring themselves to investigate whether the standard manuscript format they use is the most effective. That question of effectiveness has to do with ethical appeal, for the realm of *actio* is the realm of *ethos* much more than of *logos* or *pathos.* In presenting readers with manuscripts, writers are creating images of themselves for their readers, images that can support or sabotage their messages. If the manuscript is messy, careless, or hard to read, the writer's image will suffer. If, however, the manuscript is readable, neat, and aesthetically pleasing, it will gain the writer ethical appeal. How that ethical appeal can be achieved is the subject of this chapter. What can writers do in terms of the physical objects they present to readers that will affect readers' dispositions toward writers and their messages?

Professional printers, graphic designers, and typesetters have, of course, made these questions of printed presentation the subject of intense study. Large-circulation books and journals are carefully designed according to accepted aesthetic principles and readability criteria, and a good-size literature has evolved around book design. Much of this literature, however, is highly technical and forbidding, and almost none of it has reached the average writer, whose interests are circumscribed by the need to produce a good-looking and readable short manuscript, usually for nonpublic circulation. The growth of relatively inexpensive but sophisticated computer programs and printers means, though, that many of the decisions formerly made only by professional printers have recently devolved into the hands of average writers. As Stewart Brand said in an early edition of the *Whole Earth Catalog,* we are as gods, and we might as well get good at it.

This chapter does not propose to discuss the intricacies of desktop publishing (DTP). DTP is an area unto itself, one primarily of interest to those who really need powerful computers and large, complex programs to design all the graphic elements of public documents. This, instead, is a rhetoric of manuscripts, documents meant to be seen and judged by only a few people. We are thus concerned here with no more machinery than is in the hands of average contemporary writers—the personal computers and standard word-processing programs that we have come to take for granted in the last decade. These tools give us many new options, but they are not always well used; as one graphic designer put it about some manuscripts she has seen, "Give a neophyte a Mac, and they're all over the road with it" (Donahue). Contemporary *actio* is concerned with learning to use effectively the instruments that are being put into our hands.

TYPE AND TYPEFACES

Fascinating though it is, the question of handwritten manuscripts cannot be dealt with here; there are too many variables, and almost no public business is transacted in handwriting any longer. This chapter concentrates on typewritten and word-processed manuscripts in which the writer controls the format but can personalize it only in limited ways. An important variable here is typeface or font choice.

Until a decade ago or so, of course, there was almost no way in which a writer could have any control over typeface. American typewriters were delivered with one font—called, appropriately enough, "American Typewriter"—that could be had in the larger Pica or smaller Elite size, but that underwent no essential changes between 1900 and the present. American Typewriter, though it today evokes a sort of nostalgia, is a terrible typeface. Descended from the square-faced nineteenth-century typefaces called Egyptian, it is monospaced, mechanical, and unattractive in appearance (McKenzie 31). A number of legibility and readability studies showed that American Typewriter in both Pica and Elite forms is less legible than any other typeface except Old English (Greene; Roethlcin).

Fortunately for most of us, American Typewriter is no longer the standard default for most manuscripts. In the 1960s, typists gained access to changeable-element "goofball" or "daisywheel" typewriters like the IBM Selectric, which allowed easy changes of font, though the result was still monospaced. Today more and more writers, even student writers, have access to word-processing equipment, and it is becoming possible to personalize a typed manuscript by choosing a type font, from the literally hundreds available, that fits your needs.

There is no question about what typeface is currently the most popular for general manuscripts. Major manufacturers of computer printers report that Courier, a typeface that is a cleaner and more attractive version of American Typewriter, is the most commonly supplied font for all printers except laser printers, which allow more sophisticated typefaces (Wickenkamp). Courier has full serifs but standard line thicknesses like American Typewriter. Courier's popularity may be a function of a transitional period in our relations with the creation of manuscripts; many people still have a subliminal sense that American Typewriter is what a manuscript "looks like," and we are only slowly coming to realize that a manuscript need not always reflect the limitations of a mechanical technology from the last century.

If dot-matrix printers have the more sophisticated 24-pin print heads, they can print a number of almost-type-quality fonts. Popular for these machines are a variety of fonts patterned after Times Roman and Helvetica, the two most widely used serif and sans-serif fonts used by printers. Because those two font names are copyrighted, printer manufacturers call their proprietary fonts "Roman" or "CG Roman" and "Sans Serif," but they are very like the copyrighted fonts. Another font commonly supplied with dot-matrix printers is Prestige, which is based on American Typewriter but squarer than the old face, giving a business-like appearance without crowding letters togeth-er. After that come a variety of less-used fonts including *Script, which approximates that annoying old IBM Script face,* and ORATOR, WHICH IS A VERY LARGE FACE MEANT TO BE USED FOR READ-ALOUD MANUSCRIPTS (DEES). Some printers also come with built-in fonts for Univers, sans-serif fonts similar to Helvetica, whose simple and unadorned appearance strikes many readers as legible and unpretentious, and OCR B, a special face for optical character recognition.

When we leave the world of ink-jet and dot-matrix printers for the somewhat more rarefied land of laser printers, our choices of typeface become almost dizzyingly expanded. For those who have the resources, word-processing with a sophisticated laser printer can rival professional phototypesetting. There are hardly any families of type developed that cannot be had in versions for laser printers. Here is God's plenty indeed, and the challenge for most users is to decide which typeface will be most effective. In general, the readability of a font is in inverse proportion to its "interestingness" or visual appeal, and the old standards for laser-printed manuscripts are still Times Roman, a font developed early in this century for the London *Times,* and Century Schoolbook, based on a typeface developed in the late nineteenth century for the *Century* magazine. Here is a general table of readability versus visual appeal for the most common forms of laser-printer typeface.

Century Schoolbook	MOST READABLE
Times Roman	
Baskerville	
Garamond	
Helvetica	
Univers 55	
Palatino	
Futura	
Bodoni	
Courier	MOST VISUALLY MEMORABLE

(from McKenzie 33)

Laser printers, especially those equipped with Postscript font software, allow an almost unlimited variety of effects. There are the very respectable-looking and conservative Romans like Century and Times; there are the Old-Style types like Garamond and Baskerville, which have less contrast between thicks and thins and are still very readable; there are even "new old" fonts like

Palatino, which take some features of Old-Style type and subtly refine them. Many writers like the neatness and efficiency, which are effects of modern sans-serifs like Helvetica and Univers 55, though these fonts are not as universally beloved by readers. Some are seduced by the bold effects of such fonts as Futura and Bodoni, which have very distinguishable features. Some even want the quotidian "generic" impression created by Courier, which looks as if it had been typed on a typewriter.

Which to use? The choice is largely a personal one, but there are certain cautions to be observed. In spite of their popularity, text fonts without serifs, such as Univers 55 and the extremely popular Helvetica, are not recommended by graphic designers. The recommendation comes primarily because it is now admitted that the modern sans-serif fonts do not, as had been thought, promote readability. Though modern fonts appear attractively simple on first glance, experiments have shown that serifs are important in aiding word recognition. As Sir Cyril Burt says in *A Psychological Study of Typography:*

> What [the reader] learns to recognize are the patterns of entire words, not isolated letters. . . . Much of the rhythmic structure of each printed word arises out of the variations from thin to thick. . . . A uniform line or curve therefore deprives the reader of this feature in the pattern. Above all, as psychologists have so often pointed out, the serifs are not merely decorative. They correct the effects of irradiation (visual spread) . . . and help in combining letters into distinctive word-wholes. (8–9)

Burt goes on to say that for readability and word recognition, any serif typeface is better than a sans-serif face. (This finding gives teachers the research ammunition to ask their students not to turn in papers printed in sans-serif "draft quality," because such papers are genuinely harder to read.) Sans-serif type is more *legible* than serif type—that is, individual letters or small blocks of letters are easier to recognize—but in larger quantities is nowhere near as *readable* as serif type (Williams 55).

Burt's mention of the psychological purpose of serifs and thick–thin variations within letter forms may help to widen the use by graphic designers of modern fonts like Bodoni, which when printed with a laser printer are closer to printers' typefaces than many other type styles. As visually appealing as fonts like Bodoni are, however, they can be too much of a good thing; their heavy thicks and hairline thins can impede the horizontal flow of type necessary for easy readability (Craig 54). Heavy-faced, wide-lettered types like Basker-ville have long been known to be more legible than thin-faced and thin-lettered types and are more aesthetically pleasing than the American Typewriter-based fonts.

Final choice of typeface must largely depend on the sort of ethical appeal the writer wishes to create. Century Schoolbook's clean, cool professional look, the squared-off businesslike effect of Courier, the art-deco funkiness of Bodoni, the scientific look of Univers 55, or the "functionalist" simplicity of the Helvetica family all have their place. Each can be exploited for a subtle effect, and the choice of effect is up to the writer.

Fonts fall in and out of style, and as more people gain access to computers, the danger of poor font choice and ineffective presentation increases. Nearly all of the "cities" types (Geneva, Monaco, Paris) developed for the Apple ImageWriter are poor in quality and are best avoided. Outré typefaces to which some writers have access—script types; cursive types; large display types; reconstructed Victorian ornate types; or types like Kismet and BRADLEY , which proliferated on paperback book covers during the 1960s—are best avoided. In manuscripts, it is best to go for the tried and true.

In general, unless you are an experienced graphic designer, it is best not to use more than two different fonts per page (Donahue). Promiscuous mixing of fonts can create a visually confusing page layout, and though new technologies can tempt overuse of new possibilities, it is generally better to use only one serif and one sans-serif font per page. Avoid, however, using two different serif or two different sans-serif fonts per page. There is no real reason to do it, and it looks, as Robin Williams puts it, "tacky, unprofessional, and dumb" (57).

One area that computerization has rendered different in typography has to do with the use of underlining versus *use of italics*. Under the old typewriter dispensation, where font changes were impossible, writers evolved the convention of using underlining to signify what in composed type would have been signaled with italics. Thus, over the past century we have gotten used to seeing underlined words rather than italicized words in manuscripts when the writer meant to signal stress or give titles of works of literature or art. Even today, when word processing has made use of genuine italics easy for those with the right hardware and software, underlining is still the most common practice. Like the uses of typewriterlike fonts, underlining seems to mark us as in a transitional stage of relation to technology.

The consensus of graphic designers and typographers is that writers of manuscripts should use italics, if true italic type is available, rather than underlining (Williams 29). *Do not use merely a different font; what readers expect is a true italic font, one related to the main font being used, as this Times Roman italic font is related to the main Times Roman font in this text.* If you do not have access to a true italic font, it is better to remain with the underlining, which will not be misunderstood.

I should here mention imprint quality. The effectiveness of any typeface can be vitiated by an imprint that is not clear and dark. Where laser printers and ink-jet printers are concerned, imprint quality is seldom a problem, because these printers use no ribbons. Daisy-wheel and dot-matrix printers, on the other hand, can present genuine imprint-quality problems if their ribbons are not fresh.

Generally, a carbon ribbon is superior to a cloth ribbon if there is any choice. If you must use a cloth ribbon, changing it often is a worthwhile investment. It need hardly be mentioned that clean type on a daisy-wheel printer is absolutely *de rigeur.* Owners of cloth-ribbon printers should spend a few minutes with alcohol and retired toothbrush each year in order to avoid a truly damning effect.

Paper*

It should be admitted first that paper does not present many important options to the writer. Much of what is popularly bruited about concerning tint and gloss of paper is pure myth, and the writer needs to know only a few truths in order to choose a paper stock intelligently. Many people believe that tinted paper stock— ivory or light cream color—makes for less eyestrain and more readability. This is categorically false (Luckiesh and Moss, "Visibility and Readability"). Though pure *speed* of reading is not hampered by light tints (Stanton and Burtt), legibility tests done by a number of researchers have all concluded that the most legible format is pure black type on pure white paper. Light tints in the paper do not appreciably decrease legibility, but they do not help it, and dark-tinted paper makes reading notably more difficult. Likewise, the thickness and grade of paper used does not affect legibility; a comparison of ten grades of white paper found all equally legible (Luckiesh and Moss, "Visibility of Print").

Choice of paper is a case in which ethical appeal can be exercised mainly by avoiding negative effects. Aesthetic judgments and not legibility judgments play the largest part in reactions to paper, and a writer should know what to stay away from (Luckiesh and Moss, *Reading*). First, of course, the paper should be the standard American size, $8^{1}/_{2}'' \times 11''$. European metric sizes or $11'' \times 14''$ legal-size papers have their uses, but not outside of transatlantic correspondence or the courtroom. Lined paper, legal pad paper, graph paper, onionskin, tracing paper, and their ilk are all specialized papers and should never be used for manuscripts. They are made for other purposes, and their use in manuscripts represents the equivalent of bad table manners.

White or off-white bond paper is the best choice. Bond paper, which ranges in quality from the inexpensive utility papers used in copiers to watermarked 100 percent cotton papers, is manufactured for durability and stiffness, and today's bonds resist yellowing effectively. All bond papers have a dull finish with no glaze, and though there seem to be no legibility differences between glazed-surface papers and dull-surfaced papers, research shows that reader preference— over 75 percent of readers tested—is in favor of dull-surface paper (Paterson and Tinker 135).

---

*Headings in this chapter do not conform to volume style for reasons that become clear on p. 75 (see last sentence of first paragraph).

Writers should also avoid overly heavy paper. Bond papers are available from the light 16-lb. up to heavy 32-lb. basis weights, but the ideal weight for a manuscript paper is between 20- and 22-lb. Any bond paper heavier than 22 lbs. begins to be too thick to pass as manuscript paper, and a too-thick paper also conveys an effect of opulence and pretentiousness that no writer wants. The same thing is true of "laid" or "chained" finishes; for manuscripts, such effects are extraneous and seem contrived and, depending on your printer, heavy-finished papers may not take ink or toner well. A good woven-finish or smooth-finish bond is always a safe bet. As lovely as a 24-lb., laid-finish ivory bond like Eaton Private Stock may be, a more standard paper serves the multipage manuscript better.

If you are printing on a printer with a tractor-feed, your paper choices are circumscribed. Tractor-feed computer paper comes in two general sorts: utility paper, which can be had in 15- and 18-lb. weights, and letter paper, which is available in 18- and 20-lb. weights. It is best to avoid utility paper, which is usually lighter and manufactured for large data runs. Mechanically perforated, it does not tear apart evenly, leaving obvious tearing tabs on the sides and end. A better choice is the "letter trim" or "disaperf" paper, which is perforated by laser so that it tears apart with no obvious tabs. Letter trim paper is available in heavier weights, and a good 20-lb. disaperf bond is distinguishable from cut-sheet paper only by slightly fuzzy edges.

It should hardly need mentioning (but does) that it is the writer's task to separate the printed sheets of tractor-fed paper, to order them correctly, and to remove the "frelch" paper with the tractor holes along the sides. Unseparated pages complete with frelch are never acceptable; they constitute what is perhaps the worst *faux pas* in the realm of *actio*. Some editors will return unseparated manuscripts to the author unread. These editors are bulwarks of our culture.

If you are printing on a good laser printer, you may want to invest in special bond paper that is manufactured for laser printers. Laser paper is made extra bright and opaque, and it is available in heavier weights—up to 32 lbs.—than most bond paper. Laser paper has an extremely smooth surface so that it holds laser toner more evenly, and it is manufactured with a slight curl to it that is meant to counteract the slight curl that a laser printer's hot toner drum puts into any paper passing through it (McKenzie 154–55). For most other printers, however, a good-quality (50% rag content) $8^{1}/_{2}'' \times 11''$ smooth-finish opaque bond of 20 or 22 lb. weight in either white or off-white is the best all-around paper choice.

The necessity of transmitting your manuscript on paper that is absolutely clean, uncreased, and unmarked by fingerprints, coffee stains, blood, and such, is, of course, obvious. Editors are naturally suspicious of a manuscript begrimed by fifteen previous readings (and presumably fifteen rejections). Reprint any manuscript obviously suffering from combat fatigue.

Typography and Layout

There are many aspects of the layout of a text over which a writer has no or little control. But even in this area there are decisions to be made about such physical elements as margins, paragraph indentions, line length, subheadings, and so forth.

The first question a writer must answer is how much white space to leave on the page. The more white space, the more refined a page looks; but when printing a manuscript you may not want the amount of white space found in, say, an art book (McKenzie 21). Margins are the primary choices writers have to make in terms of the creating of white space, and they have traditionally been dealt with by setting a standard width and announcing that standard as absolute. Typographical research, however, has indicated that the standard margins may not be optimal for all manuscripts. When offered various type/white-space format options, readers most often choose margins that represent about 50 percent of the paper size (Turnbull and Baird 174).

This percentage breaks down to .71 of width of paper by .71 of height of paper if the margins are to be equal. Thus the "handbook margins" of 1½" left side and 1" right side work well enough, but the common prescription of 1" top and bottom margins is definitely too small. The minimum upper and lower margins are 1½" each, and at least another ¼" should be allotted to whichever end of the paper gets the page number (Paterson and Tinker)—usually the top. Although it has been shown that margins play no role in readability or visual fatigue (as had been supposed), their size has a keen effect on readers. Generous margins suggest openness, as does all white space; narrow margins suggest crankiness and penuriousness.

Involved in the question of margins and white space is the problem of justification of right-hand margins. This is an option that has been given to most writers only recently, with the appearance of word-processing and computerized typewriters, which can make both margins straight. The immediate tendency seems to be to use the justification feature if it is in the word-processing software—indeed, most word-processing software comes with right justification as a "default" setting that must be turned off if not desired.

Should a writer justify the right margin? In most cases, probably not. The problems inherent in justification prevent the process from being worthwhile for most manuscripts.

First, it should be noted that experiments have shown that justification of right margins does not add to legibility or reading speed (Gregory and Poulton). It is purely an aesthetic effect, and although it is an accepted effect in book printing, justification is less useful for manuscripts. The two main reasons for this are (a) the obviously "machine-printed" character it imparts to the manuscript, which may not be the effect the writer wants, and (b) problems with spacing, which can lead to a difficult-to-read layout marred by unwanted white space. The first of these reasons is self-explanatory; most writers want a clean manuscript that is not *obviously* the product of mechanical processing. The second problem with justification demands an understanding of printing conventions.

Printing typesetters, when justifying a line, use hyphenation carefully, can choose spaces between both letters and words, and can rely on *kerning*—the proportional spacing of characters in relation to each other—to make the final effect a harmonious one (Craig 170). Not all word processors and printers, however, have proportional spacing; thus each letter, whether lowercase *i* or capital *W,* takes up one-tenth or one-twelfth of an inch. Even if your machinery offers proportional spacing, most printing software is designed to justify by creating spaces between words rather than adjusting the lengths of the proportional spacing (McKenzie 39). This leads to some very noticeable spaces that break up the readability of lines and often create what printers call "rivers of white"—thick lines of white space running vertically or diagonally down the page, as in Fig. 5.1:

> Among them were: Mr. and
> Mrs. Samuel Goldwyn, Mr. and
> Mrs. Florenz Ziegfeld, Mr. and
> Mrs. Louis B. Mayer, Mr. and
> Mrs. Irvin Thalberg, Mr. and
> Mrs. Jack Mulhall, Dr. Harry
> Martin, Luella O. Parsons, Mr.
> and Mrs. Paul Zukerman, Mr.
> and Mrs. Hugh Murray, Mr. and
> Mrs. Ben Jackson, Mr. and Mrs.
> Edgar Selwyn.

FIG. 5.1. Rivers of White.

This, obviously, looks terrible. Until proportional spacing and intraword justification become common for word processors, then, it is better to pass up right-margin justification for the openness and line evenness that come with what typographers call use of "ragged right."

The importance of white space in a layout is well known, but there are only a limited number of methods for attaining it. The most obvious method is by paragraph breaks, of course; the average page of typescript has between two and four paragraph indentions. If there are fewer, the paragraphs usually appear uninterestingly lengthy; if there are more, the reader gets the impression of many ideas being presented too quickly. If, as Paul Rodgers suggests, the paragraph break is a unit of punctuation indicating, "Stop here and rest a moment," it is probably best to try to control each page's paragraph layout carefully to make the format look as inviting as possible. Skipping lines between indented paragraphs is usually not done in double-spaced formats.

With word processing, writers today are able to take full advantage of the readability advantages offered by the *typographic hierarchy:* headings, subheadings, and bullets. The use of subheadings to divide texts has long been a practice of document designers, and recent research has begun to suggest that the use of the subsections with headings can make texts of all sorts more effective (Dooling and Lachman). Not only do subheadings provide white space that opens up the manuscript's appearance, but they also have been shown to increase reader comprehension and the perception of effective organization. Indeed, dividing a text into discrete subheaded sections seems to offer many advantages and no disadvantages.

In the past, underlined subheadings, either centered or flush with the left margin, were the only choice for average writers. Today we can take advantage of different levels of subheads and bullets, done with various typographic cues. The most common are font changes and size changes, but weight or style changes like bold or italic are also possible. Careful use of cuing clarifies the scheme of a text so that readers can quickly recognize the major and subsidiary topics (McKenzie 43). A subheaded section might be considered a "metaparagraph," because subheadings seem to serve the same function as paragraphing: as rest areas for the reader's attention. In general, use short subheadings, and do not break up a heading into any more than two lines. One is better (Donahue). Though it is common to use large type size to indicate subheads, for standard-size manuscripts no type bigger than 14-point looks very good. Avoid using all capital letters as subheadings; many studies have shown that all-capital lines of type are much harder and slower reading than upper- and lowercase lines (Williams 32).

Minor Considerations

Legibility research has contributed several other suggestions to creators of manuscripts. There are, it seems, sound reasons for the old handbook injunction to use paper clips and not staples to fasten manuscript pages together. Paper curved at the angle created by a staple is harder to read due to decreased visibility of word forms (Tinker). A paper clip, on the other hand, allows the reader to deal with each page individually and read it flat. Complex mechanical clips and cute plastic clips are unnecessary. Plastic or paper folders, unless they are specifically called for, are not a good idea. They do not impress, and manuscripts in them are bulky to carry, annoying to read. The old student method of corner-fold-and-tear is obviously not recommended.

If given a choice between using Arabic and Roman numerals within a text, choice of Arabic will promote better legibility and faster reading (Perry). Bolding "peak stress words" (a peak stress word is "in each sentence that word to which the author would give maximum oral stress") in a manuscript so that they are slightly darker than surrounding words can improve reader comprehension

(Dearborn et al.; Hershberger and Terry), but today's printers bold so darkly that they radically alter the appearance of the text, and thus in this case readability works against general aesthetic appeal.

Leaving "widows and orphans"—single lines at the end of a paragraph that flow up to the top of the next page—looks messy and careless. Some software can reformat a manuscript automatically to avoid widows and orphans, but in most cases the writer will have to go through the manuscript checking by eye. The time is worthwhile. In the creation of effective manuscripts, as in so many things, neatness and care are of paramount importance.

Conclusion

The rhetoric of manuscripts is a very small part of the entire rhetorical presentation of a writer. At its best, *actio* effaces itself and allows readers to concentrate on comprehension, aware only that the texts they hold are pleasant to the eye and to the touch. The most wonderful manuscript, however, cannot turn a poor piece of writing into a good one or make a vacuous essay meaningful. The best that the suggestions here can do is prevent a good piece of writing from being sabotaged by silly or careless physical presentation. Like speakers, who are scrutinized as soon as they walk out onto the platform, writers are being sized up as soon as their manuscripts fall from a manila envelope or are pulled from a pile. Attention to the tenets of *actio* can make certain that both writer and speaker are able to present their messages in the most effective way.

Works Cited

Burt, Sir Cyril. *A Psychological Study of Typography.* Cambridge: Cambridge UP, 1959.

Craig, James. *Designing with Type.* New York: Watson-Guptill, 1980.

Dearborn, Walter F., Philip W. Johnston, and Leonard Carmichael. "Improving the Readability of Typewritten Manuscripts." *Proceedings of the National Academy of Sciences* 37 (1951): 670–72.

Dees, Edith. Telephone interview with Edith Dees, Product Manager, Epson America, Inc. Sept. 24, 1992.

Donahue, Kristi. Personal interview with typographer and graphic designer Kristi Donahue. Aug. 20, 1992.

Dooling, D. James, and Roy Lachman. "Effects of Comprehension on Retention of Prose." *Journal of Experimental Psychology* 88 (1971): 216–22.

Greene, Edward B. "The Legibility of Typewritten Material." *Journal of Applied Psychology* 17 (1933): 713–28.

Gregory, Margaret, and E. C. Poulton. "Even Versus Uneven Right-Hand Margins and the Rate of Comprehension in Reading." *Ergonomics* 13 (1970): 427–34.

Hershberger, Wayne A., and Donald F. Terry. "Typographical Cuing in Conventional and Programed Texts." *Journal of Applied Psychology* 49 (1965): 55–60.

Luckiesh, Matthew, and Frank K. Moss. "Visibility and Readability of Print on White and Tinted Papers." *Sight-Saving Review* 8 (1938): 123.

Luckiesh, Matthew, and Frank K. Moss. "The Visibility of Print on Various Qualities of Paper." *Journal of Applied Psychology* 25 (1941): 152–58.

Luckiesh, Matthew, and Frank K. Moss. *Reading as a Visual Task.* New York: Van Nostrand, 1942.

McKenzie, Bruce G. *The Hammermill Guide to Desktop Publishing in Business.* Memphis: Hammermill Papers, 1959.

Paterson, Donald G., and Miles A. Tinker. *How to Make Type Readable.* New York: Harper, 1940.

Perry, Dallis K. "Speed and Accuracy of Reading Arabic and Roman Numerals." *Journal of Applied Psychology* 36 (1952): 346–47.

Rodgers, Paul C., Jr. "A Discourse-Centered Rhetoric of the Paragraph." *College Composition and Communication* 17 (1966): 2–11.

Roethlein, Barbara E. "The Relative Legibility of Different Faces of Printing Types." *American Journal of Psychology* 23 (1912): 1–36.

Stanton, Frank N., and Harold E. Burtt. "The Influence of Surface and Tint of Paper on the Speed of Reading." *Journal of Applied Psychology* 19 (1935): 683–93.

Tinker, Miles A. "Effect of Curved Text Upon Readability of Print." *Journal of Applied Psychology* 41 (1957): 218–21.

Turnbull, Arthur T., and Russell N. Baird. *The Graphics of Communication.* New York: Holt, 1964.

Wickenkamp, Rex. Telephone interview with Rex Wickenkamp, Marketing Director, Hewlett-Packard Corp. Sept. 23, 1992.

Williams, Robin. *The Mac Is Not a Typewriter.* Santa Rosa, CA: Performance Enhancement Products, 1989.

6 The Ethics of Delivery

Sam Dragga
Texas Tech University

"For example," I said, "if you were designing the promotional materials for your company's newest machine, and the machine's specifications were relatively ordinary, you might list the specifications above a glossy picture of the new machine. If you do this," I explained, "the viewer is likely to look at the picture and ignore the words."

I stopped. It was my technical writing class. I was discussing page design techniques. And I realized the implications of my lesson: "However," I said quickly, "doing that isn't quite ethical, is it?" And with that, I launched my class on a brief and impromptu discussion of the ethics of page design.

THE REVIVAL OF THE CANON OF DELIVERY

I teach my writing students to perceive the canon of invention as analysis of aim and audience as well as information gathering, the canon of arrangement as the organization of information to achieve a clear and cohesive discourse, the canon of style as the choice of appropriate words and illustrations, the canon of memory as the process of inscribing the discourse to avoid dependence on human memory, and the canon of delivery as the displaying of typographic and illustrative characteristics on a page or screen.

Prior to the introduction of computerized word processing, graphics creation, and page design, writers virtually ignored the canon of delivery. The writer's job was to compose words. If necessary or appropriate, graphic artists, compositors, and editors designed the writer's discourse, creating illustrations, choosing sizes and styles of type, integrating the verbal and visual display. The rapid computerization of communication technologies, however, has given writers access to design decisions, reviving the canon of delivery and modifying the process of writing. This revival of delivery has given writers new rhetorical power. And with this new power to design information comes new obligations, specifically ethical obligations.

THE LIMITATIONS
OF THE AVAILABLE RESEARCH

Writers who possess the power of delivery are obliged to consider the ethical implications of their design decisions. This is difficult, however, because little research is available on this subject. In Aristotle's *Rhetoric,* the advice is brief: "We ought in fairness to fight our case with no help beyond the bare facts" (III.1). Studies of ethics typically emphasize the canons of invention, arrangement, and style because it is invention, arrangement, and style that compose the traditional territory of writers. And studies of typography, illustrations, and page design ordinarily ignore ethical issues because ethics is the traditional territory of invention, arrangement, and style.

For example, a series of articles on ethics appearing in *Technical Communication* (the journal of the Society for Technical Communication) in 1980 (Radez 5–6; Sachs 7–10; Shimberg 10–12) characterize ethics as exclusive to invention. A 1981 article on ethics by Philip Rubens in the *Journal of Technical Writing and Communication,* explaining the importance of developing a theory of ethical communication, discusses only verbal communication. A 1984 *Technical Communication* article by Mark Wicclair and David Farkas, including a series of case studies designed to stimulate discussion of ethics, emphasizes issues of invention, arrangement, and style. In *IEEE Transactions on Professional Communication,* Gregory Clark's 1987 article and William Buccholz's 1989 article also display this restricted focus. And T. R. Girill's 1987 *Technical Communication* editorial mentions graphics parenthetically: "Truthfulness requires that although we condense technical data, we should not misrepresent them to our audience (we can suppress the data points, e.g., but the curve should still have the same shape as before)" (178).

A singular exception is Louis Perica's 1972 *Technical Communication* article, which briefly addresses the ethics of visual display (5). According to Perica, architectural drawings that include prospective landscaping are ethical, unless the displayed items are unlikely to be supplied. Airbrushing photographs to "highlight essentials" is ethical; however, deleting "unsightly or unsafe items" is unethical. Double-spacing and using wide margins so that a publication occupies more pages and looks longer is ethical, as is single-spacing and using narrow margins to decrease the size of a publication. Using special sizes and styles of type, color, and glossy photographs is ethical, unless doing so obscures or omits important information. This is a brief and eclectic list of guidelines.

Although such studies of the ethics of technical communication typically ignore visual display, research on the canon of delivery gives little space to ethical issues. For example, Daniel Felker et al.'s 1981 *Guidelines for Document Designers,* Phillipa Benson's 1985 "Writing Visually: Design Considerations in Technical Publications," and Sam Dragga and Gwendolyn Gong's 1989 *Editing: The Design of Rhetoric*—though covering typography, illustrations, and page design—omit discussion of the ethics of delivery. In a 1983 *Technical Communication* article on information design, however, Robert Williams briefly and ironically addresses the issue of ethics: "An embarrassing fact can be put in the middle of a list, the longer the better. Suspect quantities can be set amid sound numbers in a table, then attention diverted by careful placement of columns, and the like" (12).

Exceptional is Edward Tufte's 1983 *The Visual Display of Quantitative Information.* This book discusses and exemplifies the issue of "graphical integrity" (53–77), clearly denounces the visual distortion of statistics as "lying graphics" (76–77), and offers several principles of ethical delivery, including proportional display, minimal design variation, minimal graphic dimensions, and clear and detailed labeling (77). Labeling itself, however, is identified as insufficient to establish graphical integrity (77).

Books designed to teach the principles and processes of technical communication give little or no coverage to the ethics of delivery. Neither Kenneth Houp and Thomas Pearsall's 1992 *Reporting Technical Information* nor Paul Anderson's 1991 *Technical Writing* discuss ethical issues. And though John Lannon's 1991 *Technical Writing,* Michael Markel's 1992 *Technical Writing: Situations and Strategies,* J. C. Mathes and Dwight Stevenson's 1991 *Designing Technical Reports,* and Leslie Olsen and Thomas Huckin's 1991 *Technical Writing and Professional Communication* do cover ethics, their emphasis is still invention, arrangement, and style. Ethical issues regarding the design of illustrations are briefly and sporadically mentioned, and the ethics of typographical display and page design are essentially ignored. For example, citing the Williams article, Lannon offers the following caution: "Unethical writers could too easily use complex tables to bury numbers that are questionable or embarrassing" (242). Regarding bar graphs, he advises us to avoid distortions of the horizontal or vertical scales, illustrates typical distortions, and declares: "Deliberate distortions are unethical because they imply conclusions contradicted by the actual data" (249). On the subject of distorted line graphs, similarly, he denounces and illustrates, arriving at the following conclusion: "Avoiding visual distortion is a matter of ethics" (254). A list of guidelines on visuals includes the following advice: "Although you are perfectly justified in presenting data in the best light, you are ethically responsible for avoiding misrepresentation" (270). On page design, again citing the Williams article, Lannon offers a single caution: "Long lists could be used by unethical writers to camouflage this or that piece of bad or embarrassing news" (288).

Lannon's coverage of ethics, however, is superior to Markel's, Mathes and Stevenson's, or Olsen and Huckin's. Citing the Perica article, Markel cautions that "it is relatively simple to manipulate drawings and photographs to influence the reader unfairly" (19). He also exemplifies unfair graphics: "A product information sheet for a computer is misleading if the accompanying photograph of the unit includes a modem when the modem is sold separately and is not part of the purchase price of the system" (19). In discussing and illustrating bar graphs, he denounces suppression of the zero point as unethical (289).

Mathes and Stevenson offer six basic guidelines on the design of graphics, but neither exemplify nor illustrate their six points. Their orientation to this issue is to perceive graphical accuracy as a question of professional skill as opposed to professional ethics: "Accuracy is the badge of the professional" (370).

According to Olsen and Huckin, "A visual aid which falsifies information or misleads your audience may hurt your reputation, since it may lead people to see you as dishonest" (168). Their discussion and illustration of this ethics of expediency covers only distortion of a bar graph through suppression of the zero point (171–72).

The failure of technical communication research to address this important issue leaves technical writing teachers without the guidance necessary to direct the ethical exercise of this new rhetorical power. And without the guidance of research, students and professionals are likely to adopt ad hoc and oftentimes erratic guidelines.

A SURVEY OF PROFESSIONALS
AND STUDENTS ON THE ETHICS
OF DELIVERY

I decided to survey practicing technical communicators as well as technical communication majors and minors regarding their opinion of various delivery situations. Ideally, using the findings of this survey, I could determine the ethical principles that guide their design decisions. Given such principles—a starting point for building a philosophy of ethical delivery—teachers of technical communication might develop ethical guidelines regarding the design of typography, illustrations, and pages.

The survey itself comprises seven questions (see Fig. 6.1). Each question is assessed on a five-point scale, and a brief explanation of each answer is solicited.

Question 1 (the compressed résumé) investigates issues of typographical display. Shrinking the type and the leading to squeeze additional information on a page is a common practice. The Perica article judges it ethical.

FIG. 6.1.   Survey of Ethical Choices on Delivery.

1. A prospective employer asks job applicants for a one-page résumé. In order to include a little more information on your one page, you slightly decrease the type size and the leading (i.e., the horizontal space between lines). Is this ethical?

1	2	3	4	5
Completely	Mostly	Ethics	Mostly	Completely
ethical	ethical	uncertain	unethical	unethical

Please explain:

2. You are preparing an annual report for the members of the American Wildlife Association. Included in the report is a pie chart displaying how contributions to the association are used. Each piece of the pie is labeled and its percentage is displayed. In order to de-emphasize the piece of the pie labeled "Administrative Costs," you color this piece green because cool colors make things look smaller. In order to emphasize the piece of the pie labeled "Wildlife Conservation Activities," you color this piece red because hot colors make things look bigger. Is this ethical?

1	2	3	4	5
Completely	Mostly	Ethics	Mostly	Completely
ethical	ethical	uncertain	unethical	unethical

Please explain:

3. You have been asked to design materials that will be used to recruit new employees. You decide to include photographs of the company's employees and its facilities. Your company has no disabled employees. You ask one of the employees to sit in a wheelchair for one of the photographs. Is this ethical?

1	2	3	4	5
Completely	Mostly	Ethics	Mostly	Completely
ethical	ethical	uncertain	unethical	unethical

Please explain:

4. You have been asked to evaluate a subordinate for possible promotion. In order to emphasize the employee's qualifications, you display these in a bulleted list. In order to de-emphasize the employee's deficiencies, you display these in a paragraph. Is this ethical?

1	2	3	4	5
Completely	Mostly	Ethics	Mostly	Completely
ethical	ethical	uncertain	unethical	unethical

Please explain:

(*Continued*)

FIG. 6.1.   (*Continued*)

5. A major client of your company has issued a request for proposals. The maximum length is 25 pages. You have written your proposal and it is 21 pages. You worry that you may be at a disadvantage if your proposal seems short. In order to make your proposal appear longer, you slightly increase the type size and the leading (i.e., the horizontal space between lines). Is this ethical?

1	2	3	4	5
Completely ethical	Mostly ethical	Ethics uncertain	Mostly unethical	Completely unethical

Please explain:

6. You are preparing materials for potential investors, including a 5-year profile of your company's sales figures. Your sales have steadily decreased every year for five years. You design a line graph to display your sales figures. You clearly label each year and the corresponding annual sales. In order to de-emphasize the decreasing sales, you reverse the chronology on the horizontal axis, from 1987, 1988, 1989, 1990, 1991 to 1991, 1990, 1989, 1988, 1987. This way the year with the lowest sales (1991) occurs first and the year with the highest sales (1987) occurs last. Thus the data line rises from left to right and gives the viewer a positive initial impression of your company. Is this ethical?

1	2	3	4	5
Completely ethical	Mostly ethical	Ethics uncertain	Mostly unethical	Completely unethical

Please explain:

7. You are designing materials for your company's newest product. Included is a detailed explanation of the product's limited warranty. In order to emphasize that the product carries a warranty, you display the word "Warranty" in a large size of type, in upper- and lowercase letters, making the word as visible and readable as possible. In order to de-emphasize the details of the warranty, you display this information in smaller type and in all capital letters, making it more difficult to read and thus more likely to be skipped. Is this ethical?

1	2	3	4	5
Completely ethical	Mostly ethical	Ethics uncertain	Mostly unethical	Completely unethical

Please explain:

Question 2 (the colored pie chart) focuses on the design of graphic illustrations, specifically using color. Without criticizing it as unethical, Lannon describes a similar technique: "If you are trying for emphasis, be aware that darker bars are seen as larger and closer and more important than lighter bars of the same size (250). Tufte, however, might consider this graphic unethical because of its unnecessary and deceptive design variation.

Question 3 (the wheelchair photograph) addresses the design of pictorial illustrations. Perica's guideline on this issue proves ambiguous.

Question 4 (the subordinate's evaluation) addresses the issue of page design. Williams and Lannon would judge this situation unethical.

Question 5 (the amplified proposal) is the opposite of Question 1 and is thus obviously a check on the consistency of the individual's ethical choices. According to Perica, amplifying a publication is ethical.

Question 6 (the reverse-chronology line graph) again focuses on the design of graphic illustrations. The little that has been written on the ethics of delivery would universally denounce this technique as deceptive. Though clearly labeled, the graphic is nevertheless a violation of the reader's expectations of a left-to-right chronological progression. In Tufte's book, thorough labeling is identified as a necessary but insufficient condition for ethical design.

Question 7 (the difficult warranty) addresses the issue of typography again. On this issue, Perica's guidelines prove ambiguous.

I chose to survey practicing technical communicators because professionals oftentimes experience ethical dilemmas on the job. Their opinions, as a consequence, would be neither academic nor naive. The professional communicators, I hypothesized, would be likely to adopt a pragmatic perspective on ethical issues, weighing the political and economic implications of their decisions and judging the seven situations according to the utility of their consequences. I distributed the survey to 33 professional technical communicators from five Dallas organizations.

I chose also to survey technical communication majors and minors to determine their perspective on the ethics of delivery. The students, I hypothesized, might be likely to ignore the practical implications of their choices and consider only the intrinsic morality of the seven situations. At the beginning of a semester, I distributed the survey to thirty-one technical writing majors and minors at Texas Tech University. All were enrolled in a senior-level course in technical and professional editing. All previously completed both a sophomore-level and a junior-level course in technical writing.

If the opinions of students and professionals differ radically on ethical issues, the teacher's job of developing and teaching delivery guidelines is itself a genuine ethical dilemma. Is it ethical to teach students to adopt the ethics of practicing technical communicators? Is it ethical to teach students to repudiate the ethics of professionals? In either situation, the student's transition to the working world is potentially complicated. If the opinions of students and professionals prove similar, however, the teacher's job of developing and teaching ethical guidelines is easier, and the student's transition to practicing technical communicator is also simplified.

SURVEY FINDINGS

Obviously, this questionnaire is a pilot investigation of the ethics of delivery and its findings are thus necessarily tentative. This questionnaire also covers only seven issues of typographical and visual display, and its findings thus yield only a starting point for comprehensive guidelines on delivery.

Table 6.1 shows the number of professional technical communicators choosing a given answer on the seven-question survey. Following is a representative sampling of the explanations offered by the professionals for their answers to each question.

Question 1 (The Compressed Résumé)

Completely ethical:
"Unless the employer has gone to the trouble of specifying fonts, leading, page size, etc., the job applicant cannot know a priori what is standard. Rather, it becomes a matter of judgment on the part of the job applicant as to what is readable and visually appealing (and how the page looks when it is copied)."
"A writer's résumé is a writing sample. It not only states credentials, but it is a visual demonstration of skill. Distortion of fact is unethical."
"To make a decision about whether to interview an applicant, the interviewer needs certain information. The applicant should provide this information in a format that is readable and accessible. If adjusting font size and white space promotes these objectives, the applicant should do it. If adjusting font size and white space defeats these objectives, the applicant should not do it. By presenting a

TABLE 6.1
Answers of 33 Professional Technical Communicators to the Survey
of Ethical Choices on Delivery

Question	Completely Ethical	Mostly Ethical	Ethics Uncertain	Mostly Unethical	Completely Unethical
1. résumé	28	1	4	0	0
2. pie chart	20	6	3	1	3
3. photo	3	1	2	0	27
4. evaluation	16	4	7	4	2
5. proposal	23	2	5	2	1
6. line graph	5	2	2	12	12
7. warranty	12	4	9	7	1
TOTAL	107	20	32	26	46

résumé that conforms to the interviewer's format constraints and communicates the information the interviewer needs, the applicant demonstrates his/her ability and willingness to meet the interviewer's needs. The interviewer evaluates this attention to his/her needs, as well as the content of the résumé, to decide whether to interview the applicant."

"The requirement was one page. How the individual chooses to present himself/herself is up to the individual. Presentation also speaks to the quality and resourcefulness of the individual. If the résumé has type that is too small, no amount of information will help."

"Requests for résumés rarely come with specifications for leading, point size, and margins. In fact, the ability to change these values can be an important tool for writers. If you squeeze too much on the page, you'll look stupid, but not unethical."

Question 2 (The Colored Pie Chart)

Completely ethical:

"It is ethical because the idea is to emphasize positive points and de-emphasize negative ones, not to hide negative ones or falsely represent positive ones. The pieces of the pie will still be of the correct size and will therefore be an accurate representation of the data, regardless of its emphasis."

"All the correct info is presented. You are stressing some points and de-stressing others. It is up to the reader to interpret the info presented. As long as all the info is presented, it's the reader's responsibility to examine it."

"I can't help it if colors make things look bigger or smaller. I'll use the knowledge to my advantage. In this case, the use of color is a persuasive technique; the color does not itself convey information in the same sense as the size of the pie slices does. The information conveyed by pie charts is only approximate in any case; more precise information is usually conveyed by the percentage labels that accompany the chart."

"Here a writer is using the tools and techniques of the trade. It is up to the reader to analyze skillfully."

Mostly ethical:

"All reports/presentations are designed to persuade the audience to the presenter's point of view. Colors enhance the persuasiveness."

Question 3 (The Wheelchair Photograph)

Completely Unethical:

"Deceiving prospective employees is totally unethical."

"This is gross misrepresentation of the facts."

"It's a blatant lie. True, it doesn't really hurt anyone, but this is false advertising. It's no longer just enhancing one fact and downplaying another; it's inventing a fact that doesn't exist. It also brings in equal employment opportunity issues and I would think it could lead to legal problems if it was discovered."

"By law, employers cannot discriminate, so nothing is gained by faking a disabled employee. The inclusion of such a picture in published materials could be seen as an attempt to defraud the government into thinking that the employer was complying. You have an obligation/responsibility to your audience. Deliberately misleading the audience is not responsible behavior."

"What interests me most is why I find this so objectionable. It has something to do with the assumption that a photograph represents literal truth. It also has something to do with the impact the misrepresentation has on the message as a whole. In the other situations, the misleading visual components are subordinate to words, and the words are the primary medium of communication. But in this case, the photograph is the primary medium of communication. As such, being inaccurate or misleading, it seems more of a lie."

Question 4 (The Subordinate's Evaluation)

Completely Ethical:

"Smart presentation of facts."

"This is no different from putting it all in paragraph form and simply using lots of adjectives to emphasize the employee's qualifications. Every review is subjective, and there is nothing wrong with using the format of the text to help make your points for you."

"The facts are not misrepresented in any way."

"Presenting information in the best possible light is what design is all about."

Ethics Uncertain:

"If asked to evaluate a subordinate, you are expected to be unbiased. Do not use bulleted lists. Display qualifications in a paragraph. Display deficiencies in another paragraph."

Question 5 (The Amplified Proposal)

Completely Ethical:

"The 25-page length is a maximum, not a minimum. The writer has already met the criteria. If he/she wants to adjust the type size and spacing a little, that is okay."

"The look and feel of a proposal is part of the selling."

"As long as no standards were given, you can adjust the type size and spacing as you think appropriate."

"How you choose to present the information in the proposal is a matter of personal preference."

"No standards were given."

Question 6 (The Reverse-Chronology Line Graph)

Completely Ethical:

"Skillful presentation of facts."

Mostly Unethical:

"This graph could easily be misinterpreted."

"While the data is still accurate, it is a clear attempt to mislead the viewer. From a distance of ten feet, would a viewer even see the dates? Probably not. The only thing worse would be to lie altogether about the decreasing sales."

Completely Unethical:

"The slope of the graph is a piece of information in the way that the color of the pie chart is not: a uniform slope means uniformly rising (or falling) sales. In this case, the slope presents a patent falsehood. Diddling with one of the axes of the graph is a flagrant lie."

"This is clearly a misrepresentation because we are taught to read from left to right and that time moves from left to right in time lines. Subliminally, the reader thinks 1987 is the beginning year."

Question 7 (The Difficult Warranty)

Completely Ethical:

"Ignorance is no excuse. The buyer beware and read carefully or give someone permission to fool you."

"Anyone who wants to read the warranty can read it."

Ethics Uncertain:

"On the one hand, it is important to include all warranty information. On the other, the warranty is designed to be very difficult to read. I would hope no designer would allow that to happen. It is poor page design."

"Readers should read the warranty anyway, but this is certainly an underhanded practice as well."

Mostly Unethical:

"It's not fair to the customer to make it difficult to read, but at least the info is given."

Table 6.2 displays the answers of the technical communication majors and minors. Following is a representative sampling of the explanations offered by the students for their answers to each question.

TABLE 6.2
Answers of 31 Technical Communication Majors and Minors
to the Survey of Ethical Choices on Delivery

Question	Completely Ethical	Mostly Ethical	Ethics Uncertain	Mostly Unethical	Completely Unethical
1. résumé	21	7	2	1	0
2. pie chart	8	12	6	4	1
3. photo	0	2	4	3	22
4. evaluation	4	14	6	6	1
5. proposal	12	10	7	2	0
6. line graph	3	5	4	14	5
7. warranty	6	6	7	11	1
TOTAL	54	56	36	41	30

Question 1 (The Compressed Résumé)

Completely Ethical:
> "I believe this is not only ethical, but also a marvelous use of technical skills to achieve the best results."

> "What difference does the type size make as long as the content includes all the necessary info about the applicant? The employer needs all the pertinent information about that applicant to make a good choice."

> "That's what computers are for!"

> "A résumé is a form of advertising. You are in essence selling yourself to the employer. If adding more info helps, do it."

> "Unless the employer asks for a specific format on the single page, the amount of information on that page is up to the applicant."

Question 2 (The Colored Pie Chart)

Completely Ethical:
> "The use of technical skills to achieve the desired end should always be a plus. As long as no changes are made in the factual realm of the document, the readers should still be able to understand it without being misdirected."

Mostly Ethical:
> "The information is presented completely with percentages. The colors only provide psychological help in de-emphasizing the numbers. If you are asked to do the job by a superior, I see very little problem."

> "You are trying to draw their attention away from the Administrative Costs, but also the numbers are clearly visible."

> "You may have tried things you think will help, but you have not actually misrepresented the information."

Ethics Uncertain:
> "It is somewhat misleading to present data in this way, but if the percentages for each piece of data are present and correct, then the chart is accurate."

Question 3 (The Wheelchair Photograph)

Completely Unethical:
> "You are painting a false picture."

> "The situation is not presented truthfully. The reader is going to perceive something that is not real."

> "That would be giving a false impression. Instead a short paragraph could be included stating that there is no discrimination against the disabled."

> "This is an outright lie. You are having an employee be something that they are not. The information would be misleading to the new employees."

> "This is completely dishonest and misleading. This could cause some controversy if the bogus situation were discovered. This could even damage a company's reputation rather than strengthen it."

Question 4 (The Subordinate's Evaluation)

Mostly Ethical:

> "The attention is drawn away from the deficiencies, but if the whole letter is read, all information is clearly stated."

> "It should be OK for a superior to highlight an employee's strong points for this purpose."

> "This is just a form of creative formatting to reach an objective."

Ethics Uncertain:

> "I'm uncertain because if the list were switched to cover the deficiencies, I'd have a problem with this technique."

Mostly Unethical:

> "You have a responsibility to your employer to allow an informed decision. By choosing this format, you make it harder to discern the full picture."

Question 5 (The Amplified Proposal)

Completely Ethical:

> "Wise use of space."

> "The spacing and the type size may be helpful because the proposal will be easier to read. I see nothing wrong with this."

Mostly Ethical:

> "Nothing is unethical about lengthening your document as long as you have not lied or misrepresented the information."

> "Presentation is a big part of a proposal and as long as you are not adding false information, adding space is fine."

Ethics Uncertain:

> "If your report is complete and well written, the number of pages will not matter because the quality will show through."

Question 6 (The Reverse-Chronology Line Graph)

Mostly Ethical:

> "This is a persuasive tactic used in many presentations. The company must present itself as strongly as it can. The client will be able to read the figures even if presented this way. The company is not lying."

Mostly Unethical:

> "This would seem unethical because you are trying to represent an increase when there actually was a decrease. Anyone just glancing at the graph would probably be misinformed."

> "Although you say the correct thing, you are misleading the reader."

> "Although all the information is correct, it is misleading to present it in this way."

Completely Unethical:

> "Don't manipulate information to give a wrong impression."

Question 7 (The Difficult Warranty)

Completely Ethical:

"The word "Warranty" is a buzz word in Advertising; it gets people to buy. If a person wants to read the warranty, he or she will regardless of whether it's in all capitals."

Mostly Ethical:

"Every product I have ever seen has been labeled like this. It is the buyer's responsibility to find out about things before the purchase."

Ethics Uncertain:

"Although you have not lied or even misrepresented the product, you are encouraging people not to read the terms of the warranty. This could come across as unethical or seem as if there is something to hide in the warranty."

Mostly Unethical:

"If it makes something difficult to read, that is unfair influence. When you buy something it should be easy to read."

"The consumers have a right to know what they are guaranteed. They should be able to read the warranty easily and be able to understand it."

DISCUSSION OF FINDINGS

According to the survey findings, professional technical writers are typically decisive regarding the ethics of delivery: Sixty-six percent of their answers were either "completely ethical" (46%) or "completely unethical" (20%). Students, however, are ordinarily tentative: Thirty-nine percent of their answers were either "completely ethical" (25%) or "completely unethical" (14%), versus the qualified yes of "mostly ethical" (26%) and the qualified no of "mostly unethical" (19%). This finding is no surprise. Although professionals are always learning, the working world emphasizes the utility of technical communication and the practical exercise of the writer's abilities, thus prizing decisive individuals. In the academic world, however, whereas students do exercise their technical communication skills, the emphasis of the classroom is always on learning. This situation elicits the individual's adoption of a cautious and deliberative orientation to professional practices, including ethical choices. That is, students are likely to perceive themselves as still learning the guidelines of their prospective profession and are, therefore, unlikely to commit themselves to a definitive position on specific ethical issues.

On the typographical display of the résumé, for example, students and professionals alike consider this practice ethical, thus subscribing to Perica's guideline; however, professionals are more likely to judge this completely ethical (85% of professionals versus 68% of students). The explanations of their answers are basically similar, with professionals and students both referring to the absence of typographical specifications and to the writers' opportunity to display their design skills.

Both students and professionals offer split decisions on the coloring of the pie chart. Adopting Lannon's perspective instead of Tufte's, 61% of the professionals consider it completely ethical and 18% consider it mostly ethical; only 26% of students consider it completely ethical, 39% consider it mostly ethical, and 19% are uncertain of the ethics of this practice. In the explanations of their answers, professionals emphasize the basic accuracy of the information and the reader's responsibility to analyze the information, whereas students focus only on the accuracy of the information.

Both students (71%) and professionals (82%) consider the wheelchair photograph completely unethical. Their explanations of their answers all criticize this practice as a distortion of the truth. Again students are more tentative: ten percent judge the photograph as mostly unethical and 13% are uncertain of the ethics.

The bulleted listing of the employee's qualifications elicits a wider variety of opinions. Students are especially tentative regarding the ethics of this practice: Whereas 48% of professionals consider the bulleted list completely ethical (thus ignoring the guidance of Williams and of Lannon), only 13% of students do. In the case of the students, 45% judge it mostly ethical, 19% are uncertain of the ethics, and 19% label it mostly unethical. Of the professionals, 12% consider it mostly ethical, 21% are uncertain, and 12% judge it mostly unethical. The professionals typically explain their answers by praising the persuasive formatting of information, whereas the explanations of the students often emphasize the inequality of the visual display.

On the amplified proposal, students are again tentative. Adopting Perica's guideline, 70% of professionals judge it completely ethical, but students split, with 39% seeing it as completely ethical, 32% labeling it mostly ethical, and 23% voicing uncertainty. In their explanations of their answers, professionals emphasize the absence of typographical specifications, whereas students discuss the basic accuracy of the information.

The reverse-chronology line graph causes substantial dissonance for both students and professionals. Following Tufte's guidelines, 36% of the professionals label this graphic completely unethical and 36% mostly unethical, but 15% consider it completely ethical. Among students, more uncertainty is evident: Sixteen percent believe this practice is completely unethical, 45% judge it mostly unethical, 13% are uncertain, and 16% claim it is mostly ethical. Both the professionals and the students explain their objections to this practice by citing the likelihood of misinterpretation.

The typographical design of the warranty causes the widest variety of opinion among both students and professionals. Of professionals 36% consider it completely ethical, 27% are uncertain, and 21% judge it mostly unethical. Among students, 35% claim it is mostly unethical, 23% are uncertain, 19% judge it mostly ethical, and 19% consider it completely ethical. Students and professionals who approve of this practice explain their answers by citing the availability of the information and the reader's responsibility to review it. Students and professionals who object to this practice explain their answers by citing the reader's right to the information.

CONCLUSIONS AND RECOMMENDATIONS

According to the findings of the ethics survey, a philosophy of ethical delivery is only beginning to develop. Students and professionals achieve consensus on only two issues: the reduction of the number of pages by means of a smaller type size and less leading (completely ethical), and the fabrication of visual information (completely unethical).

Students are dubious, however, of the ethics of persuasive coloring and the ethics of inflating the number of pages by increasing type size and leading. On such issues, this timidity is likely to diminish as students leave the academic world, acquire job experience, and adopt the practices of their professional colleagues.

Neither students nor professionals, however, have developed a consensus on the issues of graphic distortion and the utilization of spacing and typography to direct or divert the audience's attention. The writing teacher's intervention is especially critical here.

The restoration of the canon of delivery thus imposes ethical obligations on writers and on writing teachers. If students are tentative regarding the ethics of their delivery choices, it is the responsibility of writing teachers to address this subject, to assign appropriate exercises, and to bring together students and professionals to discuss the ethics of delivery, to discover specific guiding principles, and thus to develop a philosophy of ethical delivery. In doing so, writing teachers will contribute meaningfully to the practice and direction of the field of technical communication as well as to the education and professional preparation of their students. By continuing to investigate the ethics of visual and typographical display and by continuing to question the ethical choices of students and professionals, writing teachers will also assure both writers and readers that the canon of delivery genuinely serves to improve the readability, usability, and memorability of human discourse.

ACKNOWLEDGMENTS

I am grateful for the generous cooperation of Gina Burchard, U.S. Data Corporation; Linda Holsten, Micrografx, Inc.; Marilyn Lutz, Convex Computer Corporation; Wendy Smith, Lomas Information Systems; Bryan Stevens, Electronic Data Systems; and Carolyn Rude, Department of English, Texas Tech University.

WORKS CITED

Anderson, Paul V. *Technical Writing: A Reader-Centered Approach.* 2nd ed. San Diego: HBJ, 1991.
Aristotle. *Rhetoric.* Trans. W. Rhys Roberts. New York: Modern Library, 1954.

Benson, Phillipa J. "Writing Visually: Design Considerations in Technical Publications." *Technical Communication* 32 (1985): 35–39.

Buccholz, William James. "Deciphering Professional Codes of Ethics." *IEEE Transactions on Professional Communication* 32 (1989): 62–68.

Clark, Gregory. "Ethics in Technical Communication: A Rhetorical Perspective." *IEEE Transactions on Professional Communication* 30 (1987): 190–95.

Dragga, Sam, and Gwendolyn Gong. *Editing: The Design of Rhetoric.* Amityville: Baywood, 1989.

Felker, Daniel B., et al. *Guidelines for Document Designers.* Washington: American Institutes for Research, 1981.

Girill, T. R. "Technical Communication and Ethics." *Technical Communication* 34 (1987): 178–79.

Houp, Kenneth W., and Thomas E. Pearsall. *Reporting Technical Information.* 7th ed. New York: Macmillan, 1992.

Lannon, John M. *Technical Writing.* 5th ed. New York: Harper Collins, 1991.

Markel, Michael H. *Technical Writing: Situations and Strategies.* 3rd ed. New York: St. Martin's, 1992.

Mathes, J. C., and Dwight W. Stevenson. *Designing Technical Reports.* 2nd ed. New York: Macmillan, 1991.

Olsen, Leslie A., and Thomas N. Huckin. *Technical Writing and Professional Communication.* 2nd ed. New York: McGraw, 1991.

Perica, Louis. "Honesty in Technical Communication." *Technical Communication* 15 (1972): 2–6.

Radez, Frank. "STC and the Professional Ethic." *Technical Communication* 27 (1980): 5–6.

Rubens, Philip M. "Reinventing the Wheel?: Ethics for Technical Communicators." *Journal of Technical Writing and Communication* 11 (1981): 329–39.

Sachs, Harley. "Ethics and the Technical Communicator." *Technical Communication* 27 (1980): 7–10.

Shimberg, H. Lee. "Technical Communicators and Moral Ethics." *Technical Communication* 27 (1980): 10–12.

Tufte, Edward R. *The Visual Display of Quantitative Information.* Cheshire: Graphics Press, 1983.

Wicclair, Mark R., and David K. Farkas. "Ethical Reasoning in Technical Communication: A Practical Framework." *Technical Communication* 31 (1984): 15–19.

Williams, Robert I. "Playing with Format, Style, and Reader Assumptions." *Technical Communication* 30 (1983): 11–13.

7 Hypertext and the Rhetorical Canons

Jay David Bolter
Georgia Institute of Technology

Who would have thought, 40 or even 20 years ago, that the computer could have any effect on our notion of rhetoric? Yet with the advent of the word processor in the 1970s and the personal computer in the 1980s, a technology that once belonged exclusively to scientists and accountants is now widely used for writing. Students of rhetoric, literary theorists, and sociologists have begun to consider how the computer as a medium is changing rhetorical practice. One fruitful approach has been suggested by Fred Reynolds. He points out that the computer expands the ways in which materials can be delivered to the reader. As a new means of presenting or delivering text (and graphics), electronic writing compels us to reconsider the classical concept of delivery (Reynolds "Classical"; see also Sullivan, "Taking"; Welch, "Electrifying").

In order to examine the computer under the rubric of delivery, we first need to define electronic writing and to see how it differs from writing for publication in print. Our definition must take us beyond word processing. Although word processing remains the most popular use of the personal computer, it is not fully electronic writing. The word processor does demonstrate some of the qualities that the computer can lend to writing: A document in a word processor is flexible, changeable up to the time of printing. But the goal of word processing is still to produce attractive printed output. The flexibility exists only during the process of composition. Once the document is put on paper, it is no more fluid than any other printed text, and the reader of the document still confronts a fixed and finished structure of words. And because the result will be a traditional, fixed structure, writers using the word processor still conceive of their documents in traditional rhetorical terms. With the word processor the writing process has changed, but the product has not. A more significant change occurs when the computer is used both to create and to present electronic text. When a text is written to be read on the computer screen, then both writer and reader can take advantage of the flexibility of the new medium. A text that is meant to be read at the computer no longer needs to have a single, linear presentation. It can instead consist of topical units (paragraphs, sections, chapters) that are related in a variety of ways. This structure of topics is then offered to the reader, who can decide which topics to view and in what order. An electronic text that is in this sense topical and interactive is called a *hypertext*. It is hypertext, not word processing, that fully exploits the computer as a new technology for reading and writing.

The computer can combine graphics and words in the same visual field, so that the topical units of hypertext are not limited to verbal text. Graphs, pictures, and maps can be linked to verbal text and made available for the reader to explore. Personal computers have also recently acquired the capacity to display video on the screen. Thus words, graphics, animation, sound, and video can all be disposed as units in a hypertext. Such multimedia hypertexts are often called *hypermedia*. Even with the addition of graphics and video, the key qualities of hypertext are still the creation of a structure of elements and their presentation in interaction with the reader.

A good example of an illustrated hypertext is *The Dickens Web,* created by George Landow at Brown University (*Hypertext* 96ff). This pedagogical hypertext consists of primary and secondary materials useful to a student of the works of Charles Dickens. There are excerpts from Victorian texts, illustrations from editions of Dickens, short essays by Landow and other contemporary scholars (and students), timelines, and diagrams of the interrelations among these various topical elements. Each topic appears in a window on the computer screen; links to other topics are indicated (in one version) by boldface type. Wherever there is a word or phrase in boldface, the reader can follow the link simply by clicking with the mouse. A new window appears on the screen revealing the linked material. There is no necessary starting point and no definitive end to the task of reading *The Dickens Web.* But the process is not random: Structural maps show the reader what topics are contained in the web, and the reader can then pursue those topics in a variety of orders. The links indicate possible orders that the reader can follow. The text itself, what the reader sees on the screen, arises from the interaction between the link structure and the reader's decisions. There is, however, a further level of flexibility; the reader can add new topics and new links to the web. In other words the reader can join in the process of writing the evolving hypertext. So *The Dickens Web,* like other hypertexts, is never really complete as long as it attracts interested readers who wish to become writers. (See Fig. 7.1.)

A hypertext like *The Dickens Web* is a new mode of rhetorical presentation. In the technology of print, a text presents itself as a row of lines on the page, and the readers move through the text simply by turning the pages. Readers can pick up a

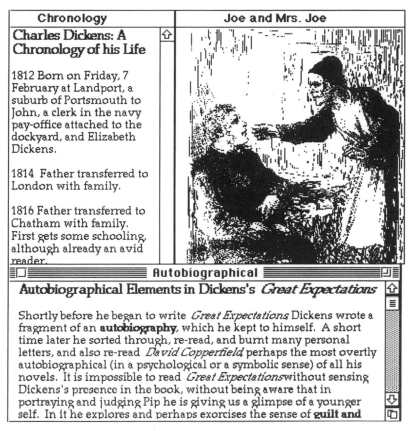

FIG. 7.1. Three overlapping windows from the hypertext *Dickens Web*. Used with the kind permission of George P. Landow.

printed book, feel its weight and the texture of its binding, open it, and put a finger on the first word of the first chapter. In an obvious sense, a printed text exists and remains the same, whether it is in the readers' hands or sitting unread on a shelf. The printed text is present with or without the readers' action. However, a hypertext is not present at all until the readers call it onto the screen. Readers can pick up a diskette that contains an electronic text, but they cannot see or touch the electronic words directly. And the light weight and plastic texture of the diskette do not convey a sense of monumentality. On a diskette or in computer memory, a hypertext is only a potential text, a structure of possibilities that readers must activate. A hypertext program mediates between the textual structure and the readers to determine which topical unit will next appear on the screen. In rhetorical terms hypertext is the mode of delivery for electronic writing. Demosthenes supposedly claimed that delivery was the most important element in oratory (and the second and the third). In electronic rhetoric, delivery once again becomes central, because the electronic text itself is defined in the act of delivery.

Hypertext moves delivery back from the margin of the rhetorical canons toward the center, and in so doing it disrupts established relationships with invention, arrangement, style, and memory. Hypertext in fact renegotiates the ratios of the five classical faculties. The current ratio with its emphasis on invention and style has been influenced, if not determined, by the dominance of print technology and the diminishing importance of oral rhetoric in our culture. Among literary theorists, rhetoric was reduced to style, in part because this faculty is most obviously useful for evaluating written texts not composed for any judicial or deliberative purpose—that is, most "high" and even popular literature. In other academic circles, rhetoric has come to be the teaching of persuasive writing with an emphasis on invention and style. Electronic technology disrupts both literary theory and composition theory. It disrupts literary theory by admitting a whole new body of materials (interactive texts) that need theoretical treatment. It disrupts composition theory by providing new facilities (for interactivity and multimedia presentation) that will need to be incorporated into the pedagogy. So it is not surprising that this new technology will revise our view of the rhetorical canons.

RENEGOTIATING THE CANONS

Consider how hypertext as a new mode of delivery redefines the other canons. To begin with, hypertext brings together the canons of delivery and arrangement, in the sense that the arrangement of a hypertext, the order in which the topics appear on the reader's screen, is determined in the act of delivery. In the developed classical system, arrangement came after invention and was in one sense the art of deciding where to place the arguments that invention had devised. Under the rubric of arrangement, Aristotle established the tradition of enumerating the parts of the speech—exordium, statement, proof, and so on—and naturally fell into explaining how to frame arguments and appeals appropriate to each part (*Art of Rhetoric* III.13–19). In the Peripatetic tradition, arrangement came to be the question of making the argument appropriate to its context in the speech. Cicero too (in *De Oratore* II.76ff) showed how arguments and emotional appeals should be honed to fit into one part of the speech or another. As early as Hermagoras, there seems to have been some confusion about where invention ended and arrangement began (see Kennedy 314–18). Thus, in various ways arrangement included the shaping as well as the placement of arguments.

With hypertext, arrangement means shaping or making the argument appropriate to its context. And hypertext further blurs the distinction between arrangement and invention. Hypertextual readers participate in invention, to the extent that they determine the argument itself based on choices made. *The Dickens Web* is at one level a myriad of essays about Dickens and Victorian England. One path through the web might constitute an essay on public health and the theme of disease in Dickens's works. Another path might explore the impact of the Industrial Revolution on contemporary fiction. A third might be a short essay with graphics on techniques of illustration in the Victorian novel. The readers' choices pull one or more of these essays out of the web. Any particular essay (path through the topics) may never have been read by any other student, and the particular path may not even have been envisioned by the authors. With its hundreds of cells and links, *The Dickens Web* contains more permutations than any one author can anticipate. Do the readers' choices then constitute arrangement or invention? In a large hypertext with many paths, arrangement is invention.

There is another sense in which hypertext redefines invention; it does so by redefining the notion of a topic. The words *topos* and *locus* in ancient rhetoric and dialectic had a variety of meanings. We recall that for Aristotle a *topos* was above all a category of argument: Some *topoi* were specific to a particular discipline; others were common to all subjects. *Topos* continued to have this meaning in other ancient writers, but it and its Latin counterpart, *locus,* also came to mean a stock phrase or rhetorical commonplace (see Kennedy 100ff; see also Carruthers 29–34, 308, 314). Even the modern sense of topic as a defined unit of discourse is not entirely absent from ancient writing. Hypertext can embody the topic in all of these senses. Hypertext is by definition topical in the sense that it requires the author and reader to conceive of text in elementary units that are located in a writing space. (Each screen or window of material constitutes such a unit in a hypertext.) A topic is a verbal or visual element that has unity or coherence: It is meaningful in a variety of contexts depending on the path that the reader follows in arriving at that topic. A topic is also a place, usually both the destination and the anchor for a number of links. Again, graphics and video can serve as topics as easily as verbal text.

Topics can also be fashioned out of topics, and we can see a string of topical units as a topic in the Aristotelian sense, a formal structure in which the links from one element to others provide rhetorical direction and force. As George Landow has argued, hypertext needs a rhetoric that facilitates the readers' understanding of the meaning of its links. When readers find a link embedded in a text, they assume that the link leads to new material that explains or elaborates the current text. The link itself raises expectations in readers, just as the footnote does in readers of a printed book. It is the task of the writer of hypertext to prepare the readers' expectations in the first topical unit and, if the readers follow the link, to satisfy those expectations in the second unit. This process, Landow suggests, calls for rhetoric of departures and arrivals ("Hypertext" 188–89). In *The Dickens Web,* readers may see a timeline on the screen with links marking various years in the timeline. The graphic structure of the timeline constitutes a rhetoric of departure: It indicates to readers that each link will give more information about a particular year in Dickens's life. A good rhetoric of arrival is perhaps more difficult, because readers may be arriving at a particular topic from a dozen different points of departure. For this reason each topic to some extent has to be self-contained in order to justify itself rhetorically.

Topics and links in a hypertext define formal shapes. For example, there is a "footnote" shape: A link leads from one topic to another, and the second topic is linked back to the first. The reader can branch to the second topic for an elaboration and then return to the first topic and proceed. This shape can be extended to create a ring of topics, in which Topic A leads to B, which leads to C, and so on, until the final topic leads back to A. A star shape would consists of one of topic with multiple branches that emanate like rays from that center. Also, there is linear presentation, in which each topic leads to the next as in a printed text. This shape can be useful for short runs in hypertext, when the author does not want to give the reader any choices—for example, in a series of screens that give instructions. In some hypertext programs these shapes are displayed to the user in the form of conceptual maps. The footnote shape and the ring are shown in the system called Storyspace.[1] (See Fig. 7.2.) Many other shapes are possible, and each will have a certain rhetorical effect. The word "shape" could be translated into Greek as *schema* and into Latin as *figura,* which reminds us that ancient theory regarded figures of thought and speech as rhetorical shapes. The rhetorical relationships defined by hypertextual links can also be considered under the rubric of style.

Ancient style was very much a matter of arrangement; the ancient theory of style was devoted to the choice and arrangement of individual words within phrases or sentences. The faculty of style was the faculty of arrangement on a smaller scale. In *De Partitione Oratoria,* for example, Cicero pointed out that arrangement, normally classed with invention, was really a part of language or style as well (i). Most, if not all, of the classical figures were instances either of substitution (of one word for another) or of rearrangement (of words). This second group included hyperbaton, anadiplosis, and hysteron proteron. All such figures become formal patterns of delivery or presentation in our extended sense, and some have explicit counterparts in hypertext.

Hyperbaton is a general figure of rearrangement. It is the departure from normal word order for rhetorical effect. (Hyperbaton characterizes the speech of Yoda in the *Star Wars* films: "Go you must, but sorry you will be.") Hyperbaton is also the controlling figure of hypertext. In the process of delivery, a hypertext makes almost constant use of hyperbaton. The topics of the hypertext appear in a variety of "unusual" orders, because there is no normal order, no single order defined and sanctioned by the author. Readers fashion hyperbaton as they read. This paradox is particularly true of narrative hypertexts, so-called interactive

---

[1]Storyspace is a computer program for building and displaying hypertexts. It was created by me, Michael Joyce, and John B. Smith and is published by Eastgate Systems, Watertown, MA.

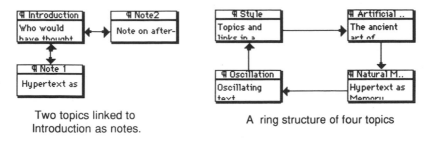

Two topics linked to
Introduction as notes.

A ring structure of four topics

FIG. 7.2.   Storyspace

fictions. In these cases the hypertext is supposed to be telling a story, but the order in which the episodes occur varies radically with each new reading. The order may never correspond to a traditional chronological telling.[2] In the hypertextual fiction *afternoon* by Michael Joyce, the principal incident is a traffic accident, and our experience of the story is largely determined by when and how the accident appears in our reading session: It may appear early, late, or not at all.

In hypertext, as in traditional writing, hyperbaton places demands on the reader. It demands a suspension not of belief, but of the desire for syntactical completion: The reader must hold one element in mind while waiting for the other elements that will complete the expression. Hyperbaton is used sparingly in traditional prose, even when the gap between suspension and completion is only a matter of a few words or phrases. Hypertextual fiction (as well as some modern and contemporary printed fiction) can require a much greater effort of suspension, for the reader may have to wait many episodes for the context of a scene or an event to become clear. It is hyperbaton that makes hypertextual fiction too demanding for many contemporary readers.

In a pedagogical hypertext, like *Dickens Web,* hyperbaton remains a defining feature, but its use is less disconcerting. Beginning with a timeline of Dickens's life and work, readers may branch first to the late novels and then back to the *Pickwick Papers.* Readers may go into detail about, say, child labor in Victorian England, without first looking at an overview of the reform movement. In other words, readers can diverge from (indeed can hardly help diverging from) an obvious or "logical" pedagogical order. But these hyperbata are chosen by readers and, if the hypertext is well organized under a rhetoric of departures and arrivals, readers should be able to maintain their orientation. Hyperbaton is the reason for creating pedagogical hypertexts or textual databases in the first place. Readers want to be able to violate the conventional order of a printed text.

---

[2]Michael Joyce's *afternoon, a story* and Stuart Moulthrop's *Victory Garden* are two recent and important examples of this growing genre. In both cases readers move through the text at their discretion, generally by selected individual words on the screen, words that "yield" to reveal new screens with new yields.

In the first chapter of this volume, Reynolds has explained how the teaching of writing has historically excluded delivery and memory as viable categories. But at least teachers of writing still think in terms of invention and arrangement. In literary criticism and theory, the narrowing has been more drastic. As Brian Vickers, Gérard Genette, and others have pointed out, all the faculties have been subordinated to style. The narrowing of style to a discussion of figures and the reduction of the number of figures began as early as the eighteenth century. In the last few decades, theorists such as de Man came to regard the elaboration of the figures of metonymy and metaphor as the central question of rhetoric (Vickers 435–80). With hypertext, however, the rubrics of style and delivery become two equally valid perspectives from which to understand the interactive experience of reading a multiply linked text.

OSCILLATING TEXT

Hypertextual presentation cannot be assimilated in every way to the ancient faculty of delivery. Hypertext systems are peculiar in that they work by a kind of oscillation. In creating a hypertext the writer moves back and forth between two different activities: adding topical materials and creating a linked structure of those materials. In adding topics, the writer can proceed as in writing for print; the product will be sentences and paragraphs that can obey traditional rhetorical practice. In linking topics, however, the writer is working in a different mode— following, for example, Landow's rhetoric of departures and arrivals. Authoring a hypertext requires oscillating between two rhetorical worlds, one familiar and one new. Sometimes these two worlds may be the domain of different authors: One could create a hypertext by copying primary and secondary texts of other printed authors and simply drawing the links. In the technology of hypertext, linking itself becomes a form of writing.

These two modes have their counterparts in the act of reading a hypertext. While reading any given topic, readers are subject to all the rhetorical devices that the writer can deploy. Both in ancient oratory and in traditional writing for print, these devices are used above all to make the text clear or transparent, where transparency is modern equivalent of the ancient virtue of clarity. The aim of the ancient orator was usually to make the audience see through the words of a speech to the matter itself. The matter or argument would of course be colored by the orator to best advantage, but the audience should not be conscious of that coloring. Similarly, the goal of transparency in modern prose is to make readers forget that they are reading a text at all. Instead of a concatenation of written words, readers should be made to look through the page to the world depicted in the text. Lucidity is also a goal in expository writing: Readers should attend to the ideas without taking too much notice of their particular verbal expression. We have all had the experience of getting lost in a printed book—reading so intensely for the story (or sometimes the argument) that we become unaware of the time, the surroundings, and even of the fact that we are turning the pages.

In reading a hypertext, however, readers must do more than merely turn pages. At the end of each topic, readers must make a decision to follow a particular link, and at the moment of decision, the text is no longer transparent. Readers become aware that they are seated before a computer and need to act in order to make the text move. In other words, the readers stop reading the words and become conscious again of the hypertext as a structure. They begin to look *at* the text rather than *through* it, and this shift in perspective, however brief, interrupts the traditional narrative flow.

A hypertext possesses an oscillating rhythm, marked by the moment when readers are called back to view the structure and decide on the next move. If a hypertext consists of extended topics, the oscillation will be relatively slow. If each topic is a single sentence or a few words, then readers will have to jump back and forth more often and more quickly. Many hypertexts vary their rhythms, sometimes requiring the readers' participation again and again in a staccato passage, whereas at other times leaving readers alone with conversation or narrative for a relatively long time. The capacity to exploit this oscillation is a central feature that distinguishes hypertext from earlier technologies of writing. Neither in print nor in manuscript did the author have a convenient way to command that the readers' attention be drawn back to the textual structure itself. (Nonetheless, the rejection of the simple canon of transparency and the oscillation between looking at and looking through have been characteristic of much modern literature and art. See Lanham 275ff, from whom I have taken this analysis.)

On the other hand, in terms of content rather than technology, the oscillation between looking at and looking through was a familiar technique in ancient rhetoric. Narration was a recognized part of oratory, and in a narrative passage the goal of the orator was to draw the scene as vividly as possible. A good orator could make the audience lose itself in the story. At other times in the speech, the orator's task would be to keep the audience aware of the circumstances of the speech itself—the trial or assembly, the audience's responsibility as jurors or participants, the orator's own position and authority. A good orator would be able to manipulate the audience by taking them back and forth, focusing now on the story behind the speech, now on the speech itself or the legal proceedings. But a good orator would never make the audience aware of the techniques of manipulation, the ways in which the orator brings about the oscillation. Ideally the audience should never realize that its focus of attention and its emotional reactions were under careful control. In ancient rhetoric, then, the rhetorical content oscillates, but the mode of delivery does not.

The ancient orator kept the audience under tight rhetorical control, and this dominance remains the goal of much contemporary writing prior to hypertext. Persuasive writing for print should be nuanced so that the reader is moved toward the goal without being conscious of the manipulation. With hypertext, however, the author must cede some control to the reader, and the ceding of control occurs precisely at the joints in the text, the moments when the reader is invited to choose a link. Such choices break the smooth rhetorical flow of the text. They constitute moments in which the reader can consider dispassionately the rhetorical structure of the text. The reader becomes aware of the text as text and of the author's attempt to structure the experience of reading. No longer lost in the text, the reader begins to look at the text in a critical way. This moment of recognition would have been a sign of failure for ancient orators, whose job it was to compel audiences to regard their speeches as the whole textual world. Especially in judicial oratory, orators never wanted their audiences to step outside and begin to consider their efforts as speeches with some points well made and others not. But that is precisely what the hypertextual author must accept: The reader will be repeatedly stepping into the ruptures of the text and examining their structure.

THE HYPERTEXTUAL VOICE

The ruptures in a hypertext also lead necessarily to a discontinuity of voice. In its nonfigurative sense, voice is of course a part of delivery, and Cicero and others discussed voice particularly in terms of the modulations appropriate for various rhetorical needs. For both Cicero and Quintilian, the purpose of delivery was to add emotional color to an argument and so make the argument persuasive (Cicero, *De Oratore* III.57ff; Quintilian XI.3.61ff). As Quintilian put it, the voice served as an intermediary to transfer the appropriate emotion from the orator to the listener (XI.3.62). The goal was a kind of emotional unity between orator and audience. Orators depicted (not necessarily cynically) certain emotions in their speeches and so called forth those emotions from their listeners. Clearly, the process of identification proceeded on the orators' terms. In hypertext the reader can identify with the author, but this identification happens because the reader begins to take control of the text and therefore to usurp the role of the author. Furthermore, in the ancient conception, delivery comes after the text is formed; it is performance in the sense that an actor performs from the script of a play. As we have seen, in hypertext there is no text prior to delivery; as an individual reading experience, the text comes into existence in the act of delivery. In this sense hypertext has more in common with extemporaneous speaking, in which there is also no text prior to the act and in which the audience can affect the text, as least through signs of approval or disapproval.

Furthermore, the ancients were generally thinking in terms of a single orator and therefore a single voice throughout the speech. But a hypertext, even by a single author, is always the work of two voices—because, at the points of linking, the (apparent) authorial voice falls silent and readers have at least a limited opportunity to raise their voices. Many hypertexts, for example *The*

Dickens Web, are collaborative. Several authors (Dickens himself, other Victorians, as well as Landow and his colleagues and students) collaborated in producing the web. And in principle each reader can join in the effort by adding new topics and links.

Hypertexts are by nature *polyvocal.* Contemporary literary critics have argued that all texts are polyvocal, but what might be metaphorically true of printed texts becomes true at an operational level for hypertext. Classical rhetorical theory was not well suited to the notion of polyvocal text. The great polyvocal (prose) text of the ancient world was the Platonic dialogue. And Plato made it clear that he shaped the dialogue form as an alternative to the univocal speech. When orators and sophists did appear in a Platonic dialogue, they often conflicted with Socrates over exactly this point. Socrates favored question and answer, whereas his opponents (Thrasymachus in *Republic* I; Gorgias, Polus, and Callicles in the *Gorgias;* Protagoras in the *Protagoras*) preferred to deliver their ideas in long univocal passages. Traditional rhetorical theory has little to say about the dialogue.

In the figurative sense, what we mean today by the voice of a text was in ancient terms *persona* or *ethos.* Aristotle himself emphasized the need for the orator to establish an ethos to lend persuasive power to the argument. And the Romans, for whom the ideal orator was a wealthy and respected patron with many clients, readily accepted the idea of ethos (see, e.g., May). But it was assumed that the orator's character would remain constant throughout the speech, although he might choose to remind the audience of various aspects of his ethos at various points in the speech. And again insofar as ethical persuasion is carried over into the modern teaching of writing, it is assumed that the writer will maintain one voice for the length of the composition. The persona may learn or grow in the course of the composition, especially in narrative writing, but the growth should be continuous. Most teachers of writing would not be well disposed to any essay that began in the voice of a young woman and then shifted abruptly to that of a middle-age man. They would demand some explanation for the shift. Yet that is precisely what happens in hypertext, and it may happen not once, but many times in the course of a reading. The discontinuities of voice are radical and are not sanctioned by traditional theory.

HYPERTEXT AS MEMORY

In this survey of the ways in which electronic writing renegotiates the ancient canons, the one faculty that we have not discussed is memory. We can begin by noting that writing has traditionally been understood as a means for extending memory. Writing extends memory by transferring verbal ideas from our minds to a visible surface. Writing externalizes language and memories embodied in language, and this externalizing was what Plato objected to in his classic argument in the *Phaedrus*. In Plato's view, by moving language out into the visible world, writing distorted and diminished the faculty of memory. Memory meant more for Plato than mere repetition; it meant possession, making an idea one's own, and neither the author nor the reader of a written text could possess that text in the proper, Platonic way. As soon as the text went out into the world, it lost its vital connection with its author. It became available to anyone who can read—a flaw for Plato, who believed that many truths needed to be reserved for an intellectual elite. For Plato the problem derived from what we would interpret as the great strength of writing: its ability to fix and preserve a text word for word. As Plato put it, if readers interrogated the text, they would only receive the same answer again and again. The text could not adjust itself to the needs and limitations of each reader, as of course an author could do when delivering a lecture from ideas held in memory.

The gap between internal memory and external recording is present whenever writing is used. And each technology of writing supports a different relationship between memory and the writing surface. The combination of the alphabet and the papyrus roll in Plato's day was a great improvement over earlier writing systems and materials used in the Near East and Egypt.[3] But the papyrus roll, on which text was written in undifferentiated columns without word division or much punctuation, did not allow easy access to passages in a long text. The ancients generally read aloud, spelling their way relatively slowly through the runs of letters on each line. The papyrus roll was therefore most convenient for the reading of whole books or works at one time. Ancient writers often trusted their memory in citing passages from works that they had previously read. The paged book, or codex, was more convenient for consulting works, and in the late Middle Ages, and especially after printing, there were many more works to consult. Page numbers, indices, and title pages facilitated such consultation. So the technology of the paged book was one in which a reader probably relied less on rote memorization and moved more easily from memory to the book. (But see Mary Carruthers, for whom even the Middle Ages constituted a "memorial culture," 8ff.)

Hypertext and electronic writing in general mean another revision of the ratio between memory and writing as extended memory (see Bolter 210–26). The electronic medium promises to expand the number of available texts, although the kinds of texts may be more mundane—sources of information rather than "great" works. Readers in the electronic medium will consult a greater number of texts and perhaps do less intensive reading of individual works. To facilitate rapid browsing and gathering, electronic databases and hypertexts will need automatic searching techniques, concept maps, and "friendly" interfaces. The

---

[3]The Egyptians had used papyrus, of course—indeed they gave their writing material to the Greeks—but their hieroglyphic system had all the visual advantages and verbal disadvantages of a hybrid, logographic-syllabic script.

real purpose of a "friendly" interface is to diminish the apparent cognitive distance between memory and the external source of information, to close the gap between the mind and the writing space. The ultimate goal would be to create a seamless connection, in which readers pass without effort from what they remember to what can be found in the writing space. The readers would then be able to "remember" all the information stored in a vast hypertextual database. This utopian goal is perhaps implicit in all writing systems; it was implicit in Theuth's original invention of writing according to Plato's myth in the *Phaedrus*. Theuth's claim to have invented an elixir of memory suggested that he saw no difference between writing in the mind and writing on papyrus. But Theuth was attacked by Thamus on the grounds that there was an important rupture that he had not taken into account. In fact, that rupture still exists with electronic writing. But, even if the gap can never be closed, it can be narrowed. The inventors and proponents of hypertext are always striving for the smoothest possible transition from internal to external memory.

The ancient art of memory was in fact another way of addressing the gap between writing and memory. It was an attempt to turn human memory into a technology like external writing. The student of memory would visualize a location such as a temple or garden and then inscribe vivid images at various places around the temple or garden. The art was a kind of mental writing, and Cicero was explicit in comparing it to writing: The memory places themselves served as the wax of a writing tablet and the images as the letters inscribed on the tablet (*De Oratore* II.86). Although it seems quaint to us today, the art was a sophisticated technique, and it did not evolve until after the technology of writing itself had begun to spread. The principal use of the art was for orators to inscribe in their minds for effective delivery speeches that they had already composed in writing. Artificial memory came after writing and as an aid to writing. However, as Cicero noted, this writing in the mind was not done with letters but with images. Artificial memory was a method for visualizing one's speech and mapping it into a mental structure. These mental maps remind us of hypertextual maps, especially the graphic structure maps that may be used in pedagogical and other hypertexts.

However, the maps of artificial memory were linear. Artificial memory was above all for remembering the order of points in a speech. Speaking was and is a rigidly linear exercise. Neither Cicero nor Quintilian suggested that the student of the art would want to move around the memorized building in a variety of different orders. Frances Yates explains how the Middle Ages put memory systems to somewhat different uses: The goal was less to memorize speeches, for until the late Middle Ages there were far fewer occasions for public speaking than in antiquity. Memory systems took on an ethical dimension and were used to focus the mind on vivid images of vice and virtue (Yates 50–81). Perhaps in that context, the student of memory could dispense with some emphasis on linearity, because the student could presumably move back and forth among the images, appreciating their individual significance as much as their order. When it was used for text, however, the chief virtue of the art of memory was its ability to reflect the linearity of the written or spoken material.

By contrast, a hypertextual structure is a new way of conceiving of the order of the text. Like the ancient art of memory, hypertext divides text into topics, but the map that results is a network of relationships, not the single line of a delivered speech. (Look again at the concept maps in Fig. 7.2.) Like the ancient memory system, the hypertextual network is operative: That is, it is meant to be used to spin out the text. But the text that it spins is not predetermined. A hypertext is a network of possible lines of thought, rather than a fixed representation of a single line.

VERBAL AND VISUAL RHETORIC

We have seen how hypertextual delivery or presentation takes on roles assigned to arrangement, invention, style, and memory in the classical canons. There is one way, too, in which hypertext seems to break out of the traditional rhetorical categories altogether. An ancient speech was primarily an oral performance, not a verbal-visual experience. The visual aspect of delivery was gesture and posture but, however much emphasis Cicero and Quintilian put on gesture, the fact remains that delivery was the delivery of the words of a speech. As we have indicated, hypertext is not necessarily only the presentation of words, but also of graphics and video. Furthermore, hypertextual documents often include graphic maps of their structure of links. A timeline in *Dickens Web* is such a map: It defines a visual space in which the reader can locate various topical units. This combination of verbal and graphic elements sets hypertext apart—not only from ancient rhetoric, but also from the traditional teaching of writing for print, where delivery must still mean the presentation of verbal ideas in the relatively modest visual space of paragraphed text.

Multimedia hypertext is closer in spirit to the medieval illuminated codex than it is either to the ancient speech or to the modern printed book. In an illuminated manuscript the decorated letters created a subtle space in which verbal text and image were perfectly merged. Meaning was conveyed visually as well as orally; the codex had to be seen to be understood. In hypertext too an image can become part of the text. For example, a map of London in the nineteenth century may serve to organize a variety of topics: Keying on Fleet Street could lead the reader to a discussion of the press, selecting Regents Park could lead to an illustrated discussion of the urban landscape design, and so on. Elements of the map become visual symbols that represent topics in a convenient two-dimensional space. These symbols are part of the text in much the same way that famous chi-rho-iota page of the Book of Kells is both image and text at the same time. As it matures, hypertext will likely draw on the visual rhetoric of the graphic artist or animator as well as the oral and verbal rhetoric of speaking and writing.

There exists, then, a tension between the visual and verbal rhetorics of hypertext. Two different modes of communication confront each other in the same space and are therefore constantly pulling the author or reader back and forth between the pole of purely alphabetic writing and the pole of the purely pictorial. Similar tensions have existed with earlier technologies, but the tension is perhaps stronger with hypertext precisely because of the unified character of the electronic writing space, the ease with which images can coexist with words on the screen. In exploring hypertext, we need to overcome the traditional Western prejudice against images and in favor of words, but we must not then forget the tremendous power of verbal communication. Achieving a new balance between verbal and visual presentation will be a principal task for writing pedagogy and rhetorical theory in the coming decades.

WORKS CITED

Aristotle. *The Art of Rhetoric*. Trans. J. H. Freese. Loeb Classical Library. Cambridge: Harvard UP, 1959.

Bolter, Jay David. *Writing Space: The Computer, Hypertext, and the History of Writing*. Hillsdale, NJ: Lawrence Erlbaum Associates, 1991.

Carruthers, Mary. *The Book of Memory: A Study of Memory in Medieval Culture*. Cambridge, Eng.: Cambridge UP, 1990.

Cicero. *De Oratore, De Partitione Oratoria*. Trans. E. W. Sutton and H. Rackham. Loeb Classical Library. Cambridge: Harvard UP 1967.

Joyce, Michael. *afternoon: a story*. Watertown: Eastgate Software, 1987.

Kennedy, George A. *The Art of Persuasion in Ancient Greece*. Princeton: Princeton UP, 1963.

Landow, George P. *The Dickens Web*. Watertown: Eastgate Software, 1992.

Landow, George P. "Hypertext in Literary Education, Criticism, and Scholarship." *Computers and the Humanities* 23 (1989): 173–98.

———. *Hypertext: The Convergence of Contemporary Theory and Technology*. Baltimore: Johns Hopkins UP, 1992.

Lanham, Richard. "The Electronic Word: Literary Study and the Digital Revolution." *New Literary History* 20 (1989): 265–90.

May, James M. *Trials of Character: The Eloquence of Ciceronian Ethos*. Chapel Hill: U of North Carolina P, 1988.

Moulthrop, Stuart. *Victory Garden*. Watertown: Eastgate Software, 1991.

Quintilian. *Instiutio Oratoria*. Trans. H. E. Butler. Loeb Classical Library. Cambridge: Harvard UP, 1922.

Reynolds, John Frederick. "Classical Rhetoric and Computer-Assisted Composition: Extra-Textual Features as 'Delivery.'" *Computer-Assisted Composition Journal* 3 (1989): 101–07.

Sullivan, Patricia. "Taking Control of the Page: Electronic Writing and Word Publishing." *Evolving Perspectives on Computers and Composition Studies: Questions for the 1990s*. Eds. Gail E. Hawisher and Cynthia L. Selfe. Urbana: NCTE, 1991. 43–64.

Vickers, Brian. *In Defence of Rhetoric*. Oxford: Clarendon, 1988.

Welch, Kathleen E. "Electrifying Classical Rhetoric: Ancient Media, Modern Technology, and Contemporary Composition." *Journal of Advanced Composition* 10 (1990): 22–38.

Yates, Frances A. *The Art of Memory*. Chicago: U of Chicago P, 1966.

8 Oral Memory and the Teaching of Literacy: Some Implications from Toni Morrison's *Song of Solomon*

Joyce Irene Middleton
University of Rochester

> *What they telling you in them schools?*
>
> -Pilate, *Song of Solomon*

"Oral memory" is a concept that refers to a means of storing cultural knowledge within the personal human memory without the aid of writing. It is not the self-conscious, artificial memory system that is more familiar to rhetoricians, *memoriae rerum* and *memoriae verborum*. That "art of memory" is strongly influenced by literacy. Many recent works of interest to the rhetoric and composition community use the phrase "oral memory," but the writers who refer to it have not defined it in any formal way (see, e.g., Brandt; Goody; Havelock; Lentz; Ong). However, through using this concept in their work, these writers make us aware of significant distinctions between oral memory and the artificial art of memory (the fourth canon of classical rhetoric). These distinctions should be clarified so that new relations between orality, literacy, and memory might be discovered and explored for the benefits that these relations would bring to the rhetoric and composition community and classroom.

In early discussions of the Western oral-literate tradition, the concept of oral memory is frequently cited as the storage mechanism of the Homeric bard. Eric Havelock's *The Greek Concept of Justice* (38–53) offers an especially useful analysis of the psychology of oral memorization. Similarly, in other ethnic, non-Western oral traditions, the human, oral memory stores and passes on cultural knowledge without ever writing it down. Using oral memory as a category of talking about language, I will show the ways in which the evolved Western literate tradition not only abandons the historical canon of memory in classical rhetoric—an inattentiveness that is fairly familiar,[1] but I will also articulate the

---

[1]Edward P. J. Corbett's revival of classical rhetoric gives minimal attention to the role of memory, the fourth canon, for today's writing students. In addition, it is the psychology community rather than the writing community that has gathered together an anthology of primary historical texts on the subject of memory (see Herrmann).

less familiar ways in which this Western literate tradition poses conflicts for cultural oral memory and orality as Toni Morrison illustrates this in *Song of Solomon*. I will also show the ways in which oral memory gave African Americans a means to acquiring literacy as illustrated in Frederick Douglass's "Narrative." This illustration reveals strong links to Havelock's arguments about orality as an essential means to literacy for all of our students. Stating that a dichotomous view of orality and literacy is a mistake, Havelock writes in a late essay that the relationship between orality and literacy is

> one of mutual, creative tension, one that has both a historical dimension—as literate societies have emerged out of oralist ones—and a contemporary one—as we seek a deeper understanding of what literacy may mean to us as it is superimposed on an orality into which we were born and which governs so much of the normal give and take of daily life. ("Oral-Literate" 11)

I will conclude this chapter with an open-ended discussion about the significance of teaching memory, orality, and literacy together, with a specific focus on two scholars, Kathleen Welch and David Bleich, who are articulating these pedagogical strategies.

ORAL MEMORY AND LITERACY: A CULTURAL CONFLICT

Of her six novels, Toni Morrison's *Song of Solomon* offers a story and language that shares an explicit interest in orality and literacy, especially "oral memory," which is a major theme in the novel. The story centers on the life of a young black man called Milkman who wanders aimlessly through his life until he discovers that his great grandfather was a flying African. This discovery gives him a focused cultural identity, a strong sense of family dignity and wisdom, and an authentic personal voice. Morrison found the myth of the flying African in a written record of folk beliefs and survival wisdom that were verbally collected from African Americans who lived on the coastal region of Georgia and South Carolina. Thus Morrison's novel, as a literacy event, retells a tale that was historically and traditionally passed on in the African-American oral tradition.

Song of Solomon shows a powerful tension between the demands and values of Western literacy and the tenacity of the African-American oral tradition. As participatory readers, we not only reevaluate the Western cultural assumptions of literacy, but we also confront the effects of these assumptions on the inner speech and psychology of the black community.

Three characters in this novel—Macon Dead II, his father "Papa" (the first Macon Dead), and Macon Dead's son Milkman (the third Macon Dead)—may be viewed as students of literacy who are involved in cultural conflicts between their inner oral memory—a strong communal value—and their outer (schooled)

literacy, which devalues oral memory. Through the experiences of these characters, Morrison asks her readers what the loss of an oral memory implies. The
underlying sense of orality here refers not to differences in dialect or grammar,
but to a set of cultural styles and ways of knowing. In addition, these characters
represent three generations and show not only the cultural conflicts, but a genera-
tional progression of these conflicts; thus they give further insight about the
values, constructions, uses, suppressions, and losses of oral memory.

As the son of an ex-slave who was legally forbidden to read and write, Macon
Dead inherited the values and learning styles of his father's oral tradition—the
dominant means of conserving the cultural knowledge of the slaves. Morrison's
novel illustrates apprenticeship learning, which is one feature of the oral tradition. Telling his story to Milkman, Macon recalls the life he shared with his
"Papa." Macon proudly tells Milkman that "I worked *right alongside* my father.
Right alongside him" (5; emphasis added). Implicitly Morrison's storyteller tells
us that Macon's oral memory was engaged through apprenticeship learning, a
common oral cultural teaching style. In *Orality and Literacy,* Walter Ong discusses the significance of apprenticeship learning in an oral tradition and contrasts this learning style with that of a literate tradition. The apprenticeship, he
says, privileges learning "by listening, by repeating what [is heard], by mastering proverbs and ways of combining and recombining them, by assimilating
other formulary materials, by participation in a kind of corporate retrospection"
(2; see also Ong 43; Burke 101). In addition, Jack Goody, in an anthropological
study, elaborates the way in which the oral-literate hierarchy devalues traditional
oral styles of learning. Discussing "Alternative Paths to Knowledge in Oral and
Literate Cultures," Goody's analysis helps us to articulate the cultural conflict in
Morrison's novel. He states that "indeed 'knowledge' and 'science' have become
almost synonymous with book-learning, to be distinguished from most productive activities which are largely learned by apprenticeship, by imitation, by
participation" (165).

Macon also remembers that because his father could not read, knew only
"what he saw and heard tell of" (52), his father etched in his mind certain
historical figures by naming the farm animals with the names of well-known
Americans, so that President Lincoln, Mary Todd, Ulysses S. Grant, and General
Lee were familiar names to Macon by the time that he attended school (52).
Macon reflects that

> his father may have called their plow horse President Lincoln as a joke, but Macon
> always thought of Lincoln with fondness since he had loved him first as a strong,
> steady, gentle, and obedient horse. He even liked General Lee, for one spring they
> slaughtered him and ate the best pork outside Virginia. (52)

In Macon's reflection we see what Walter Ong describes as "close to the human
lifeworld," a characteristic expression of orality that fuels his own retelling of
this story from his oral memory.

Macon has powerful, fond, loving memories of his father and the life they spent together before his father was murdered. But the most powerful memory—the one that supersedes his memory of his own oral tradition—is the memory that his father lost his name and lost his property because he could not read or write: "Papa couldn't read, couldn't even sign his name," he tells Milkman. "Everything bad that ever happened to him happened because he couldn't read" (53).

Thus, Macon abandons the oral tradition that he inherited from his father, breaks the bonds between himself and his African-American ancestry, and violates one of the most important codes of an oral tradition—he does not "pass it on" to his children. But his son, Milkman, now the third generation in this family, hungers for it, a hunger that manifests itself in father–son conflicts and Milkman's own rebelliousness. Through these agonistic struggles (father–son conflicts), the father surrenders his stories of his boyhood and oral tradition to Milkman. After one particular conflict, Milkman begins an apprentice-style relationship with his father, and the narrator tells us that "life improved for Milkman enormously after he began working for Macon" (56).

As a late episode in the novels shows, the cultural knowledge of Milkman's past needs to be understood in its historically oral context. One of the strongest illustrations of this need occurs during the moment when he discovers the answer to the riddle about his family's history and genealogy that a group of children are singing. Eager to remember the song, Milkman attempts to write it down, but he has no writing tools, and so he cannot record the song onto paper. Instead his circumstances require that he commit the song to his personal, oral memory. In this scene, Morrison's storyteller focuses on the significance of the *mode* of acquiring the knowledge of the riddle: It is in the form of a song, it is highly rhythmic, and it reveals balanced patterns and repetitions. Morrison's readers should also notice that the preserved song includes some words that Ong would call "archaic words": "*come boobe yalle, come boobe tambe.*" No one alive knows what they mean anymore, but they are "passed on" within the context of the song. It was a brilliant stroke for Morrison to place this song in the voices of the children. She constructs a scene in which oral memory is working, and the children naturally and unself-consciously use their memories and preserve this oral history (instead of staging a self-conscious preservation by adults that would probably carry with it an air of reverence for the acts and rituals of oral tradition).

Throughout most of the story, Milkman does not have much of an identity or voice. But we see that oral memory—both personal and collective—is essential to Milkman's ability to develop a conscious identity and to finding a personal voice. He needs to know and understand the cultural myths and patterns that will enable him to deepen his vision and to speak.

This brief illustration of oral memory in *Song of Solomon* throws into relief the cultural conflict between the African-American value for oral memory as a means of storage and transmission and the Western literate tradition.[2] Ong articulates this oral-literate distinction in his discussion of oral memorization. In contrast to the oral culture, he says that in "a literate culture, verbatim memorization is commonly done from a text, to which the memorizer returns as often as necessary to perfect and test verbatim mastery" (57). In the Western literate tradition, writing separates the knower from the known (Ong 44). Memory finds external sources for storage—such as books, libraries, and computer disks. In a recent article on memory, critic Thomas Butler notes our cultural inattention to oral memory:

> We have learned to process experience so quickly, that we are usually not even conscious of what we are doing. And we encode information according to some schema of which we are often unaware. If it be professional data we are more conscious of what we are doing, filling it with other material of the same category, updating when necessary. As for everyday life experiences, we most often have no filing system at all, leaving their later recollection to chance. (14)

Butler's observation points to our modern lack of articulated process for memory and storage, which was central not only to invention, the first canon of classical rhetoric, but also to literacy itself.

ORAL MEMORY AS A MEANS TO LITERACY: THE CASE OF FREDERICK DOUGLASS

Early histories of literacy show that oral memory was important in the tradition of schooling for rhetorical invention, the study of language, and the conventions of literacy, even with the emergence of various writing technologies. Despite the significance of oral memory to literate training, the fairly recent histories of rhetoric and literacy continue to overlook significant relationships between literacy, memory, and speech traditions. On this subject, I will use Frederick Douglass's well-known description of learning to read and write ("Narrative" 274–81) to show how these relationships formed the basis for his introduction to literacy and, later in his career, enhanced his talent for oratorical eloquence. Although Douglass is a real historical figure and Milkman is a fictional character, a significant link between them is the presence of the African-American oral tradition. Both Milkman's grandfather and Douglass were ex-slaves. But where Milkman's orality, through his father, is suppressed in relation to the Western literate tradition, Douglass's orality strengthens his access to the American literacy and schooling of his time.

---

[2]For a longer discussion of this novel, see my "Orality, Literacy, and Memory in Toni Morrison's *Song of Solomon*" in *College English* 55 (1993).

Devoting substantial time in his narrative to illustrate how he learns to read and write, Douglass not only articulates the important relationship between literacy and freedom (and illiteracy and oppression), but also shows how African-American orality and oral memory provided a central means of acquiring literacy. Learning to read was legally prohibited to slaves. But when Douglas was moved by his slaveholders to the city of Baltimore, the liberal urban setting became the site for his formal literate instruction. First the wife of his slaveholder, Mrs. Auld, unwittingly teaches him to read the "A, B, C" (274); implicit here is an orally based instruction. When Mr. Auld discovers his wife's transgression, he exclaims with alarm, "If you give a nigger an inch, he will take an ell. . . . Learning would *spoil* the best nigger in the world . . . if you teach that nigger how to read, there would be no keeping him" (274). Mr. Auld forbids his wife to give Douglass any further instruction. But she has already stirred within him a desire to increase his learning, and he must discover an independent means to acquire more lessons.

Much of Douglass's success is directly linked to the orality of the American culture of the time, what Ong would perhaps call "residual orality." Douglass's narrative mirrors the orality of the larger American culture: It is an oratorical culture, rich in speech traditions and oral rhetorical instruction (see Halloran). Oral-literate training included a focus on classical rhetorical models, especially memory, delivery, elocution, voice, gesture, figures of speech, and reading aloud. Douglass cites *The Columbian Orator* as a significant source for learning to read, noting specifically a rhetorical dialogue between a slave and his master that ends on a highly persuasive note—the freeing of the slave. Highlighting the importance of oral memory to his learning and the repetition that strengthens his memory, he states: "Every opportunity I got, I used to read this book. . . . These were choice documents to me. *I read them over and over again* with unabated interest. . . . The reading of these documents *enabled me to utter my thoughts,* and to meet the arguments brought forward to sustain slavery" (278–79; emphasis added). The reasoning skill that empowers Douglass is presented in the form of a dialogue that imitates a real setting for face-to-face argumentation and that stages the tone of an oral, agonistic verbal performance. *The Columbian Orator,* a contemporary school text, was a collection of dialogues, speeches, poems, and other models for speech making. The contents included texts by George Washington, Cato, Hugh Blair, Milton, Socrates, Cicero, and famous contemporary speakers.

The rich representation of figures of speech and tropes in Douglass's written narrative illustrates his appropriation of American oral rhetoric to tell his own story. The passage that describes his response to his slaveholder reveals Douglass's command of figures.[3] After listening to Mr. Auld's arguments about teaching slaves to read, Douglass writes:

---

[3]In his award-winning book, *The Signifying Monkey,* Henry Louis Gates, Jr., explores and analyzes the concept of signification as a central feature in African and African-American oral and

What he most dreaded, that I most desired. What he most loved, that I most hated. That which to him was a great evil, to be carefully shunned, was to me a great good, to be diligently sought; and the argument which he so warmly urged against my learning to read, only served to inspire me with a desire and determination to learn. In learning to read, I owe almost as much to the bitter opposition of my master, as to the kindly aid of my mistress. I acknowledge the benefit of both. (275)

The figures of speech that Douglass uses here show how much of his own eloquence is linked to the early American oratorical tradition. Thus the implicit orality of the school text empowers Douglass's personal oral memory in his desire to achieve literacy. Douglass had to "steal" his literacy. In contrast to the other city school boys, Douglass did not have the time to read this textbook, newspapers, or any other texts with leisure. Thus the skill for using his personal oral memory was crucial. But, as his description shows, he gains from the contemporary, residual orality in the dominant American discourse.

Douglass learns to read, but he also wants to write. He gains access to writing by drawing on the resources of his African-American oral tradition when he tricks young white boys into teaching him to write. In this episode of the narrative we see that Douglass constructs himself as a "trickster" figure. He stages contexts and uses the imagination of "playing the dozens" and signifying in order to fulfill his desire to write. First, he learns to write a few letters on his own. Continuing, he states that

after that, when I met with any boy who I knew could write, I would tell him I could write as well as he. The next word would be, "I don't believe you. Let me see you try it." I would then make the letters which I had been so fortunate as to learn, and ask him to beat that. In this way I got a good many lessons in writing, which it is quite possible I should never have gotten in any other way. (281)

The agonistic gesturing makes the frame and drama of the contest between Douglass and these boys emphatic. Writing was a prize that Douglass won through his signifying arts. In effect, Douglass's verbal performance provides an early historical image that other contemporary African-American men of eloquence (King, Jackson, Malcolm X, for example) have displayed. Douglass's narrative shows African-American orality as a means of personal empowerment,

---

literary traditions. With specific reference to Douglass's *Narrative,* Gates analyzes one of Douglass's uses of chiasmus. "You have seen how a man became a slave; you will see how a slave became a man" (Douglass 294). Discussing the importance of this passage in the tradition of slave narratives, Gates says that "Douglass's major contribution to the slave's narrative was to make chiasmus the central trope of slave narration, in which a slave-object writes himself or herself into a human-subject through the act of writing. The overarching rhetorical strategy of the slave narratives written after 1845 can be represented as a chiasmus, as repetition and reversal" (172). Also, on signification, see Smitherman.

and the consciousness of orality in American discourse enhanced his potential to achieve literacy.[4]

ORAL MEMORY IN RHETORIC
AND COMPOSITION STUDIES

Some distinctions between oral memory and the art of memory (the fourth canon in classical rhetoric) should be articulated in future studies on memory. Whereas oral memory is a conception for cultural oral traditions and, specifically, for oral epic traditions, the art of memory is a reconceived view of memory that was articulated by rhetoricians and was clearly influenced by the increased acceptance and use of literacy in Greek culture. Thus Frances Yates's seminal work, *The Art of Memory,* begins with a rhetorical, not a poetic, tradition. The very notion of memory as "inner writing" shows the early influence of literacy on the rhetorical tradition of memory. Noticing this literate influence, Goody infers that "the elaborate systems discussed by Yates appear to have been invented by a literate society" (180), not only because of the obvious metaphor of writing that is closely associated with memory, but also because of the shifting focus of memory from acoustic to visual: "Since the whole system depends upon locating visual cues, in a building, theatre, etc., speech must first be reduced from sound to visual elements before any storage can take place, and writing is one way of doing just this" (181). The evolving art of memory shows orality and literacy working together.

New textbooks and research on contemporary issues in rhetoric and literacy need to explore the significant relationships between memory, orality, and literacy. The cultural conflicts in Morrison's novel illuminate a modern problem in literate pedagogy that a few scholars in rhetoric and composition are beginning to articulate and address. Two of these writers, Kathleen Welch and David Bleich, are beginning to develop a pedagogy that links memory, orality, and literacy in the classroom. Their approaches represent a powerful response to the dichotomizing of orality and literacy.

In her book *The Contemporary Reception of Classical Rhetoric,* Kathleen Welch tells us that the deletion of memory and delivery from the five-part canon of rhetoric "has become a commonplace in rhetoric and composition studies" (96). Analyzing the significance of this deletion, Welch argues that if all composing is recursive and is not linear or divisible into discrete parts, then the five

---

[4]Formal schooling for classical rhetoric and oratory represents a patriarchal institution with a focus on training schoolboys to become men of eloquence. In this context, we see that Douglass was able to mingle with schoolboys to gain lessons and access to American discourse. This access was almost impossible for ex-slave women. In contrast to Douglass, we see that Sojourner Truth, who became a renowned American speaker, never learned to write (see Yellen 77).

canons must "work together to maintain a synergistic, mutually dependent relationship" (96). Welch observes that in a complete system of rhetoric, memory is not simply a rote activity, but is a phenomenon of personal power (98). In addition to the attention that she gives to memory as an essential canon of classical rhetoric, Welch also recognizes the crucial relationship between memory, language, and psychology. Thus, she links the study of memory to studies of "interior discourse," which is an integral feature of "oral memory." It is important, she feels, to connect inner speech (the language that is lived and felt) to outer speech in order to cultivate a synthesis between the two (162). Platonic rhetoric, Welch argues, understood this essential language process: "The signature of Platonic rhetoric," she says, "is the subjectivity of thinking rather than the objectivity of texts" (163). She concludes her arguments by linking concepts of classical rhetoric to aspects of secondary orality, or, what she calls "electrifying classical rhetoric" (143).

John Trimbur discusses a pedagogical problem that helps to illustrate Welch's argument about inner and outer speech. One of his students, "an older Black woman," had problems with one of his writing assignments because "she had been taught by her parents not to judge other people." Facing a cultural conflict, she resisted Trimbur's writing assignment that asked her to make an interpretive judgment. But through voicing her inner speech, she generated class discussion (outer speech) that helped the writing assignment to open up to her. Trimbur says "the class proposed [a topic that] seemed just enough to get her going" (217–18).

In composition studies, David Bleich also argues for teaching oral and written language together and for studying one's own language in the literacy classroom. Implicit in his interests are the resources of oral memory as the site for discovering histories of our own language. He says:

> Each person enters the classroom with a history of language use—a history which most people have *no reason for remembering in any formal way.* Once it is allowed that how we speak and write is a product of how people speak in our homes, the speech customs in our native communities and early school years, in stores, on ball fields, in the movies, people will recognize these everyday language-use occasions. If one task of the literacy classroom is to try to reconstruct that history, then many hours can be spent thinking and asking friends about what one only partially remembers. (184; emphasis added)

Given the illustration from Morrison's *Song of Solomon,* I would add to Bleich's description that this history of language ranges beyond the everyday language use into the language use of our historical communities and ancestry as well. Bleich focuses on bringing sources of cultural knowledge into the academic classroom that schooling often ignores or devalues.

Related to Bleich's pedagogical issue, Goody analyzes an oral-literate cultural conflict that literate schooling creates within a traditional oral culture. "With compulsory schooling," he says, "there is an increasing tendency at the popular urban level to see proper knowledge as coming from books alone; it is they that tell the truth, not the knowledge we obtain from our parents (i.e., the elders) or from our peers, nor yet directly from nature itself" (163). This conflict, as we have seen it illustrated by Morrison, creates an artificial dichotomy and hierarchical values that claim the superiority of knowledge from written records over that from other sources. If writing separates the knower from the known, Goody observes the cultural implications of ignoring the role of oral tradition within a tradition of literate schooling:

> [T]here is certain to be a difference in intra-familial roles, relations with the elders, compared to societies where the bulk of knowledge is passed down orally, in face-to-face contact, between members of the same household, kin-group or village. There the elders are the embodiment of wisdom; they have the largest memory stores and their own experiences reach back to the most distant points in time. (164)

Goody concludes his analysis by stating that any efforts to change this hierarchical relationship between oral and literate traditions will call for a "revaluation of forms of knowledge that are not derived from books" (164). Bleich's initiative to study one's own language underscores the action to change language use within the academy.

Bleich's use of response statements seems to accommodate his articulated teaching interests by encouraging students to recall and recreate their knowledge in their own language, drawing on the values of both orality and literacy. Related to oral memory, these response statements might ask students to consider not only the content of their memories, but how they happen to remember that content, without the use of a written record. One aspect of recalling, one feature of an encoding system that both Thomas Butler and Toni Morrison observe, is based on the synecdoche, where a part stands for a whole. Butler says that "in all such memory events we seem to be dealing with *invention*, the memory system abstracting one feature and filing in such a way that . . . it acts synecdochically, restoring the whole" (18; see also Morrison, "Memory" 386). Both Butler and Morrison also note an important relationship between emotion—"a good bonding agent"—and memory (Butler 18; Morrison, "Memory" 386). Bleich seems interested in this aspect of recalling, through which we may explore the nature of "memory events" as well as literacy events. His classroom, "a place where human relationships will govern the use and study of language" (320), also provides an active framework for recognizing emerging patterns of metadiscourse with regard to speech processes, oral memory, and literacy.

Through the collective efforts of several modern scholars who are rereading the Western rhetorical tradition—Kathleen Welch, C. Jan Swearingen, and Sharon Crowley, for example—several paradoxes and ironies have emerged. A reconsideration of the role of "oral memory" in the teaching of literacy produces yet another paradox for this history. Historians, most notably Havelock, have argued that Plato's invention of the Socratic dialectic represented his effort to shift away from the seductive poetic influence on the "oral memory" of the audience, evident through mimesis, and to cultivate a means of critical thinking that could break the "oral spell." Thus mimetic behavior would be displaced by real, active thinking. But in a current history of writing instruction, *The Methodical Memory,* Sharon Crowley observes that writing instruction in current-traditional rhetoric has taken on the appearance of little more than mimetic behavior, the activity that Plato in his oral culture struggled to confront.

New work in rhetoric and literacy must continue to explore the theoretical, psychological, and pedagogical implications for teaching oral memory, orality, and literacy together. The social and cultural implications of such pedagogy will be many and varied, and the brief illustrations from Morrison's novel and Douglass's narrative help to show the kinds of cultural conflicts and challenges that we might face and begin to recognize in our classrooms. Peter Burke's work on memory helps us to sense the broad, complex social dimension for a modern study of memory in rhetoric and composition. He says:

> Given the multiplicity of social identities, and the coexistence of rival memories, alternative memories (family memories, local memories, class memories, national memories, and so on), it is surely more fruitful to think in pluralistic terms about the uses of memories to different social groups, who may well have different views about what is significant or "worthy of memory." (107)

Morrison offers an explicit statement about memory that stimulates our thinking about memory and literacy. She states that "memory (the deliberate act of remembering) is a form of willed creation. It is not an effort to find out the way it really was—that is research. The point is to dwell on the way it appeared and why it appeared in that particular way" (385). If memory is a phenomenon of personal power, as Welch suggests, then modern rhetoric and composition classrooms must create the settings that will encourage the sharing and discovery of this power, settings that will reconstruct the significant relationships between memory, literacy, and orality in contemporary pedagogy.

WORKS CITED

Bleich, David. *The Double Perspective: Language, Literacy, and Social Relations.* New York: Oxford UP, 1988.

Brandt, Deborah. *Literacy as Involvement.* Carbondale: Southern Illinois UP, 1990.

Burke, Peter. "History as Social Memory." *Memory: History, Culture and the Mind.* New York: Blackwell, 1989.

Butler, Thomas. "Memory: A Mixed Blessing." *Memory: History, Culture and the Mind.* New York: Blackwell, 1989.

Corbett, Edward P. J. *Classical Rhetoric for the Modern Student*. 3rd ed. New York: Oxford UP, 1991.

Douglass, Frederick. "Narrative of the Life of Frederick Douglass." Ed. Henry Louis Gates, Jr. *The Classic Slave Narratives*. New York: New American Library, 1987. 244–331.

Gates, Henry Louis, Jr. *The Signifying Monkey*. New York: Oxford UP, 1988.

Goody, Jack. *The Interface between the Written and the Oral*. New York: Cambridge UP, 1987.

Halloran, S. Michael. "From Rhetoric to Composition: The Teaching of Writing in America to 1900." *A Short History of Writing Instruction*. Ed. James J. Murphy. Davis: Hermagoras, 1990.

Havelock, Eric. "The Oral-Literate Equation: A Formula for the Modern Mind." Eds. David Olson and Nancy Torrence. *Literacy and Orality*. New York: Cambridge UP, 1991.

———. *The Greek Concept of Justice: From Its Shadow in Homer to Its Substance in Plato*. Princeton: Princeton UP, 1978.

———. *Preface to Plato*. Cambridge: Harvard UP, 1963.

Hermann, Douglas J. *Memory in Historical Perspective*. New York: Springer-Verlag, 1988.

Lentz, Tony. *Orality and Literacy in Hellenic Greece*. Carbondale: Southern Illinois UP, 1989.

Morrison, Toni. "Memory, Creation, and Writing." *Thought* 59 (1984): 385–90.

———. *Song of Solomon*. New York: Signet, 1977.

Ong, Walter J. *Orality and Literacy*. New York: Methuen, 1982.

Smitherman, Geneva. *Talking and Testifying*. Detroit: Wayne State UP, 1977.

Trimbur, John. "Beyond Cognition: The Voices in Inner Speech." *Rhetoric Review* 5 (1987): 211–21.

Welch, Kathleen E. *The Contemporary Reception of Classical Rhetoric: Appropriations of Ancient Discourse*. Hillsdale, NJ: Lawrence Erlbaum Associates, 1990.

Yellen, Jean Fagan. *Women and the Sisters: The Anti-Slavery Feminists in American Culture*. New Haven: Yale UP, 1989.

9 Mass Memory: The Past in the Age of Television

David Marc
University of Southern California

> *An entrepreneurial mode of selective memory has achieved amazing commercial success.*
> —Michael Kammen, *Mystic Chords of Memory*

The relationship between human memory and documentary communication media is often analogous to that of physical labor and machine automation.[1] In some cases the communication medium does no more than make easy what would otherwise be difficult. Take the case, for example, of a TV actor using a teleprompter or cue cards while speaking lines. The printed words, not visible to the viewer, are used to promote the illusion that the actor is speaking from memory. And yet the memorization of lines, such as a TV actor might deliver in the course of a broadcast, is not a feat that would stretch the capacity of the human mind; stage actors have been doing it for centuries. The written word, whether electronically generated or hand-printed, has merely reduced labor here, in the same way that the use of a jackhammer can break up 10 square feet of concrete with less human effort than if a pickaxe were employed.

But with mental automation as with physical automation, there is an inevitable transcendence of mere improvements in speed and efficiency. Capacities for entirely new operations emerge. The combined physical power of 10 million slaves cannot hoist a rocket into outerspace. By the same token, it is one thing to memorize the Homeric epics and discuss them with others who have done likewise; it is quite another thing to have a library full of books at one's disposal that includes Homer's works annotated by dozens of readers from different centuries and differing cultures. That library is not only larger than one human memory or

---

[1]Most communication media are documentary, in that they process messages into replayable, reproducible documents. Print, film, audiotape, videotape, and computer discs all fit this description. Not all media belong in this category, however. The telephone, for example, is not by itself a documentary medium.

several, but it is qualitatively different. The print medium offers the reader an *Odyssey* that did not exist in a primarily oral culture.

Is all this to the reader's advantage? Certainly the necessity of memorizing poetry (and opinions about it) becomes less urgent as print "automates" the memorization process. As a direct result, the understanding of what poetry is— of what knowledge is—begins to shift. "An educated Greek was one who had *memorized* Homer, who could sing it or perform it," Marshall McLuhan reminded his audiences. "He was a gentleman and a free man."[2] But in the age of books, the ability to recite becomes less important than the ability to cite.

In recent years the automation of memory has accelerated wildly, finding its way into the most intimate processes of thought and expression. For example, the word-processing capacities of the personal computer with which I am writing this chapter offer the use of an internally embedded thesaurus. Before I began writing with a word processor, I used to write with an electric typewriter. During that time I estimate that I used a thesaurus approximately once every 10 times I wrote. Now, with the needed entry available at the touch of a fingertip, I tend to use the thesaurus as many as 5 or 6 times every time I write. Has my vocabulary (i.e., language recall) improved because of this? Or has my vocabulary suffered because, instead of searching my memory for synonyms, I have become dependent on an externalized automated memory, thus allowing my organic capacity for such work to atrophy? Similarly I used to know, by memory, the half-dozen or so telephone numbers I dialed most often. Now these numbers are stored in an automatic dialing memory and as a result I have forgotten many of them, forcing me to carry an address book or to call directory assistance when I need to make a call from an outside phone.

The shifting (diminishing?) role of human memory in everyday life may provide clues to the stunning problems of shrinking attention span and lack of historical consciousness that seem to be plaguing education as well as the entire sphere of public life in the United States. Ideally, the external mechanization of memory should be freeing human memory from busy work and trivia, producing greater opportunities for creative thought. But, in practice, is the automation of mundane recall activities obviating the very discipline that makes such vital creative activities as allusion, cross-referencing, suggestion, connotation, and implication impossible?

Of all the communication media that are displacing, replacing, and redefining personal thought processes in the late twentieth century, none is more ubiquitous

---

[2]This quotation is taken from a biographical PBS documentary produced by Stephanie McLuhan. Cheap printing and widespread literacy have turned books into a mass communication medium over the last 200 years. As a result, generations of students have been asked to read print documentations of stage plays that were originally written by Shakespeare for audiovisual presentation. Some readers of these books have only rarely seen a Shakespeare play produced on stage; others never at all. In any case, their understanding of what Shakespeare did must differ radically from the playwright's contemporary audience.

than television. Above and beyond all of its functions, TV is a throbbing public memory. It continuously delivers and creates history in the form of the news; it continuously represents and interprets history in the form of dramatic programming. By manufacturing norms and by announcing the parameters of acceptable manners, styles, and language usage, it stimulates and constricts behavior, setting contexts and expectations for future events. As a first step in examining how television functions as an external cultural memory for its public, it is helpful to consider the place of television in a broader historical process: the extension of documented culture to the population at large, a process that has been taking place over the last three centuries.

In his 1953 essay, "A Theory of Mass Culture," Dwight Macdonald described pre-industrial Western civilization as the sum of two complementary cultures: a *court culture* based on literacy and a *folk culture* based on oral communication (60). In the former, human memory was externalized into bibliography. Religion, mathematics, documentation of events, criticism of the arts and sciences, and other components in the making of consciousness were transmediated into print and stored in libraries. Access to these data banks was limited to a tiny, genetically determined user group of aristocratic readers. In the case of the vast illiterate majority, stories, beliefs, and skills were passed on by word of mouth in a system of integral kinship relationships. For those who could not read, memory remained essentially an organic (that is, nonautomated) process.

The ruling courts aggrandized their culture through the establishment of institutions such as universities and museums, which in turn celebrated certain authors and artists as geniuses and heroes, certain works as masterpieces, and certain media and genres as inherently superior to others. An accreting history, or cultural memory, was thus written and preserved as the "great tradition" of a society, or *Kultur* as denoted in German. As bookmaking technology progressed, the primarily oral character of traditional courtly forms, such as classical epic poetry and Renaissance stage drama, receded from cultural memory; poems and plays were documented in ink and introduced to generations of readers as print phenomena.[3] The longer-than-life endurance of books became a key element in establishing the rhetorical hegemony of what later came to be known as "high culture." By contrast, folk culture was artifactual and phenomenal, lacking verifiable or authentic texts, lacking the signatures of geniuses, and lacking clearly definable lines of rational evolutionary development.

These two socially determined constituents of feudal culture were not of course completely autonomous from each other. The matter of religion, for example, was dictated to the folk by the court, at the threat of military force if

---

[3]The career of Alexander Pope exemplifies the direction of Western high culture during the eighteenth century in this regard. Pope translated Greek and Latin poetry for English publication and edited a new edition of Shakespeare's plays. Moreover, as a poet, he employed the rhyming heroic couplet, a quintessentially oral line, in works designed specifically for print.

necessary. This was particularly important because religious belief was—and some argue still is—a basic source for all cultural expression.[4] The medieval cathedral functioned as an important cultural bridging phenomenon between the élite and the folk, acting as a communication medium for the translation of the Bible and other religious messages into nonliterate forms such as sculpture, painting, and stained glass. The cathedral also functioned, by means of its lavish architecture, as a symbol to the peasantry of the temporal power of the reader/builders.

Given the significant prescription of religion, folk cultures were able to main some degree of lateral independence from the court. Though unsigned by their illiterate *auteurs,* tales, songs, visual designs, medical remedies, and other cultural items were created, distributed, and retained in a nonliterate system of learning and remembrance. With the advent of industrialization, however, this bilateral model of culture described by Macdonald gradually disintegrated. The horizontal communication system of class equals passing on culture to class equals, both at court and on the back 40, was replaced by a vertical model that Macdonald and others called "mass culture." Under these new conditions an educated elite of cultural specialists developed. It was their task to create culture—at first in print, but later by whatever means available—to be sold at market to the newly literate urban classes. In *Literature in the Marketplace,* Per Gedin writes:

> During the eighteenth century the foundations were laid for what was later to be called "the reading public." The invention of the printing press in the fifteenth century provided the technical precondition for a much wider dispersal of the written word, but it was not until the period of blossoming capitalism in the eighteenth century that the aristocracy's exclusive privilege of education was broken. . . . The reading public developed initially through the publication of newspapers and magazines. (13)

Some hoped that the introduction of literacy to previously excluded classes would result in a general sharing of what had once been the finest of the culture of the few. In *Culture and Anarchy,* Matthew Arnold expressed the hope that "the sweetness and light of the few must be imperfect until the raw and unkindled masses of humanity are touched with sweetness and light" (69). It soon became obvious, however, that publishing-for-profit would reshape and redefine culture rather than simply distribute it more widely.

A new culture of inexpensive periodicals and books went on sale. But what memory did this culture have to draw on for its rhetoric, its metaphors, its vision of order, or its senses of the comic and the tragic?[5] What versions of etiology and

---

[4]T. S. Eliot argues the continuing significance of this point in the twentieth century in his essay "Notes Toward the Definition of Culture."

[5]Pope was a merciless critic of this bargain basement literacy in such poems as "The Dunciad" and "An Essay on Criticism."

history might give it coherence? Here was an expanding audience that had been trained to read, but had not been *educated* by any previous standard. Here was an audience that could read, but could not read classical Greek or Latin. Would or could the nascent reading classes adopt or accept the historical memory that had been developed by (and for) aristocratic readers over the ages? Might adaptations of oral folkways find their way into the print world to merge with an aristocratic world view? The progressives of the reading societies advocated the former; romantic poets, notably Wordsworth, dreamed of the latter.[6] Although a bit of both did occur, the result is better described as a *tertium quid;* new memories—what might be called mass memories—were forged for a new mass culture.

A contest for public memory took place in the book stalls that began sprouting in cities during the late eighteenth century. A prevailing recollective paradigm emerged that would remain at the heart of European politics and culture for most of the next two centuries. Thomas Paine, Karl Marx, Emile Zola, and the other writers who founded what eventually came to be known as the political Left posited an historical memory dominated by economic relations and, quite specifically, by the mechanics of economic exploitation. Pamphlets, newspapers, novels, plays, and other texts from the emerging Left subculture told a new class of urban workers that they could achieve consciousness (i.e., a grasp on reality, a sense of coherence) by *remembering* that throughout history it was their own toil, and the toil of those like them, that had laid the foundation on which all human achievement had been built. Their struggle for food, clothing, and shelter was valorized as the salient feature of the past, and the recollection of it empowered them in an ongoing struggle to throw off the yoke of their exploiters. This heritage of economic exploitation provided a moral mandate for the seizure of political power, a revolution that in any case was bound to take place as the evolving nature of work required ever increasing degrees of education among workers. The Revolution of 1917 institutionalized class memory as official history in Russia and in the republics and parties throughout the world that belonged to or supported the Soviet Union.

Right-wing response, epitomized in the work of such commentators as Arthur Gobineau, José Ortega y Gasset, and various geneticists and social Darwinists, rejected the heritage of class conflict and instead promoted racial and ethnic memory.[7] The granting of suffrage and other cultural rights to the lower classes necessitated a theory of justification for continuing upper-class privilege. To this end, the past was recuperated chiefly in tribal terms. Genetic purity was publicly recalled as an Edenic condition of communal harmony. Evil, usually associated with disorder, could not be traced to an internal exploitative class structure, but

---

[6]Wordsworth's "Preface to the Lyrical Ballads," published in 1801, is a kind of manifesto for an inclusionary aesthetic that would synthesize courtly form with folkish content in a language available to all classes of English readers.

[7]A classic statement of this position is Arthur Gobineau's "Essay on the Equality of Races" (1870).

rather to the introduction of unwholesome exogenous genetic forces. In ethnically cantonized Europe, the chief historical villains in this scenario were the Jews, portrayed as a racially identifiable minority from another continent who had penetrated the national *bund*. Gypsies and other submerged or displaced minorities, such as the Anatolian Greeks of Turkey, fit the bill in this regard as well. Entire European political parties were founded on anti-Semitic and other types of xenophobic platforms, culminating in the election to power of the National Socialists in Germany in 1933 and the subsequent establishment of fascist parties and states throughout Europe in the decade that followed.

Totalitarians of all stripes were particularly keen to use the new electronic communications media to promote or create official cultural memories for their populations. The propaganda films of Eisenstein and Reifenstel, as well as the radio addresses of Hitler and Mussolini, are all artifacts of the belief that these new media could be used efficiently as direct instruments for the inculcation of collective memory. The ideological distinctions between communist and fascist memory lessons grew increasingly elusive with the passage of time. By the 1980s, the Stalinist regime of Bulgaria was carrying on an "ethnic cleansing" campaign that required all citizens of Turkic ancestry to change their surnames to Slavic-sounding analogues.[8]

The sudden and utter ruin of European Communism in the late 1980s and the overnight outbreak of ethnic animosities and wars that ensued signaled a decisive end to the rhetorical peculiarities of the Left–Right battle for the past. In his book *The Consciousness Industry* (1974), Hans Magnus Enzensberger was among the first to look beyond this collapsing paradigm to describe a new set of conditions for the character and role of public memory in the age of television.

First of all, Enzensberger argues that the grand opposition between "High Culture" and "Low Culture," once a germinating center of Western intellectual discourse, has actually shrivelled from significance. Despite the need of many intellectuals—veterans of both Left and Right—to hang on to a concept that honors their own taste above that of nonprofessionals, the terms "high" and "low" now chiefly refer to demographic marketing niches.

Culture today is produced and distributed by a very few corporations who, through their many divisions and subsidiaries, make decisions about what culture all members of society will consume, from the top of the social ladder to the bottom. So, this logic goes, General Electric, Time-Warner, CBS, Bertelsmann Group, and other giant media conglomerates share a collective stake in presenting their publics with cultural items spawned by coherent cultural traditions. These corporations might talk to some segments of the public-cum-audience over TV networks, to other segments in printed matter, to others through audio re-

---

[8]For more information on the Bulgarian government's violent, often fatal, anti-Turkic campaign, see *The New York Times*. Front-page articles covering it appear in the *Times* on Jan. 17, Feb. 7, and Feb. 8, 1985.

cordings, and so on. But corporations control culture, Enzensberger concludes, and thus the regulation of consciousness and collective memory is firmly in their hands. Just as the garment industry reaches both high and low, from exclusive boutiques to shlocky discount stores, so has the consciousness industry achieved a comprehensive industrial oligarchy over culture at large.

Enzensberger builds this broad and general analysis on a very personal, and in some ways shocking, foundation of individual experience. He reflects on how we *like to think* that "we reign supreme in our own consciousness, that we are masters of what our minds accept or reject," that each mind is a kind of "last refuge" where the individual is still in charge of self. But this, he tells us, is an illusion. The belief in self-autonomy, where such belief still exists, is a vain faith in what he dismisses as an "imaginary fortress" (3). Unfortunately, we can no longer think of our minds as our own because mass culture, with its endless barrage of styles, suggestions, moral codes, and so on, has become the context for all of our thinking. Even to count oneself in opposition to mass culture is to participate in it.

This kind of atmospheric penetration of consciousness is different, he tells us, from the time-honored idea that "what is going in our minds . . . is a product of society" (3). It is more insidious. When communication was mostly oral and personal, there was room enough and time for the individual to make decisions about what to accept and what not to accept. Learning relationships such as student and teacher, apprentice and master, and congregant and clergy, were human relationships in which the character of the teacher could be measured against the content of the lesson. Given the nature of contemporary education— given class size alone—such relationships are rarely possible in schools today. More to the point, the information gained in schools becomes a shrinking per- centage of the whole as increasing quantities of data are industrially distributed by mass media, a situation in which interpersonal relationships are rendered structurally impossible. The transmissions of billboards, tee-shirts, radios, and television screens are, alternately and simultaneously, bits of two-dimensional wallpaper and piercing missiles of data, switching significances in relation to the murky rhythms of personal psychological predisposition.[9] McLuhan coined the term "sobconscious [sic] inklings" to describe this phenomenon.

The job of passing information, the act essential to the creation of individual consciousness, has evolved into what Enzensberger calls "the mind-making in- dustry." Furthermore, he warns us that the character of this revolutionary system is largely invisible, especially to students of modern culture who are still wed to the ideological templates of the past:

It (the consciousness industry) has developed at such a pace and assumed such

---

[9]For a sardonic picture of the osmotic effect of mass culture on the individual, see Don Delillo's novel, *White Noise*.

varied forms that it has outgrown our understanding and our control. Our current discussion of the media seems to suffer from severe theoretical limitations. Newspapers, films, television, public relations tend to be evaluated separately, in terms of their specific technologies, conditions, and possibilities. . . . Hardly anyone seems to be aware of the phenomenon as a whole. (4)

The political imagination that evolved out of the Left–Right paradigm created a vision of a power elite that uses the communication media to hypnotize people by repeatedly feeding them predigested messages. When necessary, deviance is dealt with by secret police, as in Orwell's *1984*. But Enzensberger paints a different picture of how communications media are used to rule a society. The media machines—in the form of TV, radio, movie projector, printing press—are indeed spitting out the data, but the success of the system is dependent on its ability to persuade the public to collaborate with it in the creation of a social product. Every time we dress in a certain style that we have learned (or learned to admire) from the mass media, we are socially legitimating another small piece of data to the people around us who respect us, look up to us, depend on us, are attracted to us, envy us, and so on. In this way, that particular piece of information emerges from the clutter to significance.

The old image of a one-way stream of data simply filling up millions of helpless blank minds made for an easy villain; the transmitter of data was guilty. The Left blamed big business; the Right, big government. But where actually tried, this totalitarian model has proved more or less unworkable. Instead, we might imagine an entire population milling around a smorgasbord of suggestions, tasting, sampling, and recommending the fare to each other. The caterer, the supplier of the food, hardly seems like a villain.

In the advanced capitalist countries—the United States, Canada, Japan, and the nations of Western Europe—the culture industry is not so much charged with the duty of initiating ideas as with testing their viability as attractive products. Thus if a garage band comes up with a new pop sound or a TV producer comes up with a new wrinkle in a formula drama, the task of the vast entertainment/industrial complex is not so much to evaluate the quality or the lack of quality of this invention, or its beauty or truth or lack of same, but rather to test how deeply it can penetrate the market without causing disruption of the marketplace. Demography becomes more important than either democracy or autocracy.

The same holds true in terms of collective historical memory. Writing about such media-staged events as the Statue of Liberty centennial and the bicentennial of the U.S. Constitution, Susan G. Davis commented, "The way we experience the past and present, the very experience we have to interpret, is being rebuilt for us through marketing strategies" (Kammen 669). By turning these historical memorials into corporately sponsored television programs, the selling of soft drinks, automobiles, and toothpaste is put on an equal footing with the events themselves. The Constitution guarantees the spectator's freedom of speech; Coca Cola quenches the spectator's thirst.

In societies still wed to older ideological templates, such as China and Iraq, the role of the mind industry is less subtle. Straightforward political propaganda is still commonplace. Politics is treated as if it were simply a matter of taking sides. In such societies it becomes the job of the elite to inform the mass audience as to which opinions it must subscribe to, and to warn individuals of the consequences of failing to take the government-sponsored side.

But in both parliamentary democracies and authoritarian societies, the mass media are of equal importance to the degree that systemic power has become a matter of information. Individual survival becomes dependent on the receipt of information. In the eighteenth century, if a revolution was to be successful, it had to seize control of the royal palace, as in the taking of Versailles in the French Revolution. In the nineteenth century, if a revolution was to be successful, it had to take the center of the capital city with its factories and great public squares, as in the national revolutions of 1848. But in the twentieth century, the revolutionaries must take the TV station to make a credible seizure of power.

Imagine an anchorman in military uniform appearing on CNN one evening. He greets the audience, proclaims himself the new President of the United States, and offers a list of reasons for the deposing of the elected president. Would the viewer scoff at this as nonsense, or would the very fact that this man is appearing on television lend credence to his claim? Indeed, wouldn't the burden of proof fall on the elected government to demonstrate that a coup had *not* taken place? What strategy might the elected government choose to attempt to reassert itself? It would have to "take back" CNN or make convincing counterbroadcasts over other networks. The technological miracle of international satellite transmission attests to the power of those who can manipulate it, just as the building of the cathedral and the publishing of the book did in former ages.

Of course such shocking announcements of new realities are rare on television, especially in nontotalitarian states, where TV is far more concerned with the business of continuity than the anti-business of disruption. The medium is most effective when it is integrating change into a seamless flow of consciousness, shaping and creating a public sphere for the reception of new data. Enzensberger calls the training of populations to use television this way "the industrialization of the mind." He sets down four prerequisites for rule by media to take place in a society, paraphrased here (7–9):

1. *The successful selling of the idea that intellectual enlightenment is the highest form of human achievement.* People must be convinced that improvement of their life comes not from some invisible force (such as God or spiritual principles), but out of a TV set and/or other such receiving and playback devices. In a society where theocracy rules, or maintains a large organized following, the consciousness industry is limited in its power.

States that officially subscribe to, or people who sincerely believe in sacred books or in the presence of supernatural forces are less susceptible to electronic media manipulation. Interestingly, TV programs often pay lip service to the virtues of traditional religion. The important factor, however, is whether the secular messages about consumption are more highly valued by the audience as a guide for successful living than the messages printed in the Bible or spoken from the pulpit, even the electronic pulpit. Television has presented its audience with an emphatically secular vision, offering immediate tangible results and rarely dwelling on the problem of eternity (Lidz 55).

Enzensberger's identification of traditional religious faith as the chief antagonist of mass culture has proved particularly prescient since he offered it some 20 years ago. The most serious political challenges to consumption-oriented media rule have indeed come from theocratically inspired forces. Examples include the Revolution in Iran and the rise of religious fundamentalism in several parts of the Islamic world, the renaissance of fundamentalist Protestantism in the United States, and the emergent power of the Jewish Orthodox right wing in Israeli politics. Though each of these political movements was spawned from a distinct religious tradition, each is committed to an attempt to roll back what it has defined as the secular, materialist juggernaut of electronic media influence, and to reassert the power of religion and religious leaders in everyday life. Socialist attacks on "consumerism" or on the "capitalist content" of mass culture have provoked far less interest from the public.

2. *A proclamation of equality and human rights as official rhetoric, no matter what the reality is.* In Western Europe, the touchstone of official freedom is the French Revolution; in the former Communist countries it was the Bolshevik Revolution of 1917; in the Americas, Africa, and Asia, it is the revolts that ended colonial subjugation. Whether or not people actually have these rights becomes less significant than whether they are willing to accept as "fact" the proposition that they have been guaranteed these rights through a verified historical event. In terms of collective memory, this is the most important of Enzensberger's preconditions. The past must provide a structure that makes revolutionary challenge obsolete or, better yet, absurd. The Soviet practice of committing dissenters to mental hospitals speaks to this last point.

3. *A measure of economic prosperity in the society.* The growl of a hungry stomach is still loud enough to distract a viewer from television, no matter how hypnotic the effect of the medium is imagined to be. More importantly, the ruling elite of such a society is well aware that it would be necessary to use old-fashioned force to put down a hungry population; the behavior of the hungry or of the cold is difficult or even impossible to manipulate with symbols. Avoidance of that kind of messy public violence

is among the chief advantages to government by media. This is also a reminder that media dominance is not possible in just any society. It implies an evolutionary course of national development that must be reached for it to take place.

4. *The existence of the proper technology to invade every facet of life with electronic messages.* This fourth prerequisite is related to the third. If people do not have electricity and radios and TV sets, they cannot be manipulated by electronic media. In addition to the availability of consumer goods, there must be an acceptance of consumerism as a way of life, which is not always quite so forthcoming as it may seem. This was evident in the United States during the 1950s, as the nation was emerging from a prolonged period of economic hardship and war to become the world's first TV-dominated consumer society. Marketing specialist Ernest Dichter was moved to comment that "one of the basic problems of this prosperity is to give people the sanction and justification to enjoy it and to demonstrate that the hedonistic approach to life is a moral one, not an immoral one" (Lipsitz 47).

Print plays a role in mass-mediated society, but only a limited one. During the period when its chief rival as a social memory system was oral, print was a technologically advanced medium, the medium of choice for those with the skills to use it. In terms of late twentieth-century technology, however, print proves relatively slow and inefficient. Furthermore, accessing print requires special—and increasingly elusive—conditions such as quiet and long periods of uninterrupted time. As a result, millions of people who have been taught to read and write find literacy a skill with few organic applications in their lives. How many letters have not been written because of the telephone? How many novels have not been read because of the cinema? How many newspapers have folded since the establishment of the network television system in the late 1940s? How many "how-to" manuals have been bypassed in favor of videotapes? How much reading time on trains and buses has been sacrificed to the car stereo and to looking out the window? How much reading time on airplanes has been lost to in-flight motion pictures?

It seems that in every instance where print has been forced to compete with electronic audiovisual media in an open communications market it has gone into retreat. The great exception is the schools, where print continues to dominate by means of official fiat. Yet teachers somehow continue to wonder why so many of their students have such difficulty reading and writing. As early as 1964 Marshall McLuhan provided a clue to that mystery when he observed that children who watch television "bring to print all their senses, and print rejects them. Print asks for the isolated and stripped-down visual faculty, not for the unified sensorium" (269).

If, as McLuhan implies, the synaesthetic pleasure of multimedia experience is by its very nature more attractive than the single-sense visual focus of reading, what are the consequences for human memory? For one thing, visceral reaction takes priority over the particulars of content in personal recall and this is inimical to the inculcation of cultural memory in the traditional sense. Images, styles, tones, fashions, ambiences, and manners are salient. Facts, dates, names, places, institutions, cause-and-effect theories, and other components that inform a literacy-based historical perspective are reduced to the accoutrements of an entertainment experience.[10] Unless the viewer chooses to write these things down, and thus introduce and synthesize print into the audiovisual communication process, the details necessary for reasoned argument pass by at a rhythm unimpeded by the rate or depth of the viewer's comprehension. Even when stored on videotape, factual data are extremely difficult to access. If in doubt, compare searching through the pages of a book, with its static text and its index and table of contents, to fast-forward and fast-rewind searching on a VCR in pursuit of a piece of information.[11]

In his brilliant and moving study, *Time Passages: Collective Memory and Popular Culture,* George Lipsitz finds the relationship between a personal sense of history and the electronic media "paradoxical." He observes that

> time, history and memory become qualitatively different concepts in a world where electronic mass communication is possible. Instead of relating to the past through a shared sense of place or ancestry, consumers . . . can experience a common heritage with people they have never seen; they can acquire memories of a past to which they have no geographic or biological connection. This capacity . . . to transcend time and space creates instability by disconnecting people from past traditions, but it also liberates people by making the past less determinate of experiences in the present. (viii)

Lipsitz's ambiguity goes to the heart of the matter. On the dark side, he sees the mass media as having atomized people from organic kinship relationships. Even McLuhan's celebrated 1960s image of a family gathered around the "electric hearth" seems warm and quaint today when measured against the reality of demographically balkanized family members moving to their personal TV sets at separate corners of the home in the age of wide spectrum cable. Barry Levinson's 1990 film *Avalon* is a powerful statement of the pessimistic view. Through most of the film an immigrant grandfather functions as a household shaman, telling and retelling stories of the family's American origin at the turn of the century. When television arrives at the house, however, he is gradually supplanted from

---

[10]For a somewhat hyperbolic but nevertheless cogent presentation of this argument, see Neil Postman, *Amusing Ourselves to Death.*

[11]It is worth mentioning that this problem is being addressed in a newer audiovisual technology, the video laser disc, which digitalizes content and provides a printed table of contents, thus making each information bit in the text more easily accessible.

this position. The final scene of the film takes place in a nursing home where the grandfather now lives. His son brings a young grandson to visit him on Thanksgiving Day, hoping that the old man will retell the story of his coming to America, as had been the family custom on that holiday for decades. Indeed the grandfather, despite his enfeeblement, begins to spin the magic tale, but it simply does not get the grandson's attention. The television is going, as it always is at such institutions, and the boy is fixed on the Macy's Thanksgiving Day Parade, a commercial event that is in no way connected to the original meaning of the holiday or to its special meaning for his family. How can the words of an old man compete with the audiovisual allure of marching bands and skyscraper-size cartoon characters?

The optimistic scenario that Lipsitz suggests, that mass-media dominance will release people from the bigotries and parochialisms that are passed from one generation to the next, is perhaps something more than a pipe dream but less than a redemptive hope for the future of the human race. Despite the complicity of the audience, as described by Enzensberger, it does not appear at this stage of development that the vertical system of culture made possible by mass communications technology can fulfill the biologically based emotional needs of the atomized member of the audience. The chronic epidemic of clinical depression, the rising rates of murder, suicide and random violence, the now chronic threats to the family of divorce and child abandonment, the appearance of whole new psychosomatic ailments (notably Epstein-Barr syndrome) are evidence of a population that has been disconnected from the roots of its organic capacity to remember: to recall, to reexperience, to recuperate, to recreate itself.[12] Though often and carelessly blamed for society's ills, television and other mass communications media are surely symptoms of this disconnectedness, though not necessarily causes.

And so we sit, remote control in hand, 50-channel spectrum to graze, shelves full of videotapes, AM and FM, CD player, tape deck, phonograph, telephone, FAX machine, waiting for virtual reality, searching for something to remember, nothing particular to forget.

WORKS CITED

Arnold, Matthew. *Culture and Anarchy.* (1869). Ed. J. Dover Wilson. London: Cambridge UP, 1950.
Delillo, Don. *White Noise.* New York: Viking/Penguin, 1985.
Eliot, T. S. *Christianity and Culture.* New York: Harvest, 1968.

[12]According to the *University of California at Berkeley Wellness Letter,* "Nearly 10 million Americans sought help from psychiatrists, psychologists, social workers, or hospital psychiatric clinics in 1980, the first year such a count was taken. If visits to counselors, specialists in geriatric problems and such support groups as Alcoholics Anonymous, not to mention conversations with . . . (clergy) . . . were added to the count, this total might easily double" (4).

Enzensberger, Hans Magnus. *The Consciousness Industry.* New York: Seabury, 1974.

Gedin, Per. *Literature in the Marketplace.* Trans. George Bisset. Woodstock: Overlook Press, 1977.

Gobineau, Arthur. "Essay on the Equality of Races." (1870). *Selected Political Writings of Gobineau.* Ed. and Trans. Michael D. Biddiss. New York: Harper, 1970.

Kammen, Michael. *Mystic Chords of Memory.* New York: Knopf, 1991.

Levinson, Barry. *Avalon.* Tri-Star Pictures, 1990.

Lidz, Victor. "Television and Moral Order in a Secular Age." *Media in Society: Readings in Mass Communication.* Eds. Caren J. Deming and Samuel L. Becker. Glenview: Scott, 1988.

Lipsitz, George. *Time Passages: Collective Memory and American Popular Culture.* Minneapolis: U of Minnesota P, 1990.

Macdonald, Dwight. "A Theory of Mass Culture." *Mass Culture: The Popular Arts in America.* Eds. Bernard Rosenberg and David Manning White. New York: Free, 1957.

McLuhan, H. Marshall. *Understanding Media.* New York: Signet, 1964.

McLuhan, Stephanie. *Marshall McLuhan: The Man and His Message,* by Tom Wolfe. Canadian Broadcasting Company, 1984.

Ortega y Gasset, José. *The Revolt of the Masses.* New York: Norton, 1932.

Postman, Neil. *Amusing Ourselves to Death: Public Discourse in the Age of Show Business.* New York: Viking, 1985.

University of California at Berkeley Wellness Letter IX:1 (Oct. 1992).

10

The Spoken and the Seen: Phonocentric and Ocularcentric Dimensions of Rhetorical Discourse

Bruce E. Gronbeck
University of Iowa

It is commonplace among rhetoricians to open their discussion of the fourth (or fifth) canon of rhetoric, memory, with a review of *Rhetorica Ad Herennium,* the oldest Latin treatise on rhetoric preserved whole. Dating from perhaps the second decade in the first century BCE, the treatise addressed to Gaius Herrenius is known as a handbook. The sustained discussion (Kaplan III.28–40) of a visual theory of mnemonics, whereby orators are urged to invent pictorial systems to help them remember details and attitudes, is interesting and as modern as the most recent offer to train your memory pictorially in three days. Interesting or not, however, it lacks an intellectual problematic that can engage rhetoricians.

Curiously, we start discussions of memory with the anonymous author of this Roman handbook rather than with Aristotle. I would agree with Kaplan that pseudo Cicero's pictorial system is the oldest extant set of mnemonic devices in rhetoric. I would also argue that Aristotle's *De Memoria et Reminiscentia* is a much more theoretically provocative and hence more suggestive work on memory than the Roman handbook. In his short treatise on memory and reminiscence or recollection, Aristotle is grappling with timeless questions about the source of the power of the past: How is it impressed on the mind, and how do we bring it into consciousness? While answering them, Aristotle makes some important distinctions between memory and recollection and, thereby, begins to suggest why *memoria* (*mneme* in Greek) was worth identifying as a canon of rhetoric equal in importance to the other four.[1]

---

[1] Aristotle also articulated some absolutely ridiculous notions in this treatise. He suggested dwarfs had "abnormally weak memory, as compared with their opposites, however, because of the great weight which they have resting upon the organ of perception" and that "infants and very old persons have bad memories, owing to the amount of movement going on within them; for the latter are in

In *De Memoria* Aristotle observes that "the persons who possess a retentive memory are not identical with those who excell in power of recollection" (McKeon 449b); more specifically, that "slow" people can possess a "retentive memory" but as a rule only "quick-witted and clever" people are good at recollecting. He reaches this conclusion through definition and theoretical development of the concepts in the treatise's title. Memory to Aristotle is a mechanism for the reproduction of the past; it "is, therefore, neither Perception nor Conception, but a state of affection of one of these, conditioned by lapse of time" (McKeon 449b). Key to memory, then, is "presentation," which in *De Anima* he equates with perceiving in contradistinction to thinking and discriminating. He goes so far as to harden the distinction: "For perception of the special objects of sense is always free from error, and is found in all animals, while it is possible to think falsely as well as truly, and thought is found only where there is discourse of reason as well as sensibility" (McKeon 427b). From here Aristotle moves on to imagination, ultimately arguing that both perception and imagination are sense-bound, usually focused on the visual sense—*phantasia,* a word coming from *phaos* (light) "because it is not possible to see without light" (McKeon 428b).

Recollection, in contrast, is explicitly tied to thinking and even scientific knowledge, by which Aristotle seems to mean what we would call generalized knowledge: "When (after an interval of obliviscence) one recovers some scientific knowledge which he had before, or some perception, or some other experience, the state of which we above declared to be memory, it is then, and only then, that this recovery may amount to a recollection of any of the things aforesaid" (McKeon 451b). Aristotle's discussion of recollection is confusing in its generality at key points, and the term lacks clear definition. He offers, however, a series of attributes. Recalling always is matter of reconstructing "movement" or sequences of action; recollection can involve "customary order" as well as "natural order"; promptuaries of "mnemonic *loci*" can help in the recollective process; recollection is always based on thought, and usually discriminative; recollection often is centered on temporal rather than spatial relationships. Thus, recollection "is, as it were, a mode of inference. For he who endeavors to recollect *infers* that he formerly saw, or heard, or had some such experiences, and the process by which he succeeds in recollecting is, as it were, a sort of investigation" (McKeon 451b–453a).

De Memoria is highly suggestive, if frustratingly unclear, to the student of rhetoric. The discussion of memory in *Rhetorica Ad Herennium* suggests that it is "the treasure-house of the ideas supplied by Invention" (Kaplan III.28), and hence merely an auxiliary appliance rather than a primary tool for the practicing rhetor. By the end of his discussion, pseudo-Cicero can only say: "So, since a

---

process of rapid decay, the former in process of vigorous growth; and we may add that children, until considerably advanced in years, are dwarf-like in their bodily" (McKeon 453b).

ready memory is a useful thing, you can see clearly with what great pains we must strive to acquire so useful a faculty" (Kaplan III.40). In *De Memoria*, however, we find an attempt to separate memory from recollection—the (pictorial) reproduction of the past from the reconstruction of sequences of understanding. We find separated brute representation from interpretive framing. We find the spatial-visual separated from the temporal-aural or temporal-lingual. We find the roots for a distinction important to our time: *between the ocularcentric and the logocentric or phonocentric in discourse.* My goal here is to deal with the relationships between the ocularcentric and phonocentric aspects of electronically driven rhetorical discourse. To do so, however, I must scan rhetorical history in order to foreground the issues that frame those relationships. Only then can we understand why it is that the spoken and the seen are so easily bonded in the era of electric rhetoric (Gronbeck).

MEMORY, RECOLLECTION, AND RHETORICAL DISCOURSE THROUGH THE AGES

Although I certainly do not want to assume responsibility for the construction of a history of rhetoric as seen through the distinction between memory and recollection, I do want to suggest that the question is enduring and regularly addressed in creative ways. Consider the following sample of rhetorical theorists on matters of relevance.

Longinus

In *On the Sublime* we find discussions of both the visual and the phonological as Longinus seeks to define and understand the force of the "the sublime" in discourse. His first major statement on the visual runs as follows:

> Weight, grandeur, and energy in writing are very largely produced, dear pupil, by the use of "images." (That at least is what some people call the actual mental pictures.) For the term Imagination is applied in general to an idea which enters the mind from any source and engenders speech, but the word has now come to be used predominantly of passages where, inspired by strong emotion, you seem to see what you describe and bring it vividly before the eyes of your audience. (Fyfe 171)

Late in the treatise Longinus takes up the fifth source of sublimity, arrangement of words. After a discussion of musical instruments, he says:

> We hold, then, that composition, which is a kind of melody of words—words which are part of man's nature and reach not his ears only but his very soul— stirring as it does myriad ideas of words, thoughts, things, beauty, musical charm, all of which are born and bred in us; while, moreover, by the blending of its own

manifold tones it brings into the hearts of the bystanders the speaker's actual emotion so that all who hear him share in it, and by piling phrase on phrase builds up one majestic whole—we hold, I say, that by these very means it casts a spell on us and always turns *our* thoughts toward what is majestic and dignified and sublime and all else that it embraces, winning a complete mastery over our minds. (Fyfe 235)

These passages are clearly separated from each other, the first coming when Longinus is treating ideas (*inventio*), and the second when completing his discussion of style (*elocutio*). The contrasts between them are significant, I think: Pictorial speech clearly is representational, giving presence to scenes that guide emotional response, whereas the aural rhythms of speech clearly are recollective, calling up that which is "born and bred in us." The visual to Longinus is presentistic, whereas the aural draws upon from the past, almost magically, to shape or direct present action thanks to its "complete mastery over our minds."

With the help of Vernant, Vance argues that even in the Middle Ages the commemorative process was attached to "the cult of the voice," because the past was summoned by voice and because it was out of traces (*vestigia*) of the past on our souls that the social and religious orders could be stabilized. Christ's "do this in remembrance of me [*in meam commemorationem*]" formed the apotheosis of memory. With Truth anterior to the present, the past had to be summoned vocally, just as God himself had called the world into existence phonologically (Vance 374–78). *Vestigia* were then ritualistically united with *visibilia,* the seen that comprised the presentistic aspects of secular and sacred ritual.

Longinus's attempt to argue both the spoken and the seen into his understanding of the sublime thus was extended into understandings of socioreligious performances in the medieval period. Both the spoken and the seen depended on functioning memory—though, again, through Longinus and beyond there is a significant distinction drawn between the presentational aspects of the seen and the recollective or interpretive force of the spoken.

Bacon and Campbell

The faculty psychology of Francis Bacon was perfectly made for an understanding of rhetoric that separated yet found compatible the seen and the heard. In that he separated the faculties of imagination and reason, he had clear grounds for distinguishing between them. In *The Advancement of Learning,* Bacon lays out four great intellectual arts: invention (inquiry), judgment (examination), memory (custody), and tradition (elocution). Regarding invention, he recognized two kinds: the arts of the sciences (discovering new knowledge) and the arts of speech and arguments (rediscovering or assembling old knowledge). Thus, of speech and argument he says:

> The invention of speech or argument is not properly an invention, for to *invent* is to discover that we know not, and not to recover or resummon that which we already

know: . . . So as to speak truly, it is not invention, but a remembrance or suggestion, with an application. (127)

Bacon goes on to discuss systematic research (Preparation) and topical systems
(he calls them Suggestion) as ways of combing past knowledge. After discussing
Judgment he moves on to Memory, which is divided into two parts: writing (the
use of recorded commonplaces or set passages) and memory proper, which is
subdivided into prenotion (systematic seeking of information in particular areas
of "narrow compass") and emblem: "Emblem reduceth conceits intellectual to
images sensible, which strike the memory more; out of which axioms may be
drawn much better [in] practice than that in use" (136).

Bacon then comes to the fourth intellectual art, Tradition. He divides it into
three parts: the organ of tradition, or speech/writing; the method of tradition, or
magistrial and probationary patterns of organization; and the illustration of tradition, "comprehended in that science which we call *rhetoric, or art of eloquence;*
a science excellent and excellently well laboured" (146). He offers one of the
most famous definitions of rhetoric in the Western world: "The duty and office of
rhetoric is, to apply reason to imagination for the better moving of the will"
(146). This definition is urged "for the end of logic is, to teach a form of
argument to secure reason, and not to entrap it; the end of morality is to procure
the affections to obey reason, and not to invade it; the end of rhetoric is, to fill the
imagination to second reason, and not to oppress it" (146).

In so prominently featuring the imaginative, Bacon understands that he risks
the censure of Plato, so he responds: "As Plato said elegantly, *That virtue, if she
could be seen, would move great love and affection;* so seeing that she cannot be
showed to sense by corporal shape, the next degree is to show her to the imagination in lively representation: for to show her to reason only in subtilty [sic] of
argument, was a thing ever derided in Chrysippus and many of the Stoics; who
thought to thrust virtue upon men by sharp disputations and conclusions, which
have no sympathy with the will of man" (147). The argument gets even more
complicated:

Reason would become captive and servile, if eloquence of persuasions did not
practise and win the imagination from the affections' part, and contract a confeder-
acy between the reason and imagination against the affections; for the affections
themselves carry ever an appetite to good, as reason doth. The difference is, that
the affection beholdeth merely the present; reason beholdeth the future and sum of
time. And therefore the present filling the imagination more, reason is commonly
vanquished; but after that force of eloquence and persuasion hath made things
future and remote appear as present, then upon the revolt of the imagination reason
prevaileth. (147–48)

This may be enough to demonstrate the complex exploration of the spoken
and the seen in Bacon. Recollection is central to his theory of rhetoric. He
indentifies multiple triggers to recollection: (a) (Re)Invention is marked verbally

in speech and argument, and hence is fundamentally oral or heard; (b) memory proper can be searched systematically (in what seems to be an extension of Aristotle's thoughts about memory) or it can be raised emblematically—that is, via visual images; and (c) rhetoric is defined cognitively as an illustrative art in that the imagination, an ocularcentric faculty, is the energizer of reason and a defender against rampant affections. In such a theory, subject matter (invented material) is rehearsed verbally, by the voice and concepts that use the classical topical system to retrieve that which is known, whereas style (the clothing of subject matter)—especially tropes—is imagaic and hence operates visually, by depiction constructing visions of proper and improper thought and action.[2]

Baconian thought permeates rhetorical theorizing well into the nineteenth century. A significant case in point is George Campbell, whose *The Philosophy of Rhetoric* is the most sophisticated statement on rhetoric doctrine deriving from the age of enlightenment. Grounded in associational psychology overlaid on the remnants of a Baconian theory of faculties, Campbell's treatise posits the central epistemological problem in rhetoric as one of creating lively or vivid ideas discursively. He assumed that there are three sources of ideas—sensations, memory, and the imagination. Because language is not sensible, it must work with ideas of the memory and, especially, the imagination, whose ideas are the least vivid. How can the orator use language to create lively ideas of the imagination (Bitzer xxii)?

Of the ends of rhetoric—"every speech being intended to enlighten the understanding, to please the imagination, to move the passions, or to influence the will" (1)—Campbell has this to say initially about pleasing the imagination:

> The imagination is addressed by exhibiting to it a lively and beautiful representation of a suitable object. As in this exhibition, the task of the orator may, in some sort, be said, like that of the painter, to consist in imitation, the merit of the work results entirely from these two sources; dignity, as well in the subject or thing imitated, as in the manner of imitation; and resemblance, in the portrait or performance. (3)

By chapter 7, section II, "Men Considered as Endowed with Imagination," Campbell is ready to argue that the qualities in ideas "which principally gratify the fancy [imagination]" are vivacity, beauty, sublimity, and novelty (73). He then engages a tortuous discussion of the difference between lively ideas of ratiocination and lively ideas of imagination; he tries to demonstrate that visual-

---

[2]The actual separation between *inventio* and *elocutio,* of course, is not really so neat as Bacon's division of the arts intellectual suggests. The "Coulours of Good and Evil," while being stylistically sophisticated disquisitions on virtue and vice, contribute as much substantively as linguistically to rhetorical discourse. Likewise, the *antitheta,* Bacon's stock of pro-and-con arguments, are not only sources of argument but also depend for their force on proper linguistic construction. Historically, the separation of *inventio* and *elocutio* can never really sustain a split between content and form; talking is not that simple.

ization allows for a judgment of similitude or comparison—which, he is convinced, is what gives imagination (recollective images) its power to shape our perception of present circumstances (74).

The discussion of memory likewise is in two sections. In chapter 5, while discussing common sense, Campbell asserts a connection between memory and experience: It is memory that gives experience the power to govern especially moral decisions; in that rhetoric is primarily concerned with moral topics and evidence broadly understood, common sense's empowerment by remembered experience is central to his theory of rhetoric. Consider:

> Remembrance instantly succeeds sensation, insomuch that memory becomes the sole repository of the knowledge received from sense; knowledge which, without this repository, would be as instantaneously lost as it is gotten, and could be of no service to the mind. Our sensations would be no better than the fleeting pictures of a moving object on a camera obscura, which leave not the least vestiges behind them. Memory, therefore, is the only original voucher extant of those past realities for which we had once the evidence of sense. . . . My memory, furnish[es] me with numerous examples, which, though different in every other particular, are similar in this, that they present a body moving downwards, till obstructed either by the ground or by some intervenient object. Hence, my first notion of gravitation. (47)

In the chapter 7 discussion of "Men Considered as Endowed with Memory," Campbell makes memory the servant of the other great faculties—understanding, imagination, the passions, and the will. And then, throwing away the classical topical system, he follows David Hume in finding memory as the faculty that newly combines previous experiences via the principles of resemblance, causality, or natural relation (76–77).

To Campbell, then, although memory is important to all faculties, it is the primary mechanism for rehearsing experience, which, in turn, is our primary source of moral evidence. As our experiences (remembered sensations) are combined and recombined commonsensically, we are able to construct principles that govern our arguments. By attacking the topical system (part of the "science of *logomacy*," 69),[3] Campbell initially has no mechanisms for cueing psychological operations. By book II (Chap. 10), however, he explores the "artificial and arbitrary" connections between words and things, and has this to say:

> [T]hough this connexion hath not its foundation in the nature of things, but in the conventions of men, its effect upon the mind is much the same. For having often had occasion to observe particular words used as signs of particular things, we hence contract a habit of associating the sign with the thing signified, insomuch that either, being presented to the mind, frequently introduces or occasions the appre-

---

[3]Whereas Campbell attacks the topical system, a year later Joseph Priestley embraces it, though strictly as a mnemonic system.

hension of the other. . . . Thus, certain sounds, and the ideas of things not naturally related to them, come to be as strongly linked in our conceptions, as the ideas
of things naturally related to one another. (258)

Memory of past experiences thus can be cued either by apprehension of
the things themselves or—more usefully so far as rhetorical discourse is concerned—by language, even "certain sounds," as Campbell notes. In contrast,
once again, recollection and imaginative reconstruction are as visualistic as the
imitations of painters; imagination is the source of "portrait or performance."
The spoken (verbalized) and the seen (visualized) are separable yet related opera-
tors in rhetorical discourse.

One last observation regarding Campbell must be made. In identifying four
ends for discourse, he sets the stage for generic theories. He explicitly associates
addresses to the imagination with poetry—narration and description with epic
poetry and tragedy (3). It will not be long after Campbell until addresses to the
understanding are viewed as informative or argumentative; to the imagination,
poetic; and to the will, persuasive. The 19th-century rhetorics (handbooks of
composition) get their generic organizational patterns from Campbell. The effect
of such genre-alizing is to separate temporarily theoretical development of the
seen and the heard, of the imagination and the understanding. That separation
holds for the most part well into the twentieth century.

Schwartz

We should stop to consider I. A. Richards's doctrine of the "interanimation of
words," wherein he discusses relationships between word sounds and meaning,
as well as his theory of metaphor, wherein his theory of the "transactions between contexts" features recollection as the source of power. More provocative
among twentieth-century theorists of the spoken and the seen, however, is Tony
Schwartz. Schwartz is important because of the identification he forges between
the seen and the heard. To Schwartz, a specialist in advertising and political
campaigning, the post-literate age is characterized by its lack of reliance on
reading and writing; it rather features both sound and sight, the oral and the
pictorial. He captures the difference in an aphorism: "Electronic media are *received* media. Print is a *perceived* medium" (Schwartz, *Media,* 17). The aphorism signals a distinction between what he sees as the immediacy of apprehension
of electronic media vis-à-vis mediation required to assemble and then react to
literate discourses.

Schwartz is best known for his talk about sound, about what he called *The
Responsive Chord* (1973). Aural and pictorial stimuli to Schwartz have an instan-
taneousness of apprehension that is impossible with print:

A spoken word never exists in time. It exists only as a series of vibrations. A
television picture never exists on the tube. It exists only as a construct of moving

light dots. The brain puts together the product of seeing and hearing television, and this process takes place at a phenomenal speed. It is true that a person also assembles in his brain [the] words that he reads, but those words always stay on the page to be viewed. (19–20)

Schwartz's so-called resonance theory of communication is aurally tuned. An electronic oral medium "concentrates," he says in *Responsive Chord,* "on evoking responses from people by attuning the message to their prior experience" (20). Pictorial media such as television, however, also work evocatively to Schwartz, for "with electronic media we now 'see' by the same process by which we have always heard" (22). Print and other verbal media, in contrast, are not evocative but externally oriented. "Content" is carried from one brain to another via a transportation system, "via mail delivery, Western Union, book shipment, newspaper distribution"—that is, "across a gap" (20). A transportation theory accounts for literate communication; a resonance theory, for post-literate communication. Post-literate communication relies on "replay," as did pre-literate societies with their tale telling, liturgies, minstrels, and ballads (26). The ability of electronic media to connect memory with new information for millions of people, argues Schwartz, simultaneously is democratizing and empowering (95–122).

What is fascinating in these ideas is the direct connection between the phonocentric and the ocularcentric; they are more or less merged in their electronic versions. They both are grounded in a kind of recollection or resonance, attaching the past and the present for the guiding of the future.

The journey from Aristotle to Schwartz has a good many more stops than we have made in this review. Whereas *memoria* as a canon or office of rhetoric disappears, *memoria et reminiscentia* in an Aristotelian sense are subjects never far from the central concerns of rhetoric theory. What is instructive about the journey is the regular discussion of both the spoken and the seen in treatises fundamentally treating oral discourse, as well as the varied attempts to posit relationships between them. Even though theoretical grounds vary—from Aristotle's and Longinus's capacities to Bacon's faculties to Campbell's ends to Schwartz's senses—the attraction of accounting for the power of both the spoken and the seen through theories of memory and recollection is everpresent. Why that is so is theorized by Walter Ong.

WALTER ONG AND THE AGE
OF SECONDARY ORALITY

Tony Schwartz dedicated *Media: The Second God* (1981) to Marshall McLuhan; Walter Ong was McLuhan's student at St. Louis University in the late 1930s. Ong belongs to a group of scholars who have worked on what are called the orality-literacy theorems, which were grounded and then extended in McLuhan's

The Gutenberg Galaxy (1962). The theorems were developed in a group of books that came out together in the early 1960s (reviewed in Havelock, *Muse* chap. 3). The orality-literacy theorems generally posit a simultaneous evolution of dominant media of communication, sociocultural structures, and sense of consciousness in the West. As the Judeo-Christian civilizations moved from oral to manuscript to print to electronic cultures, profound changes in both social structure and sense of self accompanied those shifts. Most thoroughly researched and interpreted are differences between oral and literate cultures (Havelock, *Preface, Muse;* McLuhan, *Gutenberg;* Goody and Watt; Ong, *Ramus, Rhetoric, Orality*). Although "oral residues" (Ong, *Rhetoric*) continue into the print era, literacy allows the reorganization of societies around abstracted rules, constitutions, and the emergence of a sense of private self.

A special problem for scholars of the orality-literacy theorems is the electronic age. Havelock was a classicist; Ong is a professor of literature and psychology; Goody and Watt have strong anthropological leanings. At the end of his life, McLuhan was working on "laws of the media," though only fragments of the work were posthumously published (*Laws*). Ong at least has gotten a start on that analysis, though much remains to be done. Ong has suggested that the electronic age is one dominated by "secondary orality." He says:

> The new orality has striking resemblances to the old in its participatory mystique, its fostering of a communal sense, its concentration on the present moment, and even its use of formulas (Ong 1971, pp. 284–303; 1977, pp. 16–49, 305–41). But it is essentially a more deliberate and self-conscious orality, based permanently on the use of writing and print, which are essential for the manufacture and operation of the equipment and for its use as well. . . . Secondary orality generates a strong group sense . . . McLuhan's 'global village.' . . . Secondary orality promotes spontaneity because through analytical reflection we have decided that spontaneity is a good thing. . . . Electronic media do not tolerate a show of open antagonism. (*Orality* 136–37)

Ong goes so far as to flirt with postmodernist thought at the end of *Hopkins, the Self, and God* (1986), because it allows him more access to the "I" of self in the contemporary age, though he generally backs off such considerations. He does praise Derrida for his phonocentric analyses of written (logocentric) language (166), but without commitment to the deconstructionist project, either. I would suggest that Ong is attracted to neither French postmodernism nor French deconstruction because of the union he is seeking in the concept of secondary orality between the spoken and the seen.

The pedestal concept is Ong's understanding of oral culture and consciousness. In primary oral culture—a society that has known no literate mode of communication—thought and expression have a series of identifiable features to Ong. They are: (a) additive rather than subordinative, with details or items piled one on the other; (b) aggregative rather than analytic, with ideas clustered on cliches and axioms that aid memory; (c) redundant or "copious," with much repetition of the just-said to keep hearers and speakers on the same track; (d) conservative or traditionalist, with the society's primary commitments frozen in narratives and aphorisms that can be memorized and repeated easily to the next generation, because there is no other way of keeping cultural history; (e) concrete in its processing of the lifeworld because the only way to test knowledge claims in nonabstract ways is referentially; (f) agonistically toned, with the testing process executed in verbal combat; (g) empathetic and participatory rather than objectively distanced, with involving, personalized formulaic expressions rather than the objectification of life that can accompany writing and printing; (h) homeostatic, with oral societies living in a kind of permanent present, sloughing off the old that does not serve the here-and-now but retaining what is useful; and (i) situational rather than abstract, for oral communicators cannot keep in memory the sort of abstractions that can be recorded on paper (*Orality* 36–57).[4]

Ong's vision of oral societies is rooted in the works of Lord and Parry, and then expanded by his own interpretations of anthropological studies of preliterate cultures. Ong contrasts such societies with literate societies. Writing/print brings with it much more than mere ways of recording oral speech. Writing restructures consciousness, in the title of chapter 4 of *Orality and Literacy*. Writing is a technology, an artificiality that exteriorizes thought; alienates the self from nature and (by allowing for individuation) from other selves; allows for the development of lists, facts, science, and other marks of the exteriorization of knowledge; distances people by interposing texts between them—texts that, as Plato noted, cannot respond when interrogated; permitted the development of a nonrhetorical feminine style in discourse; and even provided conditions for reorganized societies (Ong, *passim*).

Electronic media—and Ong includes the telegraph, telephone, radio, sound motion pictures, television, and computers—compose a further stage in humanity's evolution. As early as 1971 he wrote: "Secondary orality is founded on—though it departs from—the individualized introversion of the age of writing, print, and rationalism which intervened between it and primary orality and which remains a part of us. History is deposited permanently, but not unalterably, as personality structure" (*Rhetoric* 285).

Here is a hermeneutic understanding of communication media, one wherein the past is re-represented, albeit in determinatively altered forms in current practice. Here is a definition of what it means to call a discourse "aggregative" and "conservative": Both oral and much televisual discourse aggregates or assembles pieces of conventional wisdom, stories or anecdotes, and materials (rhymes, tales) memorized by society's youth, re-presenting such materials in both primetime programs and the best televised political performances. (Critics of Ronald Reagan never tire of pointing to his strongly oral style and polished,

---

[4]John Schaeffer relates these features of oral discourse to a doctrine of common sense, *sensus communis*, as the foundation of Western understandings of community.

subtly emotional delivery that exemplify rhetorical perfection in the age of television [Gold; Jamieson].)

We are not, of course, living through a return to oral culture. As the passage from "The Literate Orality of Popular Culture" (*Rhetoric*) quoted earlier indicates, we have not shed writing, print, and rationalism. The analyticity of print is embossed on our brainpans, as Ong explains when discussing televised political debates:

> On television contending presidential candidates do not stomp about a platform flailing their arms or even stand out in the open, like earlier orators metonymically claiming possession of a field, but install themselves behind protective lecterns for genteel exchanges of words projecting images of their self-contained selves instead of pacing up and down a rostrum flailing verbally at one another. . . . Writing governs our oral delivery as never before, and since, as has been seen, writing is interiorizing and nonforensic, the agonistic edge of orality is dulled. ("McLuhan" 142)

Ong thus holds to no simply linear model of evolution. Although he believes that humankind has always valued historicity—the cyclicity and recycling of human experiences—he also realizes that with the spread of writing we could invent history proper, the recording of chronicles and their interpretation (*Interfaces* 74–77; *Orality* 96–101). Hence, both histories and historicity—that is, both our view of sequences in past events as well as our inward sense of relived experiences—produce a noetic state in which technologically sophisticated media do not reproduce orality but rather create a secondary orality. Our societies exist as the global villages McLuhan and Fiore depicted, but in few ways imitating preliterate life.

This is about as far as Walter Ong has gone with the notion of secondary orality. Given our review of the spoken and the seen in rhetorical history and the regular tension between the recollected and the remembered, perhaps we can extend the notion a bit further. Let us begin with the proportion or tetrad around which we have been circulating:

THE VISUALIZED:THE REMEMBERED::
THE SPOKEN:THE RECOLLECTED

Isolating and then assembling the elements of this construction, I think, lead to the following positions:

1. The recollected is the repository of a society's stock of knowledge—its collective beliefs, attitudes, values. The recollected has been stamped on society's children at the youngest ages, especially in formal and informal ways (Hall, *Silent*).

2. The spoken is so closely tied to the recollected because most of our cultural learning (enculturation) occurs aurally: admonition from parents and other authority figures, face-to-face interchange with friends who teach us the Rules of the Game and hence even the idea of social rules and roles.

3. Part of the power of the spoken is its immediacy, the directness and intimacy of the connections between speaker and hearer, the physical continuity between the emitted and the received sound waves, the anatomical inflexions of voice that carry subtle emotions simply inexpressible in mere words communicated literally.

4. The remembered is the repository of an individual's life events—that person's pleasurable and painful experiences.

5. If Aristotle and his successors right up to Freud are correct, such experiences are often recalled visually, in images, acted-out stories, or happenings. Human memory is both personal and visually biased.

6. The recollected and the remembered—as well as, then, the spoken and the visualized—are complementary in that their union completes the joining of the social and the personal in human affairs.

The sixth proposition brings us to the phonocentric and ocularcentric aspects of rhetorical discourse. It carries us, I would hope, past the territory traversed by the rhetoricians who attached recollection/speech to *inventio* and remembrance/vision to *elocutio*. And it is in the union, not separation, of the phonocentric and the ocularcentric in televisual discourse, especially, where we find the sociocultural force of "secondary orality."

Just as all but hermits have complete lives only in the amalgamation of sociality and psychology, existence as a self within social nets, so is rhetorical discursivity a matter of social meaning and individual interpretation. In negotiation theories of discourse of the like espoused by John Fiske, the languages of texts are decoded (Hall, "Encoding") or made meaningful (Fiske) by situated audiences. Whereas the semiotics depends on socially shared codes and signification processes, interpretation depends on the life experiences of the reader-listener-viewer. The communication process is never completed until the messages, the tellings or showing, are retrofitted by an audience. And that audience is always limited in its interpretive abilities by its life histories—what it shares (recollects) with others and what it knows (remembers) from its lived experiences.

By analogy, therefore, it is perfectly natural to expect effective rhetorical discourse to array both recollections and memories, material from both the orally biased dominion of acculturated wisdom and the visually biased dominion of personal knowledge. From the beginnings of serious theorizations about human communication—from Aristotle and his fellow Greeks, from the Romans following Cicero—the search for the best way to articulate relationships between the spoken and the seen, in both oral and written discourse, has been a high-priority task.

In this, the age of secondary orality, of discourses where the spoken and the seen are co-present as media or codes, we have arrived at a historical juncture where the recollected and the remembered now can be literally fused in a unitary discourse. Remnants of the literate, of course, are always there, as Ong noted when discussing presidential debates. Not only is there a literate residue in today's televisual discourses, but we often find unmistakable signs of its presence in oral discourse: introductions, bodies, and conclusions (rational segmentation); propositions with supporting materials (linear logics); formal sentence structures that could have flowed only from literate minds (complex syntax); bouquets of facts and figures arrayed in the middle of policy speeches (scientistic aggregations of information).

Yet, what is generally conceded to be the most powerful televisual discourse relies less on logocentric than on a fusion of phonocentric and ocularcentric codings. Consider a famous political ad from the 1988 presidential campaign (Fig. 10.1). Logologically, the advertisement consists of six factual statements

VIDEO	AUDIO
A guard with a rifle climbs circular stairs to a prison watchtower. The words "The Dukakis Furlough Program" are superimposed on the bottom of the prison visual.	Dissonant sounds are heard—a drum, a synthesizer droning of an up-and-down tone. A voice-over male says, "As governor, Michael Dukakis vetoed sentences for drug dealers."
A guard with a gun walks along a barbed wire fence.	The tone gets louder, with a beat added. "He vetoed the death penalty."
A revolving door formed by bars rotates as men in prison clothing walk in and out the door in a long line. The words "268 Escaped" are superimposed.	"His revolving-door prison policy gave weekend furloughs to first-degree murderers not eligible for parole." The droning sound and beat become louder.
The camera comes in for a closer shot of the prisoners in slow motion revolving through the door.	"While out, many committed other crimes like kidnapping and rape."
Words "And Many Are Still At Large" is superimposed.	"And many are still at large." Drone gives way to a high-pitched hum.
Picture of a guard on a roof with a watchtower in the background.	"Now Michael Dukakis says he wants to do for America what he's done for Massachusetts."
A small color picture of Bush, with words "Paid for by Bush/Quayle 88."	"America can't afford that risk!" Tones become more pronounced and then disappear.

FIG. 10.1.   Bush's Revolving Door Ad.

and one interpretive sentence ("America can't afford that risk!"). Those six factual statements refer to three actions by Michael Dukakis, one implication of his actions (first-degree murderers were furloughed), two descriptions of furloughed prisoners, and only one negatively evaluative adjective ("revolving-door" policy). One number and two descriptive statements also appear on screen.

The linguistic signs convey a sense of facticity and rational description of actions and their real-world consequences. The rhetorical force of the ad—the reason it created a controversy—comes from the fusion of its audio and video codes. Visually, the ad opens with the sun setting over the hills presumably surrounding the valley in which the prison stands. With night comes the darkness that is the criminal's natural environment. While guards seemingly control the prison from above, from the watchtower that signals oversight, the prisoners below move into and immediately out of that prison through revolving bars. As we return to society's penal representative standing on the roof, we know he guards no one. In the darkness, our incarceral institutions have emptied themselves and endangered the citizenry.

Simultaneously coded aurally are electronic drum beats that gain in strength as the ad runs, a synthesized sine-wave tone that intrudes more forcibly as time passes, and then a high-pitched hum much like the oscilloscope's high flat tone that is sounded in the operating room when the patient dies. The calm, matter-of-fact voice of the narrator thus is mixed with recollections triggered by stereotypic electronic sounds—sounds associated, thanks to televised crime shows and detective movies, with impending danger (drums), conflict (toned sine waves), and death (high, thin flat tones). The logocentric is tempered by or even subordinated to the phonocentric.

Danger, conflict, and death thus belie the calm of the logologically descriptive words and, fused with the pictures of prisonerless prisons, they transport us into a postmodern world of deceptive appearances, the simulcra (Baudrillard). The ad is modernist enough, of course, to suggest that the agent of the deception is Michael Dukakis. None of the charges against Dukakis are articulated as such. They come, rather, from emphasizing the audio and video codes and then unitizing them: The phonocentric and ocularcentric rehearse our recollections and memories intertextually, creating ideas never articulated linguistically. The Revolving Door ad is television in its most potent construction.

PARTING THOUGHTS

French social critic Jacques Ellul has spent much of the last 20 years attacking *la technique*, technology that creates and controls the environments within which we live our lives. The latest in a series of his books, *The Humiliation of the Word* (1985), argues the proposition that we have allowed the visual to triumph over the spoken and written. Yet, in asserting that the visual is not a language per se, not until it is encoded by voice and word, Ellul in an odd way adds force to this analysis. His argument, in spite of his distaste for the visual, comes close to that of Rick Altman, who suggests that it is sound that provides television flow with "discursification":

> By bringing a specially made image together at this specific time with a spectator especially desirous of seeing that very image, the sound has succeeded in involving both the spectator and the image in the discursive circuit it directs. . . . Only when the sound track succeeds in bringing image and spectator together do they fulfill their mission. (50, 51)

The arguments I have been advancing, of course, are not yet finished. The tetrad THE VISUALIZED:THE REMEMBERED::THE SPOKEN:THE REC-OLLECTED needs further theoretical grounding, and its utility should be demonstrated with texts less obviously phono- and ocularcentric than a political advertisement. Yet, I am convinced that with the tetrad and via analyses of the texts of electric rhetoric, we will come to appreciate the genius of Walter Ong and his conceptualization of secondary orality. As well, we will recanonize *memoria* and rebeatify Aristotle for the sheer wisdom lying behind *De Memoria et Reminiscentia*. In uniting memory and recollection, the spoken and the seen, the psychological and the social, we will explore the wholeness of rhetorical discursivity at the dawn of the twenty-first century.

ACKNOWLEDGMENTS

Special thanks to Iowa's Center for Advanced Studies, as well as its staff members Jay Semel and Lorna Olson, for the facilities to think these odd thoughts. Thanks as well go to my peers Rick Altman and Donovan Ochs, who took time to give me reactions from their respective intellectual worlds.

WORKS CITED

Altman, Rick. "Television/Sound." *Studies in Entertainment: Critical Approaches to Mass Culture.* Ed. T. Modelski. Bloomington: Indiana UP, 1986.

Bacon, Francis. *The Advancement of Learning.* New York: Dutton, 1915.

Baudrillard, Jean. "Simulcra and Simulations." *Selected Writings.* Ed. Mark Poster. Stanford: Stanford UP, 1988. 119–48.

Bitzer, Lloyd. *The Philosophy of Rhetoric* by George Campbell. Carbondale: Southern Illinois UP, 1963.

Ellul, Jacques. *The Humiliation of the Word.* Trans. Joyce M. Hanks. Grand Rapids: Eerdmans, 1985.

Fiske, John. *Television Culture.* London: Methuen, 1987.

Fyfe, W. H., trans. "'Longinus' On the Sublime." *Aristotle; "Longinus": Demetrius.* Loeb Classical

Library. Cambridge: Harvard UP, 1960.

Gold, Ellen Reid. "Ronald Reagan and the Oral Tradition." *Central States Speech Journal* 39 (1988): 159–76.

Goody, Jack, and Ian Watt. "The Consequences of Literacy." *Literacy in Traditional Societies.* Cambridge, Eng.: Cambridge UP, 1968. 27–68.

Gronbeck, Bruce E. "Electric Rhetoric: The Changing Forms of American Political Discourse." *Vichiana,* 3rd series, 1st year. Napoli, Italy: Loffredo Editore, 1990. 141–61.

Hall, Edward. *The Silent Language.* Garden City: Doubleday, 1959.

Hall, Stuart. "Encoding/Decoding." *Culture, Media, Language.* Eds. Stuart Hall et al. London: Hutchinson, 1980.

Havelock, Eric A. *The Muse Learns to Write: Reflections on Orality and Literacy from Antiquity to the Present.* New Haven: Yale UP, 1986.

———. *Preface to Plato.* Cambridge: Harvard UP, 1963.

Jamieson, Kathleen Hall. *Eloquence in an Electronic Age: The Transformation of Political Speechmaking.* New York: Oxford UP, 1988.

Kaplan, Harry, trans. *Rhetorica Ad Herennium.* Loeb Classical Library. Cambridge: Harvard UP, 1954.

Lord, Albert B. *The Singer of Tales.* Cambridge: Harvard UP, 1960.

McKeon, Richard, ed. *The Basic Works of Aristotle.* New York: Random, 1941.

McLuhan, Marshall. *The Gutenberg Galaxy: The Making of Typographic Man.* Toronto: U of Toronto P, 1962.

———. *Laws of the Media: The New Science.* Toronto: U of Toronto P, 1988.

McLuhan, Marshall, and Quentin Fiore. *War and Peace in the Global Village.* New York: Bantam, 1968.

Ong, Walter J. *Hopkins, the Self, and God.* Toronto: U of Toronto P, 1986.

———. *Interfaces of the Word: Studies in the Evolution of Consciousness and Culture.* Ithaca: Cornell UP, 1977.

———. "McLuhan as Teacher: The Future is a Thing of the Past." *Journal of Communication* 31 (1981): 129–35.

———. *Orality and Literacy: The Technologizing of the Word.* London: Methuen, 1982.

———. *Ramus, Method, and the Decay of Dialogue: From the Art of Discourse to the Art of Reason.* Cambridge: Harvard UP, 1958.

———. *Rhetoric, Romance, and Technology: Studies in the Interaction of Expression and Culture.* Ithaca: Cornell UP, 1971.

Parry, Adam, ed. *The Making of Homeric Verse: The Collected Papers of Milman Parry.* Oxford, Eng.: Oxford UP, 1971.

Priestley, Joseph. *A Course of Lectures on Oratory and Criticism.* Eds. Vincent M. Bevilacqua and Richard Murphy. Carbondale: Southern Illinois UP.

Richards, I. A. *The Philosophy of Rhetoric.* New York: Oxford UP, 1965.

Schaeffer, John. *Sensus Communis: Vico, Rhetoric, and the Limits of Relativism.* Durham: Duke UP, 1990.

Schwartz, Tony. *Media: The Second God.* New York: Random, 1981.

———. *The Responsive Chord.* Garden City: Doubleday, 1973.

Vance, Eugene. "Roland and the Poetics of Memory." *Textual Strategies: Perspectives in Post-Structuralist Criticism.* Ed. Josue V. Harari. Ithaca: Cornell UP, 1979.

Vernant, Jean Pierre. *Mythe et pensée chez les grecs.* Paris: Maspéro, 1965.

11 A Special Afterword to Graduate Students in Rhetoric

Sheri L. Helsley
Old Dominion University

During my undergraduate years at the University of Virginia, like most of my friends I had no clear sense of what I wanted to do with myself and, consequently, what I wanted to study. So I listened to my advisors, took classes that interested me, and just hoped I would find my niche somewhere. I ended up double-majoring in philosophy and foreign affairs, and even spent a semester abroad studying the European Economic Community with a British member of the European Parliament. After graduation I boarded a plane to Tokyo, where I taught for several years. While I was in Japan, I decided that I probably ought to get a master's degree. But in what? Because what I most enjoyed was reading, writing, and teaching, I picked English. Then, during my first year of graduate work at Old Dominion University, I stumbled into a classical rhetoric seminar on the advice of one of my professors, and there I found my niche.

In that seminar, which had drawn students with interests ranging from journalism and advertising to literary theory and the teaching of composition, we were all asked to grapple with the sophists, Plato, Aristotle, the orality/literacy hypothesis, and contemporary applications of classical rhetorical theory. All of us found startling correlations between the issues that were hotly debated then and those that continue to be debated today. We all discovered that in the current debate about how best to teach oral and written communication, as well as the ongoing critical dialogue about the ethics of commercial/political advertising, the interpretation of literature, the credibility of information sources, and the anxieties of living in an electronic age, we could find new power in ancient sources. By positioning these areas of inquiry within a context and a tradition anchored in classical rhetoric, we learned not only how to deploy the available means of persuasion but also how to see them in action around us every day.

For me personally, the most obvious and immediate application of classical rhetoric was in my teaching of first-year composition. Like most inexperienced graduate teaching assistants, I had begun with the assumption (perhaps unconsciously) that I should teach the way I had been taught. I had diligently mapped out the steps of the writing process as I understood it, and I had urged my students to be creative and critical writers while laying out prescriptive rules I had always assumed writers should follow. I talked extensively about invention, arrangement, and style issues, completely dismissed rhetorical memory, and treated delivery as conforming to specific teacher-provided manuscript conventions. What I came to realize, though, through studying classical rhetoric and reexamining its five canons, was that by simplistically interpreting memory and delivery I was dismissing or marginalizing 40% of a five-part construct.

As Fred Reynolds soon prompted me to see, though, there are really a variety of ways that both teachers and students can employ the classical canon of memory in their thinking about rhetoric, composition, and communication. Most treatments of classical rhetoric dismiss memory by translating it as memorizing, and so it is understandable that most new teachers of rhetoric and composition might be tempted to consider it irrelevant. This simplistic approach to memory issues, however, like so many treatments of classical rhetoric, is certainly open to debate and alternative interpretation. Flower and Hayes's work on short- and long-term memory in the composing process opens up one alternative possibility. But other alternatives as well—memory as memorableness, memory as mnemonic techniques, and memory as psychology, for example—can offer both teachers and students access to the power of this rhetorical canon, and can provide them with insights that might otherwise be missed.

Similarly, I learned that interpreting delivery as prescriptive manuscript conventions, or relevant only to oral communication, limits students' choices in analyzing and producing texts. Rhetorical delivery is enormously important in an electronic age. Word processing and desktop publishing, for example, are now readily available to student writers, and classical rhetoric prompts us to address the use and adaptation of these powerful post-typewriter presentation technologies. When we interpret delivery as presentation or secondary orality, we do important things for ourselves and our students. We restore the recursiveness and synthesis originally envisioned in the interaction of the five rhetorical canons. We move into important discussions of inevitable technologies and new structures of consciousness in the electronic age. We expose our students to the power of presentation in both encoding and decoding—an issue that has been largely ignored in contemporary education.

Memory and delivery, like many of the concepts in classical rhetoric, can be especially difficult and challenging because so many different translations, interpretations, and misrepresentations are available. Whereas some may see this as limiting, or as a reason for avoiding or dismissing classical rhetoric itself, I have come to see it as intellectually exciting. I now see rhetorical memory and delivery as ambiguous zones that are unusually rich with opportunities for important new scholarly work by graduate students in composition, speech communication, media studies, and rhetoric. I have come to believe that by embracing the ambiguities, exploring the debates, and studying the uses of classical rhetoric both inside and outside the classroom, others like me will also find their niche.

About the Contributors

Virginia Allen is associate professor of English and secondary education at Iowa State University, where she teaches courses in rhetoric and composition, linguistics, science fiction, and pedagogy. She holds a BA in philosophy from Florida State University, an MA in English from Chicago State University, and a PhD in English education from Florida State University. In addition to having written numerous articles and book reviews, she is the author, with Merriellyn Kett, of *College Writing Skills* (Merrill, 1981) and *How to Avoid Sexism: A Guide for Writers, Editors, and Publishers* (Ragan, 1978). She currently serves as associate editor of *Vitae Scholasticae: The Bulletin of Educational Biography*.

Jay David Bolter is professor of literature, communication, and culture at the Georgia Institute of Technology. He holds a BA in Greek from the University of Toronto, and an MS in computer science and a PhD in classics from the University of North Carolina, where he previously held a dual appointment as associate professor of classics and computer science. He has written extensively on the relationship between computers, hypertext, and classical studies, and is the author of *Turing's Man: Western Culture in the Computer Age* (University of North Carolina Press, 1984) and the widely acclaimed *Writing Space: The Computer, Hypertext, and the History of Writing* (Lawrence Erlbaum Associates, 1991).

Robert J. Connors is associate professor of English at the University of New Hampshire. He earned a BA in English from the University of Massachusetts, and an MA and PhD in English from Ohio State University. Widely published in composition theory and the history of rhetoric, he received CCCC's Braddock Memorial Award in 1982 and MLA's Mina P. Shaughnessy Prize in 1985. He currently serves on CCCC's executive committee, as well as the editorial boards of five journals. He is co-author, with Andrea Lunsford, of *The St. Martin's Handbook* (1992); with Cheryl Glenn, of *The St. Martin's Guide to Teaching Writing* (1992); and, with Lunsford and Lisa Ede, of *Essays on Classical Rhetoric and Modern Discourse* (Southern Illinois University Press, 1984).

Sharon Crowley is professor of English at Northern Arizona University, where she teaches courses in rhetorical theory and literary theory. She received BA and MA degrees in English from the University of Nebraska, and a PhD in English from the University of Northern Colorado. From 1989 to 1992 she chaired CCCC's National Committee on Professional Standards in Postsecondary Writing Instruction. She has written dozens of articles and reviews, and is the author of *A Teacher's Introduction to Deconstruction* (NCTE, 1989), as well as *The Methodical Memory: Invention in Current-Traditional Rhetoric* (Southern Illinois University Press, 1990), which won the W. Ross Winterowd Award for Most Outstanding Book in Composition Theory in 1990.

Sam Dragga is associate professor of English at Texas Tech University, where he teaches courses in technical and professional writing. He holds a BA in English from the University of Dayton, and an MA and PhD in English from Ohio University. He is a member of the executive board of the Association of Teachers of Technical Writing and is the author, with Gwendolyn Gong, of *Editing: The Design of Rhetoric* (Baywood, 1989), which won NCTE's award for Best Book in Technical and Scientific Communication in 1989. He has written extensively on technical communication issues, and his "Responding to Technical Writing" won ATTW's Best Article Award in 1991. Gong and Dragga's book *A Writer's Repertoire* is forthcoming from HarperCollins.

Bruce E. Gronbeck is professor of communication studies at the University of Iowa, where he specializes in cultural studies, politics, and media criticism. He received his BA from Concordia College, and his MA and PhD in speech from the University of Iowa, where he served as department chair from 1985 to 1991. He has received numerous grants, honors, and awards, including 10 visiting appointments, one honorary doctorate, and a prestigious Fulbright Lectureship in Sweden in 1992. He has written 7 books and more than 60 articles on rhetorical and media criticism, including the recent *Media, Consciousness, and Culture* (Sage, 1991) and the forthcoming *Sociocultural Dimensions of Rhetoric and Communication*.

Sheri L. Helsley is a graduate teaching assistant and the co-chair of the graduate student caucus in the Department of English at Old Dominion University in Norfolk, Virginia. She received a BA in philosophy and foreign affairs from the University of Virginia, and an MA in the teaching of English from Old Dominion University. In the fall of 1993 she will begin doctoral work in rhetoric at Ohio State University.

Winifred Bryan Horner is professor of English and Radford Chair of Rhetoric and Composition at Texas Christian University. She earned her BA in English from Washington University; her MA in English from the University of Missouri, where she chaired lower division studies and directed composition; and her PhD in English from the University of Michigan. She has been president of the Rhetoric Society of America and the National Council of Writing Program Administrators, chair of the writing division of MLA, and a member of the executive committees of NCTE and the International Society for the History of Rhetoric. She has published 12 books, received many honors and awards, and served on the boards of 5 journals.

David Marc is visiting professor at the Annenberg School for Communication at the University of Southern California, where he teaches seminars on humanities techniques for the study of mass communications. He received BA and MA degrees in English from SUNY Binghamton, and a PhD in American studies from the University of Iowa. He is the author of *Demographic Vistas: Television in American Culture* (University of Pennsylvania Press, 1984), *Comic Visions: Television Comedy and American Culture* (Routledge, 1989), and *Prime Time, Prime Movers* (Little Brown, 1992). He has been a media critic for *The Village Voice,* and has appeared on "The Today Show," "Sixty Minutes," and "The CBS Evening News."

Joyce Irene Middleton is assistant professor of English at the University of Rochester, where she teaches courses in composition theory and African-American writers. She received her BA, MA, and PhD degrees in English from the University of Maryland at

College Park, where she received numerous academic honors and awards, including several Ford Foundation awards and a Postdoctoral Fellowship for Black American Scholars. She has written extensively on the relationship between orality, literacy, and memory, and her book *The Art of Memory in Toni Morrison's Song of Solomon* is in progress.

John Frederick Reynolds is associate professor of English and director of professional writing at Old Dominion University, where he teaches courses in composition, rhetoric, criticism, and pedagogy. He holds BA, MA, and MA degrees in speech communication and English from Midwestern State University, and a PhD in composition studies from the University of Oklahoma. He has written extensively on classical rhetoric in contemporary composition and is the author, with David Mair and Pamela Fischer, of *Writing and Reading Mental Health Records: Issues and Analysis* (Sage, 1992). He currently serves as membership director for the Rhetoric Society of America, and Book Review Editor for the *Journal of Advanced Composition.*

Kathleen E. Welch is associate professor of English at the University of Oklahoma, where she specializes in rhetorical theory and composition. She received a BA in English from Augustana College, and an MA and PhD in English from the University of Iowa. She has been president of the Association of Teachers of Advanced Composition, and is currently president-elect of the Rhetoric Society of America and president of the Coalition of Women Scholars in the History of Rhetoric and Composition. She is the author of *The Contemporary Reception of Classical Rhetoric: Appropriations of Ancient Discourse* (Lawrence Erlbaum Associates, 1990) and is currently writing *Classical Rhetoric, Literacy, and Secondary Orality.*

As of September 1, 1993, Sharon Crowley is professor of English at the University of Iowa, David Marc is associate professor of critical studies at UCLA, and Winifred Horner is Cecil and Ida P. Green Distinguished Professor Emeritus at Texas Christian University.

Author Index

Page numbers in *italics* denote complete bibliographic information

Subject Index